Educating
Mentally Retarded Persons
in the Mainstream

Educating Mentally Retarded Persons in the Mainstream is the inaugural volume of the new Perspectives on Handicapping Conditions Series, edited by Jay Gottlieb, Ph.D. The second proposed volume in this series, now in preparation, is:

Developmental Theory and Research in Learning Disabilities edited by *Jay Gottlieb, Ph.D.* and *Stephen Strichart, Ph.D.*

Perspectives on Handicapping Conditions Series

Educating Mentally Retarded Persons in the Mainstream

Edited by
Jay Gottlieb, Ph.D.
Department of Educational Psychology
New York University

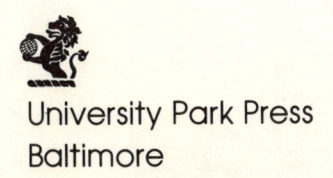

University Park Press
Baltimore

UNIVERSITY PARK PRESS
International Publishers in Science, Medicine, and Education
233 East Redwood Street
Baltimore, Maryland 21202

Copyright © 1980 by University Park Press

Composed by University Park Press, Typesetting Division
Manufactured in the United States of America by The Maple Press Company

All rights, including that of translation into other languages, reserved. Photomechanical reproduction (photocopy, microcopy) of this book or parts thereof without special permission of the publisher is prohibited.

Library of Congress Cataloging in Publication Data
Main entry under title:
Educating mentally retarded persons in mainstream.
   (Perspectives on handicapping conditions series)
   1. Mentally handicapped children—Education—Addresses, essays, lectures. 2. Mainstreaming in education—Addresses, essays, lectures. I. Gottlieb, Jay, 1942– II. Series.
LC4601.E29   371.9'28   79-20014
ISBN 0-8391-1522-9

Contents

Contributors vii
Foreword ix
Preface xiii

SECTION I   THE CLASSROOM TEACHER AND MAINSTREAMING: A REVIEW

    Chapter 1   **Attitudes of Teachers Toward Mainstreaming Retarded Children** *Judith L. Baker and Jay Gottlieb* 3

    Chapter 2   **Teacher Expectancies and Their Implications for Teaching Retarded Students** *Nancy D. Safer* 24

SECTION II   METHODOLOGICAL CONSIDERATIONS IN EVALUATING MAINSTREAM PROGRAMS

    Chapter 3   **Evaluating Programs for Educating Mentally Retarded Persons: Changing Paradigms** *Fred A. Crowell* 47

    Chapter 4   **Evaluating Educational Changes with Single-Subject Designs** *Alan C. Repp and John Lloyd* 73

SECTION III   RESEARCH ON MAINSTREAMING

    Chapter 5   **Educational Provisions for Young Children With Down's Syndrome** *John E. Rynders and J. Margaret Horrobin* 109

    Chapter 6   **Research in Large-Scale Curriculum Development for Mildly Retarded Children** *I. Leon Smith* 148

    Chapter 7   **Regular Class Education of EMR Students, From Efficacy to Mainstreaming: A Review of Issues and Research** *C. Edward Meyers, Donald L. MacMillan, and Roland K. Yoshida* 176

    Chapter 8   **Students' and Teachers' Perceptions of the Mentally Retarded Child** *Gary N. Siperstein and John J. Bak* 207

    Chapter 9   **Advocacy Through the Eyes of Citizens** *Stephen S. Strichart and Jay Gottlieb* 231

SECTION IV   CLASSROOM APPLICATIONS
            Chapter 10   **Using Research Findings for Classroom Programming** *Edward L. Meyen and Warren J. White* 253
            Index 281

Contributors

John J. Bak, B.A.
Center for Human Services
University of Massachusetts/Boston
100 Arlington Street
Boston, Massachusetts 02125

Judith L. Baker, Ph.D.
Department of Learning and
  Development
Northern Illinois University
DeKalb, Illinois 60115

Fred A. Crowell
Program Evaluator
Specialized Training Program
Center on Human Development
University of Oregon
Eugene, Oregon 97403

Jay Gottlieb, Ph.D.
Department of Educational
  Psychology
New York University
New York, New York 10003

**J. Margaret Horrobin, M.B.,
  Ch.B., D.C.H.**
Group Health Plan Incorporated
6845 Lee Avenue North
Minneapolis, Minnesota 55429

John Lloyd, Ph.D.
Department of Special Education
University of Virginia
Charlottsville, Virginia 22903

Donald L. MacMillan, Ed.D.
Professor of Education
University of California
Riverside, California 92521

Edward L. Meyen, Ph.D.,
Chairman
Department of Special Education
University of Kansas
Lawrence, Kansas 66044

C. Edward Meyers, Ph.D.
Neuropsychiatric Institute, UCLA
Research Group at Pacific State
  Hospital
Pomona, California 91766

Alan C. Repp, Ph.D.
Department of Special Education
Northern Illinois University
DeKalb, Illinois 60115

John E. Rynders, Ph.D.
Department of Psychoeducational
  Studies
Pattee Hall
150 Pillsbury Drive, S.E.
Minneapolis, Minnesota 55455

Nancy D. Safer, Ed.D.
Program Support Branch
Division of Assistance to States
Bureau of Education for the
  Handicapped
400 Maryland Avenue, S.W.
Washington, D.C. 20202

Gary N. Siperstein, Ph.D.
Center for Human Services
University of Massachusetts/Boston
100 Arlington Street
Boston, Massachusetts 02125

I. Leon Smith, Ph.D.
Professional Examination Service
475 Riverside Drive
New York, New York 10027

Stephen S. Strichart, Ph.D.
Division of Psycho-Educational
  Services
Florida International University
Tamiami Trail
Miami, Florida 33199

Roland K. Yoshida, Ph.D.
Bureau of Education for the
  Handicapped
Division of Assistance to States
6th and D Streets, S.W.
Washington, D.C. 20202

Warren J. White, M.S.Ed.
Research Assistant
Department of Special Education
University of Kansas
Lawrence, Kansas 66044

Foreword

Few would argue against the notion that change and innovation have a difficult, if not graceless, time of getting into educational systems. Similarly, few would disagree that once in the system, the nature of change and innovation and their effects are subject to extremes in interpretation and implementation. Gottlieb and his colleagues illustrate this state of affairs with clarity. But they bring more than information to the fore; they have confronted readers with a consciousness-raising experience. On the one hand, the array of chapters and their topics display a sizeable number of the variables crucial to the implementation of the least restrictive environment (LRE) requirement of Public Law 94-142. On the other hand, the chapters show what can and often does happen when conditions of implementation are treated superficially and/or capriciously. The centerpiece of this treatment is the conclusion drawn in the chapter by Meyers, MacMillan, and Yoshida with regard to the decertification program in California. While stated in a low-key manner, the conclusion seethes with indignation and outrage. It is worth quoting here because it is representative of the results of a Procrustean approach to change and innovation so common to education. They say that "the majority of the decertified were 'successfully' returned to regular programs in California in spite of inept or absent transition programs. However, this definition of success is one of survival, the academic D [decertified] students' gap generally remained 3 or more years behind placement, and placement was nearly 2 years below age expectancy. Given an acceptance of the survival definition of successful decertification, then the return was not a bad decision."

Stated in quantitative language, the full irony of the writers' conclusion may escape the reader even though the quality of life of the students is implicit. One only has to read the chapters on teacher expectancies, attitudes, and students' and teachers' perceptions of the retarded child for an appreciation of what classroom life must be like for the retarded student and for a projection of the type of person he/she will become in the years beyond school.

Given the foregoing, it would be easy to come to the conclusion, and I am sure that some readers will so conclude, that mainstreaming as an option in arriving at the least restrictive environment is a lost cause. To do so would be as much an oversimplification as concluding from other data in the book that mainstreaming is the only option.

It is within this context that Gottlieb and his colleagues provide a broad and lucid consciousness-raising experience. We must recognize, however, that the authors, individually or collectively, do not take a pro or con stand on the issue. I am sure that they could have, but they resisted in favor of making us aware of certain variables crucial to the decision to mainstream or not to mainstream and, having done so, go on to show the complexity of these variables.

Despite the contemporary nature of this book, it reminds us that there is a history of mainstreaming that we must be aware of before we take a firm stand on the issue. Even though many educators behave as though mainstreaming is a phenomenon of the late 1970s, the fact is that untold numbers of teachers of special classes for the retarded have been mainstreaming certain students, probably from the day the first special class came into being. I can tell you from first-hand experience that many of these teachers could and can confirm the contents of this book. They would probably stumble over the language and technology in the chapters on evaluation but not over the rationale and objectives.

These teachers would confirm facts that are implicit in the book. For example, they would say that some students are good candidates for mainstreaming and they could tell you why. These teachers would discuss, with specific regular class placement in mind, the social sophistication of the student and his/her work habits in academic and other pursuits because they believe it is necessary to thoroughly study a student before assigning him/her to a class. This approach to laying the foundation of mainstreaming reduces the probability of false positives. Having made the placement, these teachers do not turn their backs on their students. They are constantly in touch with the regular class teachers and confront problems early. Remedies are attempted and when it is clear that all or some important elements of the decision were faulty, the plan is aborted so that, as one teacher said, nobody gets hurt.

It does not take much to see that these teachers are not just competent at mainstreaming individual children but have, in an overlooked sense, already mainstreamed their entire class within the corpus of the school. Consider the kind of rapport the teacher of the special class needs to maintain with colleagues of regular classes in order to obtain the knowledge and feeling that leads to the placement of students. This could not come about without mutual respect, understanding, and acceptance. These are, in the final analysis, the foundations for mainstreaming.

These experiences, and they have been numerous, indicate that relegating the self-contained class to second place in a hierarchy of placement choices is unwarranted. As I read the LRE requirement in PL 94-142, it says, in effect, *all other factors being equal,* placement in a regular class is the first order desirable. As Gottlieb and his colleagues show clearly, all factors are not equal nor is there a likelihood that they ever will be.

Why do so many school districts persist in a wholesale abandonment of special classes in favor of regular class placement? This book indicates clearly that this is far from a rhetorical question. In part, at least, the stampede away from the special class as a placement option is provoked by a widespread readiness to ignore history and to look upon the special class as necessarily a segregated setting. The fact is, many authoritative people use the terms *special class* and *segregated class* interchangeably with such frequency that the term *special class* has become a metaphor for isolated, second rate education. On the other hand, I am confident that we would get a diametrically opposed view from those students who have been the victims of precipitate placement. Many of the chapters in this book indicate that this would be a sizeable proportion of the mainstreamed student body.

I think there are three reasons for the abrupt swing from conventional practices to mainstreaming in special education. First, for any one or combination of reasons, we too often oversimplify complex problems and devise quick and relatively easy solutions at the program level. It may be a spectacular court case, pressure from a small, but vocal, group in the community, a popular movement in the field that has a lot of emotional appeal, or a hurried interpretation of a government mandate. Whatever the reason may be, the fact that there is little accountability at the program level and an essentially silent constituency in the classroom makes it possible to carry out drastic change quickly. Rarely do decision makers pay anywhere near the price their teachers and students do when plans do not work out as intended.

Second, even though education as a process is an evolving phenomenon, we rarely engage in long-range study, planning, and experimentation. It would be difficult to find a research project discussed in this book with a life of more than 3 years. When you take into account that this time includes tooling-up time at one end and data analysis and reporting at the other, it turns out that a 3-year project includes 18-20 months, at best, of actual study. The studies evaluating mainstreaming are good examples of necessarily long-term studies done on a short-term basis.

Finally, there is the circularity of the phenomenological approach to determining the independent and, particularly the dependent, variables in researching practical or classroom level problems. It goes something like this. The researcher hears about problems in the classroom and decides to study them toward the end of one or more solutions. What he or she is saying in effect is "since you the educator have expressed the fact of the problem in some way, it must necessarily be a real problem; you are the expert so you should know." The researcher then tackles the problem thereby lending credibility to the stature of the problem in the first instance. The educator's assessment of the problem is confirmed; would so competent and enlightened a researcher spend time and effort on an inconsequential issue? This leads the educator to redouble efforts with the dependent variable as the focus. And so it goes.

In great part, the circularity starts with the educator who, for some reason, reduces the goals and objectives of education to a narrow few, such as academic achievement. To a lesser degree, researchers contribute to the circularity by succumbing to the convenience of readily available measures and methodologies and by shying away from independent and dependent variables that are relatively difficult to identify and measure.

I was impressed by the way the chapters by Baker and Gottlieb; Safer; and Meyers, MacMillan, and Yoshida portray the effects of the phenomenological approach while those by Rynders and Horrobin; Smith; Siperstein and Bak; Strichart and Gottlieb; and Meyen and White include many of the dependent variables that go unexamined or, at best, less than rigorously researched. The chapters by Crowell and by Repp and Lloyd provide interesting and substantive avenues for achieving the kind of balanced approach to educational research that will interrupt the underproductive circularity currently in style.

Of course, the key to recognizing the impact of the phenomenological approach to research is inherent in how you read this book. If you see it as a handy compendium of topics and literature reviews, a reference based on a reported state of the art, the probability is good that many undercurrents in the implementation of PL 94-142 will go undetected. If, on the other hand, you ruminate about the source of teachers' expectations instead of simply accepting them, you will provoke such questions as: is there any concordance between the goals and objectives of education and the range and/or focus of teachers expectations? Might not research on teacher expectancies and attitudes be more informative if it took into account the justification or misguidedness of expectancies and attitudes in the first instance? Wouldn't this lead to the kinds of inservice education, for example, that would lead to a reshaping of classroom actions, "better" results, and, therefore, more educationally valid data?

Similarly, in reading the accounts of the assessment of the effectiveness of mainstreaming, if we took the next step beyond accepting changes in measures of central tendency and focus on main effects by taking into account the children perched two or three standard deviations beyond the mean, might this not provoke such questions as: how does the validity or relevance of teachers' expectancies and attitudes effect the results? What are the characteristics of students who did more than survive the decertification program? What would have been the outcome of the studies reported by Meyers, MacMillan, and Yoshida, if responsible leadership had read the chapters by Meyen and White and by Siperstein and Bak before acting? Having done so and acted accordingly, what will a replication of the research reported by Strichart and Gottlieb have to say?

Obviously, I have exposed my biases. A book that reports on the results of "practical" research ought to have implications for change in policies and practices that lead to greater efficacy at the various levels of treatment and treatment-related pursuits. Happily, this book does so if properly read.

It has been said that education is the process whereby actions based on information that is subjectively reasonable to the actor become converted to actions based on information that is objectively reasonable. This book goes a long way toward meeting the criteria implicit in such a view of education as both a social institution and a process. The effects of proceeding along subjectively reasonable lines in mainstreaming, for example, are clearly documented. Of equal importance, the data and experiences fundamental to policies and procedures leading to objectively reasonable actions are here for administrators, teachers, teacher educators, psychologists, and researchers of all theoretical persuasions to read and act on. In this sense, this book can be a sound and enlightening experience.

Herbert Goldstein
Department of Educational Psychology
New York University

Preface

This book is the first in a series dealing with the multifaceted nature of handicapping conditions. As with all upcoming volumes in the series, this one attempts to balance review chapters with chapters that present original data. The purpose of the data-based chapters is to allow investigators freedom to present a sizeable body of their research in a sufficiently straightforward fashion so that it can be understood by advanced undergraduate or beginning graduate students in education. The investigators were asked by the editor to elaborate their data in a way that they could not otherwise do if they were to submit the research to professional journals.

Beyond the purpose of enabling investigators latitude to present their research in a single place so that it can be more easily digested by the interested reader, the series has another purpose: to acquaint students in special education with the empirical underpinning to special education. All too often, students are not required to read current journals, and when they are required to do so, they cannot understand the highly technical nature of the report writing. Students then become disenchanted with research, which only serves to reinforce their initial feelings that research is not relevant.

It is critically important that students become aware of the empirical nature of special education, especially when we are in the midst of a period in which decisions are made either politically or judicially, or because a group of "experts" are convinced of the righteousness of their convictions. There are certainly enough institutions in society that are eager to impose their views on the education of handicapped children. We need more effective champions of data-based decisions.

The present volume deals with the education of mentally retarded persons in the mainstream. The term *mainstream* is treated in a broad sense with its meaning ranging from curriculum materials geared for special education children in the regular classroom, as in the chapter by Smith, to the community involvement of retarded persons with the help of citizen advocates, as discussed by Strichart and Gottlieb. Similarly, mainstreaming affects handicapped people of all ages, from the adults, who constituted part of the sample of the Strichart and Gottlieb report, to the young children with Down's syndrome, reported on by Rynders and Horrobin. More traditional meanings of mainstreaming are presented in the chapters by Meyers, MacMillan, and Yoshida, and by Siperstein and Bak.

In addition to the chapters that present original data, there are two chapters concerning ways to evaluate mainstreaming programs. Crowell presents a broad view of mainstreaming programs and the multidimensional ways that are needed to evaluate them adequately. Repp and Lloyd, on the other hand, deal on a more microscopic level of analysis: the individual child.

Finally, the two review chapters focus on different aspects of the teacher. Emphasis was placed on the teacher because he/she is the single most important influence of whether the handicapped child will receive an appropriate education in the mainstream of the school. Considerably more research and, ultimately inservice training will have to be directed to the teacher if, in fact, an appropriate education is to be provided to handicapped children.

Subsequent volumes to this series will appear periodically. Each will be divided between reviews of the current status of the field and original research contributions. The exact balance between review and research will vary with the volume.

I would like to thank Ms. Joan Sanow of University Park Press for attending to the many details that arise during the course of editing a volume. More importantly, I would like to thank her for supporting the idea of a series of books on the education of handicapped children. Also, I would like to thank Jan Romanski for typing parts of the manuscript. Finally, my wife, Barbara, provided the encouragement to undertake this project in the first place.

**Educating
Mentally Retarded Persons
in the Mainstream**

I

The Classroom Teacher and Mainstreaming: A Review

CHAPTER 1

Attitudes of Teachers Toward Mainstreaming Retarded Children

Judith L. Baker and Jay Gottlieb

This chapter is concerned primarily with the attitudes of classroom teachers toward mentally retarded children. Attention is focused on the attitudes of regular education teachers for several reasons. The main reason is that, as a result of federal legislation (Education for All Handicapped Children Act, PL 94-142), increasingly more handicapped children are being educated in regular classrooms with teachers who have limited experience in dealing with their problems. Because teachers are known to influence the behavior of children in many ways (e.g., see Brophy & Good, 1974), it is important to acquire detailed information about the likely consequences to handicapped children of being placed in classrooms with teachers who have limited information and expertise regarding their problems. To date, the bulk of empirical literature on this topic has dealt with the positive and negative aspects of teachers' attitudes; far less information has been generated on the educational implications of positive and/or negative attitudes. Until there is a better understanding of how teachers' attitudes affect the everyday education that handicapped children receive, teachers may not be providing them with the appropriate education to which they are entitled under federal mandate. Few would deny, however, that an understanding and accepting teacher is an important component of an appropriate education *for any child*. How much more important is it for handicapped children who already face a plethora of problems without having to concern themselves with doubts as to the degree of their teachers' understanding of their problems?

The literature on attitudes of teachers toward educable mentally retarded (EMR) children is approached from the vantage of mainstreamed education, or placement in the least restrictive environment, an educational concern at the heart of PL 94-142. Perhaps more than any other aspect of PL 94-142, the mandate to place handicapped children in the least restrictive environment has caused teachers and administrators to be wary of forthcoming trends in special education and to close their eyes to the problem in the hope that it will disappear. The overwhelming extent to which schools are presently ignoring the problem of placing EMR children in regular classes is evident from data obtained in a recent unpublished survey in Illinois conducted in the fall, 1978, which indicated that, of 108 elementary school classes for EMR children, 104 educated them in self-contained classes while only 4 established resource programs for EMR children. One reason for the continued segregation of EMR children may be the beliefs and attitudes of the teachers.

Before a variety of issues related to teachers' attitudes regarding the placement of handicapped children in their classes is discussed, a brief background to the topic is presented in order to set the stage for the discussion that follows.

BACKGROUND CONSIDERATIONS

The fact that mentally retarded pupils are problematic for regular classroom teachers predates the mainstream movement. The creation and proliferation of segregated classes for mentally retarded children were as much a result of the desire of classroom teachers to rid themselves of troublesome children as it was a desire to provide these children with an educational climate and curriculum that were better suited to their unique needs (Esten, 1900). When it is considered that, at the turn of the century, an average of 33% of all children who attended regular grades were academically retarded (Ayres, 1909), it is not surprising that special classes for the most serious of the "laggards" proliferated very quickly. Those who remained in regular classes "constitute serious problems for the teachers. They are misfits in the classes, require special attention if they are to do satisfactory work and render more difficult the work with the other children" (Ayres, 1909, p. 3). It was to the advantage of the classroom teachers to be able to exclude the misfits so that they could concentrate on the other children.

As a result of classroom teachers' eagerness not to teach children who were retarded, the educational establishment pictured mentally retarded children as requiring a specialized curriculum, taught by specially trained teachers, in classes that had fewer children than were ordinarily enrolled in regular classes. In order to legitimize the claims that mentally retarded children were "different," the schools made considerable use of the newly imported IQ test, which had been brought into the United States at the beginning of the 1920s.

The separation of mentally retarded children from regular education continued unabated until the late 1960s, at which time a special education system that originally evolved as much to calm classroom teachers as to accommodate the unique needs of retarded children was suddenly seen as undemocratic and exclusionary. The same special classrooms that for years had been hailed as the appropriate placement for slow learning children who could not compete in the regular class were now cast in the role of villain for failing to promote the academic achievement of mentally retarded children and causing them to be stigmatized. In a period of a few years, an educational system that had developed and evolved over a period of approximately 60 years was undergoing a complete metamorphosis. Why? What events were responsible for the sudden change in a long-standing history of special educational practice?

A rapid change in the social climate of the United States marked the beginning of the end of segregated education for many handicapped children. Under the momentum generated by the civil rights movement, special education was subjected to varied presses from which it had previously been immune. The most damaging of these presses was the fact that minority group children were overrepresented in special classes (Mercer, 1973). Special education school administrators were hard pressed to justify continuing classes that were proven to be racially imbalanced at a time in history when the courts were striking down all institutions that had perpetuated racial segregation.

As part of the overall movement by the courts to abolish racial segregation, the case of *Hobson* v. *Hansen* (1967) struck a direct blow to education by ruling that homogeneously tracked classrooms that resulted in a concentration of minority group children in low-track classes were unconstitutional. The *Hobson* case, together with a number of other precedent-setting legal decisions (e.g., *Diana, Larry Mills, PARC*) resulted in court orders that forced school administrators to alter traditional placement and identification practices that were prevalent in special education.

Although the courts were the prime movers in changing traditional special education practices, they were certainly not the only movers. One of the primary reasons for the court's ascendancy in decision making that affects special education was the failure of special educators to demonstrate that the educational system they created is advantageous to handicapped children. Specifically, educators could not produce data to indicate that children who attended special classes achieved more than children who did not (Kirk, 1964). Most of the data indicated that mentally retarded children who attended special classes did not achieve as well as comparable retarded children who remained in the regular grades. The failure to demonstrate the superiority of special classes vis-à-vis academic achievement, coupled with the prevailing view that special classes were stigmatizing to children who attended them (Dunn, 1968), lent support to the movement to abolish segregated class education for mildly retarded children.

The combination of successful legal challenges to existing special education practices and the failure of educators to prove that segregated education was advantageous to handicapped children provided the impetus for the passage of PL 94-142.

Public Law 94-142 is expected to alter radically the manner in which special education services are typically delivered to educable mentally retarded as well as to other handicapped children. The law mandates that all handicapped children are to receive their education in the least restrictive setting that can accommodate their individual needs. Handicapped children are to be educated with nonhandicapped peers to the maximum extent possible. Although the law does not require mainstreaming of all handicapped children, it does state that handicapped children are to be removed from regular education only if it can be shown that the nature and severity of their handicap are such that their needs cannot be met in that setting with the assistance of supplemental aids and services. Handicapped children having many different learning problems may be expected to participate in regular classes for at least a minor part of the school day because criteria for removal from regular classes are not entirely clear and because any removal must be justified. The removal of a handicapped child from a regular classroom may be difficult to justify and administratively troublesome.

The integration of handicapped children into regular classes places regular education teachers in new roles of responsibility. Teachers' attitudes toward integration are expected to influence the extent to which handicapped children become not only physically integrated, but integral members of regular classes, benefiting academically, socially, and emotionally from the experience.

In the section that follows several topics are addressed that are important to understanding regular teachers' attitudes toward integration of retarded children. First, the results of studies that indicate the degree of positiveness of regular teachers' attitudes toward mainstreaming are examined. A concern is raised as to whether or not an extremely positive attitude is necessarily desirable. The second section focuses on several areas hypothesized to underlie regular teachers' attitudes toward integration and their willingness to accept handicapped children into their classes.

REGULAR TEACHERS' ATTITUDES TOWARD MAINSTREAMING EMR PUPILS

In order to assess whether regular class teachers are likely to accept or welcome back retarded pupils, results of studies that have investigated teachers' attitudes toward integration of mildly handicapped children, as well as studies that focused specifically on teachers' attitudes toward integration of retarded pupils, are reviewed. It has often been assumed that there is a strong positive relationship between teachers' evaluations of the appropriateness of mainstreaming in general and the level of acceptance they feel toward the integration of exceptional children into their own classes. Consequently, in a number of studies teachers were questioned to reveal the extent to which they favored mainstreaming of exceptional children.

Two basic approaches are used to acquire information on teachers' acceptance of mainstreaming. One approach presents them with several statements posited to tap attitudes toward mainstreaming and asks them to indicate whether they agreed or disagreed with the content of the statements. The other method provides teachers with descriptions of exceptional children having various learning problems and asks what they consider to be the most appropriate placement for these children.

Regular teachers' attitudes concerning the appropriateness of integration for EMR children, as well as for learning disabled and emotionally disturbed children, were examined by Shotel, Iano, and McGettigan (1972). Regular education teachers were asked whether they agreed or disagreed that most children of each exceptionality should generally be in regular class for most of the day and attend special classes or resource rooms for part of the day. The attitudes of two groups of teachers were examined: an experimental group who, at the beginning of the study, were about to participate in mainstreaming programs, and a control group who taught in schools having only self-contained special education programs. Attitudes toward integration were assessed both at the beginning and at the end of the school year.

Although a majority of teachers in both groups disagreed with the proposition that most EMR children should be placed in a regular classroom with special education class support, there was a significant difference between the initial attitudes of the two teacher groups. This difference, however, disappeared over the year of the study. Prior to their mainstreaming experience, experimental teachers expressed significantly less negative attitudes than the control group (63% versus 93% who disagreed with the mainstreaming statement). After working with handicapped children for a year, the proportion of the experimental group not favoring integration for most EMR children increased to 87%, while the control group did not change appreciably. This finding suggests that some experimental group teachers were initially optimistic about the integration of EMR children, but they found EMR children more difficult to integrate than they had anticipated. Shotel et al. (1972) believed that pre-mainstreaming meetings concerned with the philosophy and goals of mainstreaming may have influenced the initial attitudes of experimental teachers; some teachers may have attempted to assume very positive attitudes toward mainstreaming in order to cooperate with the aims of the new program. The researchers were told by a number of teachers whom they questioned informally at the completion of the study that many of the mainstreamed EMR children simply did not integrate well, either academically or socially, into their classes.

The results of the Shotel et al. (1972) study show that regular teachers are quite unified in their belief that mainstreaming, even with special education support, is not the most appropriate placement for many EMR children. We cannot assume, however, that these findings mean that regular teachers are generally negative toward the mainstreaming of EMR children. It is quite possible that classroom teachers feel regular class placement is the ideal alternative for some EMR children, but that it is inappropriate for others. Data from Project PRIME (Programmed Re-entry into Mainstream Education; Baker, Safer, & Guskin, in press), a large-scale descriptive correlational study of mainstreaming in Texas, as well as data from a study by Gickling and Theobold (1975), provide evidence supporting this contention.

All the regular education teachers involved in Project PRIME had one or more handicapped children integrated into their classes, at least one of whom had been identified as EMR. Some of the teachers were experiencing their first year of mainstreaming, but many had taught handicapped children for longer periods of time. When the teachers were asked whether they considered serving mildly handicapped pupils in the regular classroom a good idea for most, some, a few, or not any handicapped children the average teacher responded that it was a good idea for some children. In addition, when provided with written descriptions of children having various cognitive and social problems, the regular class teachers felt that a regular classroom with either special materials or resource room services available was the most appropriate placement for these children. Thus, the Project PRIME regular class teachers, while not overwhelmingly positive toward integration, did feel that it was appropriate for some handicapped students, and that many cognitive and social problems could be handled adequately in the regular classroom, particularly if some kind of special education services was available to assist them.

Additional evidence on regular teachers' feelings about the appropriateness of mainstreaming is offered by Gickling and Theobold (1975). These researchers questioned regular education personnel (regular education teachers, $N=183$; and regular education supervisors/administrators, $N=47$) from Tennessee before the advent of mainstreaming in that state. When asked about the manner of delivery of special education services that they favored for the future, 86% of the regular education personnel indicated that they strongly recommended the use of resource rooms for mildly handicapped children. Thus, a large majority of regular education personnel favored the integration of mildly handicapped children into regular classes with resource room support. Fifty percent (50%) of the regular education personnel, however, also strongly endorsed the use of self-contained classes for mildly handicapped children. Obviously, many participants in the study strongly recommended both options. These results then, together with those of Project PRIME, indicate many teachers do not totally favor either integration or segregation of mildly handicapped children. If a continuum is visualized, with one end of the continuum representing the belief that all mildly handicapped children should be segregated and the other end of the continuum representing the belief that all mildly handicapped children should be integrated, the data suggest that many teachers' attitudes would be located near the center of the continuum, a moderate attitude that favors integration for some children and segregation for others.

The results of the Shotel et al. (1972) study indicate that most regular teachers are not at the extreme positive end of the continuum, particularly once they have taught handicapped children. Whether or not regular teachers' lack of an extremely positive attitude toward integration of retarded children poses problems for the successful enactment of mainstreaming for these children has not been fully explored. Although there is little question that an extremely negative attitude toward integration is not desirable, the degree of acceptance that is most desirable is not known. The relationships between teachers' levels of attitude and their corresponding behavior at the different levels must be studied in order to answer this question.

Some researchers maintain that the most desirable attitude for a teacher to have is one that reflects an accurate assessment of the probability of exceptional children's benefiting from regular class placement, and that neither an extremely negative nor an extremely positive attitude meets this criterion (Haring, Stern, & Cruickshank, 1958). Haring et al. found that some teachers who became more accepting of integration as the result of an inservice workshop also became overzealous; that is, they favored the integration of children whom experts thought were better served in self-contained classes. They also found that teachers who did not change or who became more negative in attitude toward integration tended to reject the integration of children whom experts thought could be well served in regular classes.

Haring et al. (1958), of course, believed that the opinions of a selected group of experts reflected realistic perceptions of the appropriateness of integration for exceptional children. Unfortunately, since little research has been conducted to demonstrate for whom and under what conditions mainstreaming is a viable alternative, there is room for debate as to what constitutes a realistic attitude toward integration. Still, there is considerable agreement that mainstreaming is not appropriate for all mildly handicapped children so that extreme attitudes are not likely to represent realistic assessments of what is best. Thus, more moderate attitudes that favor neither integration nor segregation wholeheartedly may, in fact, be more desirable than extremely positive attitudes.

The primary concern, of course, is with the extent of regular teachers' acceptance of integration of exceptional children into their own classes. Gickling and Theobold (1975) asked regular educational personnel if they thought that regular teachers would accept special education students if there were a movement to eliminate self-contained classes. Although a majority (59%) indicated that regular education teachers would accept exceptional children, a large minority did not agree. Furthermore, half of the regular education personnel reported that they believed that regular education teachers would feel imposed upon if asked to help special education students. Because this study was conducted before the involvement of any of the participants in mainstreaming programs, their expectations of regular education teachers may have been more negative than warranted.

A number of factors are likely to underlie teachers' feelings about integration into their classes and their willingness to accept exceptional children. In the following section, several factors hypothesized to be relevant to teachers' attitudes toward the integration of retarded children into their classes are explored.

FACTORS RELATED TO
TEACHERS' ATTITUDES TOWARD INTEGRATION OF EMR CHILDREN

Regular education teachers' feelings or beliefs in several different areas are thought to influence their degree of acceptance of mainstreaming of retarded children. In particular, the following are important components of regular teachers' attitudes toward the integration of retarded children: 1) their knowledge of retarded children's academic and social behaviors, 2) their feelings about their own competence to teach retarded children, 3) their expectations of receiving assistance in teaching retarded pupils from valued supportive services, 4) their beliefs concerning the advantages and disadvantages of different educational placements for retarded children, and 5) their attitudes toward other teaching-related matters.

Knowledge of Teachers
Regarding the Behavior of Retarded Children

One may speculate that many of the regular classroom teachers' fears about handicapped children stem from limited information or misinformation, and that their expectations would be more realistic if they acquire additional experience or training with handicapped children. The belief that regular education teachers have limited information about handicapped children was documented in Project PRIME, where it was found that few regular class teachers had taken special education coursework, or even had had contact with handicapped children before the introduction of mainstreamed education in their schools (J. Agard, personal communication). A major goal of most inservice training programs for regular teachers involved in mainstreaming is to increase their knowledge about exceptional children. While this is largely viewed as a means to ensure that regular teachers are better able to meet the educational needs of exceptional children, it is also seen as a way of promoting more positive attitudes toward integration, since unfounded negative expectations could be corrected.

Regular class teachers who expect retarded children to be basically similar to normal children should not expect mainstreaming to cause serious problems in their classrooms and should have relatively positive attitudes toward integrating retarded children. However, teachers who expect retarded children to be very different from normal children, e.g., extremely antisocial or inattentive to academic tasks, should expect mainstreaming of retarded children to create countless problems in their classes and should be much less enthusiastic about the mainstreaming of retarded pupils.

One way to validate the assertion regarding hypothesized negative attitudes among teachers who expect retarded children to misbehave unduly or to be extremely incapable of academic attainments is to compare teachers' attitudes toward educable mentally retarded and trainable mentally retarded (TMR) children. Trainable children, who are less capable than educable children of grasping academic content, should be recipients of less favorable teacher attitudes. This hypothesis was supported in a study by Siperstein and Gottlieb (1978), who reported that teachers are more accepting of integrating EMR than TMR children, thus providing indirect support for the contention that teachers' expectations of the ability of retarded children relate to their attitudes toward integration of retarded children.

Certain expectations that regular class teachers have for retarded children are often based on limited information or misinformation. For instance, it has commonly been believed that one reason that regular classroom teachers tend to be reluctant to accept retarded children in their classes is their fear that the children will misbehave and disrupt their class routine. A recent survey of 54 regular classroom teachers (Gottlieb & Many, 1979) revealed that 24% of the respondents believed that retarded children would disrupt their classes, and an additional 18% were uncertain. Yet, the meager data available suggest that mainstreamed retarded children do not behave any differently than other children in the regular class (Gampel, Gottlieb, & Harrison, 1974).

The relationship between knowledge acquisition and attitude change, however, does not appear to be simple or automatic. Haring et al. (1958) found that an inservice workshop resulted in significant improvement in teachers' knowledge and understanding of exceptional children, but that increased knowledge did not necessarily result in increased acceptance of integration. Unexpectedly, these researchers found that only those teachers from schools having many handicapped children showed significant increases in acceptance of integration. This finding led Haring et al. (1958) to conclude that information about exceptional children may be more likely to promote positive attitude change in teachers having concurrent involvement with handicapped children than in teachers without such involvement.

Although it has seldom been an object of concern, some regular teachers, because of a lack of knowledge and experience with retarded persons, are likely to be unrealistically optimistic about the potential of retarded pupils. These teachers expect more from retarded pupils than the pupils are capable of giving. For these teachers, becoming more knowledgeable means becoming more negative in expectations, and possibly less positive in attitude toward integration. Apparently some of the teachers who participated in the study by Shotel et al. (1972) underwent this type of change. Shotel et al. found, for example, that the proportion of teachers who agreed that, with appropriate help, retarded pupils could function socially at age (or grade) level decreased significantly over an initial year of mainstreaming experience. Teachers' optimism concerning the appropriateness of regular class placement with resource room support for most retarded children also decreased significantly during this time period. It seems likely that many of the teachers questioned by Shotel et al. who lowered their expectations concerning the social potential of EMR children were the ones who changed their opinions about the advisability of mainstreaming most retarded pupils. If so, increase in knowledge, in this case knowledge acquired through teaching experience, may be related to negative attitude change by some teachers.

TEACHERS' FEELINGS OF COMPETENCE TO TEACH RETARDED CHILDREN

Most teachers derive considerable satisfaction from feeling that they do their job well and that the children in their care grow academically and socially because of their teaching skills. The prospect of having to instruct children whom they feel unqualified and unprepared to teach can be personally threatening. Thus, teachers' feelings concerning their competence or skill to instruct retarded children have been thought to contribute to their attitude toward integration (Gickling & Theobold, 1975; Shotel et al., 1972).

There is little doubt that regular teachers lack confidence in their ability to teach retarded children. Only 15% of the regular education personnel questioned by Gickling and Theobold (1975) agreed that the regular classroom teacher feels he/she has the skills to help special education students. Similar findings with specific reference to EMR students were reported by Shotel et al. (1972). Only 10% of a group of regular teachers about to participate in mainstreaming programs agreed that elementary education teachers generally have the training and competency to teach (meet the educational needs of) EMR children when supportive services are not available. It is not surprising that these regular teachers did not feel competent since over 99% also felt that special methods were required to teach most EMR children. After a year of mainstreaming experience, no significant change occurred in regular teachers' feelings concerning the competence needed to teach retarded children without supportive services, or in the need for special teaching methods. However, more of the regular teachers (32%) agreed that elementary teachers did have the necessary teaching skills if they were provided with supportive services. Furthermore, the percentage of teachers in agreement increased significantly ($p < 0.05$) after their initial year of teaching exceptional children. This suggests that the availability of supportive services is likely to be an additional influence on teachers' attitudes toward the integration of retarded pupils.

The data reported by Gickling and Theobold (1975) and Shotel et al. (1972) regarding teachers' expressed feelings of competence to teach handicapped children were collected either prior to the passage of PL 94-142 or prior to its full impact being felt in the schools. How do teachers presently feel regarding their competence to teach handicapped children now that PL 94-142 has been in effect for a few years?

In a recent survey, Gottlieb and Many (1979) asked regular ($N=54$) and special education ($N=56$) teachers the extent to which they agreed that retarded children could receive an appropriate education in the regular classroom. Of the regular education group, 37% agreed that retarded children could receive an appropriate education in the regular class, and 37% disagreed. The remaining quarter of the sample were uncertain. Interestingly, more special than regular education teachers agreed that retarded children could receive an appropriate education in the regular classroom. Forty-five percent (45%) of the special education teachers ($N=56$) stated that they disagreed that retarded children would be unable to receive an appropriate education in the regular classroom. Twenty-nine percent (29%) of the special education teachers agreed that retarded children would be unable to receive an appropriate education in regular classes. The remaining 26% were uncertain.

When asked directly whether most regular education teachers have the skills to teach handicapped children, 63% of the regular education teachers agreed that they did not have the skills. Half of the special education teachers agreed. These data indicate that 3 years after PL 94-142 was passed, a majority of teachers still feel ill-equipped to instruct handicapped children in the regular classrooms.

Availability of Supportive Services

If regular education teachers can be supplied with supportive services that they feel are necessary to assist them in educating mentally retarded pupils, the teachers should be more willing to accept retarded pupils into their classes. Although it is not known how teachers rank services in terms of relative importance, it was found in Project PRIME that teachers tended to value the services that they did receive and that teachers often suggested that the services that they did not receive would have been helpful to eliminate mainstreaming problems had they been available (Baker et al., in press).

A variety of services could be of benefit to regular teachers, filling a number of needs that occur or become exacerbated because of integration. Inservice training, resource room services, special education in-class consultants, special materials, and teachers' aides may all be important types of supportive services. We are not aware of any research that has systematically supplied regular classroom teachers with a variety of instructional and behavior management support, and assessed subsequent changes either in teachers' attitudes toward mainstreaming or toward exceptional children. Clearly, there is a need for this kind of research.

The need that teachers have for support is almost self-evident. But what kind of support? Principals ranked inservice training as the number one need of regular teachers involved in mainstreaming programs (Payne & Murray, 1974). Through inservice training, teachers can be provided information on retarded children's characteristics and methods for their instruction. Data reviewed previously suggested that few regular teachers are likely to have had any prior special education training and that nearly all think that special methods are necessary to teach retarded pupils. Although inservice training would seem to be essential for these reasons, only 44% of the regular teachers involved in Project PRIME reported having received any special education inservice training. Thirty-eight percent (38%) of the teachers indicated that inservice training probably would have eliminated some of the mainstreaming-related problems that occurred in their classes.

On what topics should the inservice training focus? One important topic is materials development. Teachers are in unanimous agreement that special materials are needed to teach EMR pupils (Shotel et al., 1972). However, only 38% of the Project PRIME regular teachers reported having received special materials for the retarded pupils in their classes. In addition, more than half of the teachers (58%) suggested that more or better curriculum materials would have eliminated mainstreaming-related problems.

In addition to the need to review materials development techniques as one component of an inservice training program, another need is instruction in the proper use of teacher aides, when they are available. Project PRIME teachers seldom had teaching aides (only 7% reported having the assistance of an aide); yet this was the form of assistance that the greatest proportion of regular teachers (68%) thought would have been helpful to them. The most common problem Project PRIME regular class teachers attributed to mainstreaming was a reduction in the time available for working individually with students. Since the average regular class teacher in Project PRIME was teaching 30 children, 4 of whom were handicapped, this problem is certainly understandable. Undoubtedly, an aide was seen by many teachers as a means to provide them with the time to meet more adequately the individual needs of both handicapped and nonhandicapped children.

Without doubt, classroom teachers of retarded children are at least as much in need of help from supportive services as are special education teachers, and possibly may require more support. Results of Project PRIME, however, suggest that special class teachers are much more likely than regular class teachers to be provided certain critical services such as special materials and teachers' aides. According to teachers' reports, 87% of the special resource teachers involved in Project PRIME, in contrast to 38% of the regular teachers, received special materials, and 59% of the special resource teachers, in contrast to 7% of the regular teachers, had the assistance of a teacher's aide. Disproportionate availability of supportive services to special education teachers can hardly be expected to increase regular teachers' acceptance of integration. On the contrary, regular teachers cannot be expected to be highly enthusiastic about mainstreaming under these conditions. School administrators may have to give more careful thought to resource allocation than they have in the past.

Teachers' Views About the Advantages and Disadvantages of Different Placements for Retarded Children

If one accepts that most regular teachers are sincerely concerned about the welfare of children, then it is reasonable to expect that their beliefs concerning the relative advantages and disadvantages of integrated (full- or part-time in regular class) and segregated (full-time in self-contained special class) placements for EMR children influence their attitudes toward integration of retarded children. Teachers will not favor an educational placement that they believe is not conducive to the academic, social, or emotional growth of retarded children. To the knowledge of these authors, regular teachers' beliefs concerning advantages and disadvantages of alternative placements for retarded pupils have not been explored. One study, however, which examined regular teachers' feelings about special class placement for mildly handicapped children, sheds some light on this area (Gickling & Theobold, 1975).

Many of the regular teachers questioned by Gickling and Theobold (1975) agreed that there were social disadvantages for mildly handicapped children who were placed in self-contained classes. About half of the teachers (48%) felt that being in a special self-contained class restricted the chance for a handicapped student to participate fully in school activities, such as clubs and sports, that were normally available to regular class students. More than half of the regular class teachers (61%) thought that a child was more likely to be seen as different if placed in a self-contained class rather than remaining in a regular class, and 56% of the teachers agreed that a child is socially isolated from peers when placed in a self-contained class. Furthermore, a majority of the teachers (70%) did not feel that special education placement practices had been free of socioeconomic and racial discrimination. Thus, on each question related to possible social disadvantages or discrimination as a result of self-contained class placement, half or more of the teachers believed that these actually were negative features of this placement. In addition, a minority of regular class teachers (39%) agreed that self-contained classes adequately provided academic services for the mildly handicapped and did not require change.

A vast majority of the regular education personnel (86%) who took part in the Gickling and Theobold (1975) study strongly recommended the use of resource rooms for mildly handicapped children in the future, thus indicating their support of regular class placement for at least part of the school day. A smaller percentage favored the use of self-contained classes. Teachers' perceptions of disadvantages stemming from self-contained placement seem to be a likely contributor to their personal endorsement of the resource room concept for at least some mildly handicapped children.

Teachers' perceptions of advantages and disadvantages of segregated and integrated placement and the relative importance that they place on each for EMR pupils need to be explored. The regular class teachers who participated in the Gickling and Theobold (1975) study were employed in schools that had not yet practiced mainstreaming. Conceivably, their beliefs might differ from those of teachers who are involved in mainstreaming. In addition, teachers' perceptions of advantages and disadvantages and their relative weightings of importance may differ according to the handicapping condition of the children under consideration. It seems likely, however, that teachers' beliefs about practices that could result in the greatest benefit to EMR children will influence their beliefs about educational placements.

General Educational Attitudes

It has been suggested that regular education teachers are likely to differ from special education teachers in educational attitudes (Greene, 1971), and that regular teachers' educational attitudes are likely to influence their attitudes toward integration (Baker et al., in press). Greene (1971) expected that special education teachers would score higher than regular teachers on a test designed to measure flexibility and progressivism since he believed that an orientation toward change was required of teachers serving exceptional children. However, no support for this expectation was garnered from a study that used the Minnesota Teacher Attitude Inventory to measure the educational attitudes of future special education and elementary education teachers (Greene & Retish, 1973). Furthermore, in Project PRIME (Baker et al., in press) it was found that the mean scores of regular and self-contained special teachers on three measures of educational attitudes (Importance of a Warm, Supportive Environment; Importance of a Structured, Controlled Environment; and

Belief in Traditional Authority) were very similar. Thus, the contention that regular and special teachers differ in educational attitudes is not supported by the results of these studies. Support can be found, however, for the hypothesis that regular teachers' educational attitudes influence attitudes toward integration (Baker et al., in press).

Empirical findings of Project PRIME suggest that regular teachers having certain educational orientations are more likely to be accepting of mainstreaming (Baker et al., in press). In that study, a set consisting of the three educational attitudes in Project PRIME were found to account for a significant amount of variance in each of four measures of attitudes toward integration (Attitude toward Integration of Children with Cognitive Problems, Attitude toward Integration of Children with Social Problems, Appropriateness of Mainstreaming, and Problems Attributed to Mainstreaming). An examination of bivariate correlations between educational attitudes and mainstreaming attitudes revealed that those teachers who rated a structured, controlled environment as being important tended to be negative toward integration and reported having had more problems due to mainstreaming. Similarly, teachers who believed most strongly in traditional authority tended to be less accepting of the integration of handicapped children. These results suggest that regular teachers' educational attitudes may be an additional component of their attitudes toward integration. Specifically, teachers who consider maintaining a high level of structure and control in the classroom, or who strongly believe in traditional authoritarian conceptions of education, are unlikely to favor integration for retarded children.

Having reviewed some of the literature on classroom teachers' attitudes toward mainstreaming retarded children, several points are evident. First, this body of research has produced a series of disjointed studies that has lacked even the slightest semblance of continuity. The research that has been conducted has not been guided by any model that would suggest important variables requiring study. By and large, the literature on teachers' attitudes has focused on general issues, such as whether teachers favored mainstreaming. The literature also touched briefly on the type of children for whom mainstreaming was desirable. A great many questions remain, however. The following section indicates some of the areas where additional study is required.

RESEARCH NEEDS

Research on the attitudes of regular classroom teachers toward EMR children, or any handicapped children, is in its infancy. A number of critical questions that bear directly on mainstreaming efforts and handicapped children have not even begun to be explored. This section raises a number of questions that are presently unanswered.

One line of research questioning concerns the dimensions of teachers' attitudes. As indicated earlier in this chapter, most of the research on teachers' attitudes toward handicapped children has focused on the positive or negative aspects of attitudes. Examination of the general evaluative aspect of attitudes may be necessary to our understanding of teachers, but it is hardly sufficient. A number of other dimensions must be studied including the specificity of the attitude. To what extent are teachers' attitudes influenced by specific situational factors that vary across time and place? For example, is the teacher as equally adamant that a handicapped child should not be mainstreamed for physical education as for social studies? Or is the teacher inimical to mainstreaming handicapped children even after the child was provided with instruction designed to prepare him/her for his/her mainstreaming experience? Attitudes that are invariant across settings may be more recalcitrant to modification, and teachers who possess such attitudes may not make likely candidates to develop a mainstream program.

Another approach to the multidimensional study of teachers' attitudes was developed for general education by Silberman (1969) who identified four kinds of teacher attitudes: attachment, indifference, concern, and rejection. In an extension of Silberman's study, Jenkins (1972) believed that the four attitudes would be reflected by teachers' perceptions of children's behavior, as well as actual differences in the behavior, as recorded by observers. For the most part, Jenkins (1972) observed that children in each of the four attitude groups did not differ significantly in their classroom behavior. Yet, when teachers were asked their perceptions of the children's behavior, their responses indicated discrimination of three of the four attitude groups. Teachers did not differentiate their perceptions of children whom they *rejected* from those about whom they were *concerned,* however.

Jenkins' (1972) findings have important implication for the study of regular classroom teachers' attitudes toward EMR children. The findings suggest that there is not a one-to-one correspondence between the perceptions of teachers and the behavior that children actually exhibit. Therefore, attempts to change the behavior of mentally retarded children in order to make them more acceptable to the teacher may not be effective because the change may not be perceived by the teacher. If the teacher does not perceive behavior change when it does occur, future attempts to change the behavior of mentally retarded children may have to employ as a criterion of success the extent to which others in the environment perceive changes in behavior, not whether outside observers can reliably detect the changes.

Although the case with which teachers' perceptions can be changed is not known, it is known that they relate to the social status of mainstreamed mentally retarded pupils. In a study of 324 mainstreamed EMR children, Gottlieb, Semmel, and Veldman (1978) correlated teachers' perceptions of EMR children's academic competence and misbehavior with peers' sociometric ratings of the EMR children. The responses of approximately 1,200 teachers and 8,000 nonhandicapped pupils were examined to obtain a portrait of the way that the retarded child is viewed by others in his mainstreamed environment. Gottlieb et al. (1978) found that teachers' perceptions of EMR children's academic competence and misbehavior correlated significantly with peers' sociometric responses. In fact, teachers' perceptions of behavior correlated more strongly with sociometric status than peers' perceptions of behavior, even though peers provided the sociometric ratings. Although not definitive, these data suggest that teachers' perceptions of retarded children may exert a powerful influence on their social status in the regular classroom.

In their study of teachers' and peers' perceptions of EMR children, Gottlieb et al. (1978) also found that specific teacher perceptions were significantly correlated with specific aspects of social status. Teachers' perceptions of retarded children's academic competence correlated significantly with the social acceptance; perceptions of misbehavior, on the other hand, correlated most strongly with social rejection. The nature of the significant correlations indicates that future attempts to improve the social status of EMR children may have to pay careful attention to the kind of sociometric improvement that is desired and to the type of behavior displayed by the retarded child that may require change.

Another area requiring study is the behavior that teachers exhibit in their daily interactions with retarded children. Knowing that a classroom teacher harbors negative attitudes tells little about his behavior toward the handicapped child. What kind of behavior do teachers exhibit?

If categories of inappropriate behavior toward handicapped children exhibited by teachers can be identified, their style of interaction with the children may be able to be modified. Although little information regarding teacher behavior toward handicapped children is available, Brophy and Good (1974) suggest a variety of behaviors that may be pertinent. Each of these behaviors of classroom teachers may not only express their feelings about handicapped children; they may also be detected by other students in the class who may then use the information as the basis to form their own impressions of the child. A slightly modified version of the behaviors listed by Brophy and Good (1974) includes:

1. Waiting less time (or more time) for the retarded child to respond to a question

2. Praising marginal or incorrect responses (which accentuate the child's inability to his peers)
3. Criticizing child for a wrong response (which may discourage the retarded child from attempting to answer)
4. Demanding less from retarded child
5. Reprimanding child for an inappropriate behavior to a greater extent than nonhandicapped children are reprimanded
6. Calling on retarded children less frequently than nonhandicapped classmates

Although there are a variety of other behaviors that Brophy and Good (1974) list, the behaviors listed above may be used by the teacher to indicate his feelings toward a mentally retarded child. Each of these behaviors that the teacher exhibits may reinforce the retarded child's feelings of academic inadequacy and may indicate to the child's classmates that he/she is different from them and is to be treated differently.

It is quite possible that many teachers who exhibit one or more of the behaviors listed may not be aware that they behave differently to the retarded child than to the other children. It is equally possible that some of these behaviors may be appropriate instructional strategies (such as praising a marginally correct response of a retarded child who is afraid to take risks). However, the teacher should be made aware that to the extent that he/she treats retarded children differently from the other children, he/she is highlighting this fact to the other children in class. When other children determine that the teacher maintains different standards for acceptable behavior for one child, they may also judge the child by different standards. The children may either reject the retarded child or offer him/her sympathy; neither reaction is likely to enhance the retarded child's self-image.

Yet another area in need of answers is the type of general instructional strategies that the teacher employs when the retarded child is in the regular class. What kind of groups does the teacher plan? With which other children is the retarded child grouped? What kind of educational materials does the teacher employ? Is the retarded child expected to learn from materials that are too infantile for his/her chronological age? Does the teacher have any back-up lessons if the child loses interest or is unable to achieve at an expected level? Does the retarded child share in the classroom rewards, such as being a monitor, collecting books, and so forth? In sum, information describing the everyday experiences that the classroom teacher provides for the mentally retarded child in the class is required.

There is little doubt that the way that a teacher structures the classroom affects the well-being of the retarded child. Teachers who adopt a laissez-faire approach to the mainstreaming of retarded children often witness that the children are rejected by their classmates and generally occupy a grossly inferior position in the social hierarchy of the peer group. On the other hand, teachers who are able to develop structured activities that include the retarded child as an integral member of the classroom group are able to improve the extent to which the retarded child is socially accepted by his nonhandicapped peers. For example, Ballard, Corman, Gottlieb, and Kaufman (1977) reported significant improvement in the social status of mainstreamed EMR children when the regular class teacher was provided inservice training on how to structure minimally academic group work designed to involve the EMR child in a meaningful way. The study conducted by Ballard et al. (1977) was performed in the regular classroom and lasted for approximately 13 weeks, indicating that a teacher who chooses to develop ongoing activities designed to improve the social status of EMR children is likely to succeed. Similar findings were reported by Lilly's (1970) study of children who were poorly accepted.

It must not be forgotten that educators study the attitudes of teachers to gain some insights into the adequacy of educational programming they are apt to provide retarded children in their classes. To date, the study of teachers' affective feelings toward handicapped children has been exclusively concentrated on. It is time that the instructional behavior that teachers display during their everyday performance in class is examined directly.

REFERENCES

Ayres, L. *Laggards in our schools.* New York: Charities Publication Committee, 1909.

Baker, J. L., Safer, N., & Guskin, S. L. Participant Composition. In M. J. Kaufman, J. A. Agard, & M. I. Semmel (Eds.), *Mainstreaming: Learners and their environments.* Baltimore: University Park Press, in press.

Ballard, M., Corman, L., Gottlieb, J., & Kaufman, M. J. Improving the social status of mainstreamed retarded children. *Journal of Educational Psychology,* 1977, *69,* 605-611.

Brophy, J. E., & Good, T. L. *Teacher-student relationships.* New York: Holt, 1974.

Dunn, L. M. Special education for the mildly retarded—Is much of it justifiable? *Exceptional Children,* 1968, *34,* 5-22.

Esten, R. A. Backward children in the public schools. *Journal of Psychoaesthentics,* 1900, *5,* 10-16.

Gampel, D. H., Gottlieb, J., & Harrison, R. H. Comparison of the classroom behavior of special-class EMR, integrated EMR, low IQ, and nonretarded children. *American Journal of Mental Deficiency,* 1974, *79,* 16-21.

Gickling, E. R., & Theobold, J. T. Mainstreaming: Affect or effect. *Journal of Special Education,* 1975, *9,* 317-328.

Gottlieb, J., & Many, M. Special and regular education teachers' attitudes toward mainstreaming. Unpublished manuscript, 1979.

Gottlieb, J., Semmel, M. I., & Veldman, D. J. Correlates of social status among mainstreamed mentally retarded children. *Journal of Educational Psychology,* 1978, *70,* 396-405.

Greene, M. A., & Retish, P. M. A comparative study of attitudes among students in special education and regular education. *Training School Bulletin,* 1973, *70,* 10-14.

Haring, N. G., Stern, G. G., & Cruickshank, W. M. *Attitudes of educators toward exceptional children.* Syracuse: Syracuse University Press, 1958.

Jenkins, B. Teachers' views of particular students and their behavior in the classroom. Unpublished doctoral dissertation, The University of Chicago, 1972.

Kirk, S. A. Research in education. In H. A. Stevens & R. Heber (Eds.), *Mental retardation.* Chicago: The University of Chicago Press, 1964.

Lilly, M. S. Special education: A teapot in a tempest. *Exceptional Children,* 1970, *37,* 43-48.

Mercer, J. R. *Labeling the mentally retarded.* Berkeley: University of California Press, 1973.

Payne, R., & Murray, C. Principals' attitudes toward integration of the handicapped. *Exceptional Children,* 1974, *41,* 123-126.

Shotel, J. R., Iano, R. P., & McGettigan, J. F. Teacher attitudes associated with the integration of handicapped children. *Exceptional Children,* 1972, *38,* 677-683.

Silberman, M. Behavioral expression of teachers' attitudes toward elementary school students. *Journal of Educational Psychology,* 1969, *60,* 402-407.

Siperstein, G. N., & Gottlieb, J. Parents' and teachers' attitudes toward mildly and severely retarded children. *Mental Retardation,* 1978, *16,* 321-322.

CHAPTER 2

Teacher Expectancies and Their Implications for Teaching Retarded Students

Nancy D. Safer

The retarded child is a low academic achiever, by definition. Failure to achieve in academic areas, or failure to achieve at an acceptable rate usually leads to the child's referral, diagnosis, and labeling. Generally, once a child has been identified as retarded, expectancies for his/her rate of cognitive growth and ultimate achievement level are reduced to a level in keeping with the rate of cognitive development he/she has previously demonstrated. Often, however, the child does not even perform at a level, or attain the skills and concepts, that might be anticipated given his/her cognitive stage and rate of development. In the past this has frequently been attributed to inherent defects in the cognitive structures of the retarded—defects so serious that they prevent the retarded individual from performing as well as a normal individual at a similar stage of development (Zigler, 1969).

Some theorists, however, have suggested that the lowered levels of achievement of the retarded student result from social, emotional, or motivational factors in the child's environment (Zigler, 1966, 1969; Mac-

---

This article was written by Nancy D. Safer in her private capacity. No official support or endorsement by the U.S. Office of Education is intended or should be inferred.

Millan, 1971, 1977). An even broader perspective has been taken by writers, such as Dexter (1958) or Bartel and Guskin (1971), who have suggested that handicapping conditions and retardation are social phenomena related to the values of a particular society. According to Dexter (1958), those persons judged mentally defective in most societies are those who fail to learn the "right meanings of events, symbols, or things." Because of this failure they are assigned the role of handicapped or retarded and are treated differently. Bartel and Guskin (1971) point out that the role of handicapped person, like other social roles, carries with it certain role expectations, or expectations of particular behaviors to be found in the role. They suggest that those expectations are transmitted to the handicapped person by other people; thus the handicapped person is initiated into his/her role. In recent years particular attention has been paid to the relationship of teacher expectancies to the achievement and adjustment of handicapped students. Johnson (1962) attributed the poorer achievement of special class retarded students in part to the reduced level of demands that their special class teachers made of them. Several authors (Larsen, 1975; MacMillan, 1977; Yoshida, 1976) have considered the potentially negative effect that the low achievement of the retarded child and the label *mentally retarded* can have on teacher expectancies. Larsen (1975) has even suggested that low or biased expectancies may cause the child to perform at a low level and to be labeled retarded. This chapter considers several questions related to teacher expectancies and/or bias. Specifically, the following questions are examined: What is teacher expectancy and/or bias? How do teacher expectancies and/or bias work, and do teacher expectancies affect student outcomes? Do teachers hold negative or biased expectancies for handicapped students? Can biased teacher behavior be changed? Implications for teachers of the mentally retarded are also discussed.

WHAT IS TEACHER EXPECTANCY AND/OR BIAS?

According to Brophy and Good (1974), teacher expectancies are inferences teachers make about the present and future achievement, abilities, and behavior of their students. Expectancies can be general, pertaining to the entire class or to large subgroupings of the class, or they can be specific, pertaining to individual students. Expectancies are clearly a normal part of human interactions and teaching. Unless a teacher makes some inferences about individual students, or the class as a whole, planning a year's curriculum, ordering materials, or even selecting day-to-day activities becomes impossible. For example, a third grade teacher, when planning for the upcoming year, may expect that most of his/her pupils will be reading at a beginning third grade level, and thus order third grade readers and base the year's activities on that expectancy. Pupil records, conversations with other teachers, or initial interactions with students, may suggest that some students are not reading at a beginning third grade level, so the teacher may order some different materials and plan different activities for those students, based on the levels at which he/she expects them to function. Again, these expectancies are a normal and necessary part of the teaching/planning process. They are the teacher's best guess as to how pupils are going to function during the year.

As might be predicted, sometimes teacher expectancies are wrong. The child who could not learn to read the year before suddenly catches on and moves ahead; the child who could not stay in his/her seat in the past matures over the summer and settles down; the child who is shy and somewhat apprehensive about the new classroom setting becomes accustomed to it and is more relaxed. Theoretically, these changes should not cause a problem. The teacher, acting on new information, can adjust his/her expectancies accordingly. Concern has been expressed in recent years, however, that this adjustment of expectancies does not always occur—that sometimes teachers form initial expectancies that are erroneous and do not change them in light of new, disconfirming information. Instead, they interact with students as if the initial expectancies were accurate and fixed. There are a number of ways this can occur. For some teachers a particular piece of information about a student could be so salient, or could come from a source so "expert" in the teacher's mind, that he/she ignores or discounts contrary behavioral information. Another possibility is that some teachers are not flexible and having once "classified" a child in a certain way simply fail to note changes in the child. In these instances the teacher's expectancies are biased—that is, the teacher's perception of and expectancies for a student or students are not consistent with objective information (Dusek, 1975).

HOW DO TEACHER EXPECTANCIES AND/OR BIAS WORK?

The concern that has been expressed related to biased expectancies is that they may become "self-fulfilling prophecies." This concept, originally suggested by Merton (1957), formed the theoretical basis of the most widely cited teacher expectancy study, conducted by Rosenthal and Jacobson (1968). These researchers attempted to manipulate teacher expectancies by reporting to teachers that certain students, who were actually randomly selected, should "bloom" intellectually during the year. At the end of the school year they found that indeed the "bloomers" showed a significant gain in IQ over the control group. They attributed this gain to the effects of biased teacher expectancies.

The methodology of the Rosenthal and Jacobson study has received much criticism. For example, Claiborn (1969) pointed out that the differences between the experimental and control groups could largely be explained by changes in only one first grade class. Thorndike (1968) questioned the validity of the dependent measure for younger students. Furthermore, attempts to replicate the specific study have been largely unsuccessful (Claiborn, 1969; Dusek & O'Connell, 1973; Fleming & Anttonen, 1971; Jose & Cody, 1971; Kester & Letchworth, 1972; Mendels & Flanders, 1973). Despite this criticism, the concepts of teacher expectancy and teacher bias have generated much interest, and a number of other studies designed to examine specific aspects of expectancy have been carried out. These studies and other writings have suggested some of the ways in which expectancy effects may operate.

Those who argue for teacher expectancy effects make several critical assumptions. They assume that teachers have different expectancies for students they perceive differently, that teachers behave in accordance with their expectancies for different students, that teachers behave differently toward students for whom they have different expectancies, and that these differences in behavior affect students. A fair amount of research has been carried out to examine these assumptions. Brophy and Good (1970) asked first grade teachers to rank their students in terms of achievement and then observed the teachers' behavior toward the high and low ranked students. They found significant differences between the experiences of the high and low ranked students. Teachers favored high ranked students by demanding and reinforcing good performance. High ranked students raised their hands more often, responded more frequently in class, and received more frequent praise following a correct response. Low ranked students, on the other hand, were less likely than the high ranked students to be praised following a correct response and generally received less feedback. Teachers were less persistent in "staying with" the low ranked students to elicit a correct response. Following an incorrect response, teachers would immediately move on to another pupil. This study has been followed up using different schools and different grades. In general, across teachers, the results were not replicated (Brophy & Good, 1974). Great variability was found, however, among teachers. This variability is discussed later in this section.

Work by Silberman (1969) and follow-up studies of that work (Good & Brophy, 1972a) are also pertinent to considerations of teacher behavior toward students for whom they have different expectancies. These studies examined teacher behavior toward students whom the teacher had placed in what the researchers later labeled "attachment," "concern," "indifference," and "rejection" groups. Students in the "attachment" group were generally bright, hard-working students for whom the teacher had high expectations of progress. Students in both the "concern" and "rejection" groups were low achievers from whom the teacher expected low levels of progress. The "rejection" students, however, tended to have behavior problems (mischievous, disruptive behavior) as well as low levels of achievement. "Concern" students, on the other hand, tended to be cooperative (Willis & Brophy, 1974). It was found that "concern" students received more teacher contact, more explicit feedback, and more praise than students in any of the other groups. Teachers tended to carefully monitor these students. "Rejection" students were given fewer response opportunities and received more criticism from the teacher when they did respond. Although "attachment" students were students for whom teachers held high expectancies, and were students preferred by teachers, contrary to the findings of the original Brophy and Good (1970) study, they were not found to receive preferential treatment.

A different aspect of teacher behavior related to expectancies was examined by several studies carried out in tutoring settings (Beez, 1970; Brown, 1969; Rubovits & Maehr, 1971). In these studies, tutors in college teacher training programs were given fake psychological information about children, which they were told predicted either good or poor school performance. The results showed that the tutors tried to teach more concepts to the students for whom they had high expectations than to students for whom they had low expectations for performance, although in actuality the groups did not differ in terms of achievement potential. It was also found that tutor-student interaction was qualitatively more negative with students in the low group.

The results of these studies, taken as a whole, suggest that teachers do have different expectancies for different students and that at least some teachers behave differently toward students for whom they have different expectancies. The specifics related to those differences appear somewhat more complex than was initially suspected. The original Rosenthal and Jacobson study (1968), a number of follow-up studies, and the original work by Brophy and Good (1970) have assumed that where expectancy effects existed, there was a fairly simplistic relationship between teacher expectancies and teacher behavior, with teachers attending more to high ranked students—providing them with more response opportunities, more feedback, and more praise; staying with them longer to elicit a correct response; and attempting to teach them more. Although this was found in the initial Brophy and Good study (1970) and to some extent in the tutoring studies, other studies have not confirmed this relationship. In fact, the Silberman (1969) study and its follow-ups have shown some teachers giving more praise to, monitoring progress more closely of, providing more response opportunities to, and staying longer with low achieving students in the "concern" group than the high achieving students in the "attachment" group. These studies did, however, show low achieving students with behavior problems to receive more criticism and fewer opportunities to respond.

These discrepancies may be explained, in part, by the variability among teachers reported by Brophy and Good (1974). As was previously mentioned, in follow-up studies to their initial first grade study, Brophy and Good found teachers to be highly variable, and found some teachers for whom extreme behavioral differences were observed, favoring students from whom high levels of achievement were expected.

As a result of their observations, Brophy and Good (1974) suggested three types of teachers in terms of expectancies: proactive, reactive, and overreactive. Proactive teachers have accurate and flexible expectancies for their students and use their expectancies to plan an individualized program for these students. Such teachers maintain the initiative in structuring teacher-student interactions. Thus, they might initiate more contacts with low achievers—ask them questions, "stay with" them until they get the correct answers, or monitor their work—to compensate for their greater need for help and for the tendency of high achievers to dominate in the classroom.

According to Brophy and Good (1974), reactive teachers also have accurate and flexible expectations. They do not favor students for whom they have high expectations in teacher initiated teacher-student interactions. On the other hand, they do nothing to compensate for the tendency of high achievers to dominate. For example, they might allow high achievers to call out correct answers, would not particularly solicit responses from low achievers, or, having solicited a response, would not necessarily stay with the student until he/she got the correct response, but would move on. As a result, high achievers would get a higher proportion of praise for correct responses, more opportunities to respond, etc.

Overreactive teachers are teachers who are conditioned by, and even exacerbate, student differences by favoring students for whom they have high expectations and rejecting or giving up easily on poor performers. According to Brophy and Good, such teachers are likely to make overt comments that communicate their low expectations to students. It also seems likely that such teachers might allow their low expectations for certain students to bias their judgment as to how much and what those students were capable of learning, causing them to underestimate the amount and type of material to present to them. The behavior of such teachers, and the expectancies upon which it is based are not consistent with objective information as to how much or what the low achievers are actually capable of learning. Thus, Brophy and Good's (1974) typology would suggest that teachers not only behave differently toward students for whom they have different expectations, but also that teacher behavior may be biased and inappropriate toward students for whom they hold inaccurate, inflexible expectations.

Variations in teacher behavior toward different students are only important, however, if they somehow affect the students. To date, the link between teacher expectancies and student behavior has not really been well established. As was pointed out earlier, results of the Rosenthal and Jacobson (1968) study have been questioned because of the study's methodology and because studies attempting to replicate the study have failed to confirm the results (Claiborn, 1969; Dusek & O'Connell, 1973; Jose & Cody, 1971). Although the tutoring study by Beez (1970) showed that students for whom tutors held high expectations actually learned more, this finding has also been difficult to replicate (MacMillan, 1977).

There may be several reasons why studies have failed to demonstrate the effects of teacher expectancies on student behavior. First, studies have been limited to an examination of the effects of teacher expectancies on intelligence or achievement, although presumably a number of student characteristics such as self-concept, social acceptance, attitude toward school, etc., could be affected. In addition, most studies have relied on artificially created teacher expectancies by providing teachers with false information. Yoshida (1976) has suggested that teachers rely more on their own criteria and actual contact with students in forming expectancies than on contrived statements. He cites several studies (Dusek & O'Connell, 1973; Foster, Ysseldyke, & Reese, 1975; Salvia, Clark, & Ysseldyke, 1973; Yoshida & Meyers, 1975) that support this contention. Yoshida (1976) also stated that the Dusek and O'Connell study shows that students whom teachers rank low in terms of class standing can still make an expected amount of progress in academic studies during the year. Unfortunately, this study did not gather observational data that could be used to show how teachers interacted with students for whom they held lower expectancies. Furthermore, none of the observation studies that have been carried out has looked at student outcomes. Thus, currently no body of research exists that links teacher expectancies to teacher behavior and ultimately to student outcomes.

Research and theory in other areas suggest that differences in teacher behavior related to their expectancies should affect student outcomes. Self-concept theory stresses the role of interpersonal interactions in shaping a child's self-concept and subsequent behavior (Sullivan, 1953). Children who perceive themselves viewed negatively by others will tend to behave inappropriately, thereby promoting both negative self-evaluations and further negative evaluations by others. Self-concept theory also suggests that children with poor academic self-concepts may try to avoid academic situations (McCandless, 1973). Thus, according to these theories, children who perceive that their teachers view them negatively and expect poor performance may incorporate that information into their self-concepts. Behaving in accordance with this negative self-image, they will perform poorly, thus reinforcing both the negative self-concept and the negative teacher expectancy. In addition, such children may begin to withdraw from the academic setting by not paying attention and not participating, or by misbehaving. This theory is consistent with that of Finn (1972) who has explained the teacher expectancy effect by suggesting that self-expectations are determinants of performance and that the child's self-expectations come from knowledge of his/her own abilities plus distortions. Distortions are viewed as coming from the expectations and reactions of others. According to Finn, the child integrates his/her self-concept and the perceptions of others to form a behavior regulating the concept of potential achievement. Thus, when the perception of an important other, such as the teacher, is negative, it can be expected to lower the child's concept of potential achievement and ultimately to lower performance. Since self-concept has not been examined in the teacher expectancy studies that have been carried out to date, its role as a mediator between teacher expectations and student performance remains unexplored. However, it has been shown that some teachers overtly communicate their poor expectations, give more criticism to poorer students, or reject and give up easily on them. It seems reasonable to expect that these behaviors would negatively affect the students' self-concept. Furthermore, past research has found students with poor self-concepts to perform less well academically than students with positive self-concepts (Brookover, Patterson, & Thomas, 1962; Dennerell, 1971; Ruckhaber, 1966).

Several theorists have also considered relationships between student participation, active student learning or opportunity to learn, and student achievement (Bloom, 1971; Carroll, 1962, 1963; Harnischfeger & Wiley, 1976). These theorists generally contend that one determinant of achievement is the amount of time spent in active learning. Similarly, after reviewing the research on teacher behavior/student achievement, Rosenshine and Furst (1971) concluded that student opportunity to learn instructional material was important in determining student achievement. Several of the studies reported in this chapter, however, suggested that some teachers, especially those that Brophy and Good (1974) labeled overreactive favored the high achievers in their interactions, "stayed with" high achievers longer when they did not initially respond correctly to a question, and underestimated the amount "poor students" were capable of learning. This was particularly true for low achievers who tended to misbehave. It seems clear that in such classes poorer students would be actively engaged in academic teacher-student interactions less often (although teachers might be more often engaged in management interactions, especially with students they viewed as behavior problems). It is also clear that students cannot learn what is not presented. Thus, to the degree that the assignments and materials presented to poorer students underestimate their capabilities, those pupils will make slower progress. Both these factors suggest that in the classrooms of some teachers, those teachers Brophy and Good labeled overreactive, poorer students may actually have less opportunity to learn than students for whom teachers hold high expectations.

Further consideration of the literature suggests that for poorer students less opportunity to learn may exist in classes of reactive teachers as well. It should be recalled that the reactive teachers observed by Brophy and Good (1974) did nothing about the tendency of high ranked students to dominate in the classroom. It seems likely, then, that in such classes poorer students would receive less opportunity for active participation and engagement because of the high ranked students' tendency to raise their hands more often, or call out answers. In this instance the failure of the teachers to treat students differentially based on their expectancies for them results in an inappropriate treatment—to be treated equally can be biasing if students are unequal.

Although to date research studies have not been carried out that link teacher expectancies to student outcomes, there is evidence that suggests that at least some teachers treat students for whom they hold different expectancies differently. Furthermore, there is reason to believe differential teacher behaviors may sometimes result in lower self-concepts for students for whom low expectancies are held and in differential opportunities to learn. Clearly there is a need for further research to examine the links between teacher expectancies, teacher behaviors, and student outcomes. At the same time, the research that has been carried out to date would seem to have particular relevance and implications for teachers of handicapped students. The following sections consider those implications.

DO TEACHERS HOLD NEGATIVE OR BIASED EXPECTANCIES FOR HANDICAPPED STUDENTS?

The previous section suggests that some teachers behave differently toward pupils for whom they hold different expectancies and that there is reason to believe those differences in behavior can adversely affect the students for whom negative expectancies are held. There has been much speculation as to what factors lead to different expectancies for various students. Larsen (1975), for example, states that ethnicity, sex, social class, physical attractiveness, neatness, and language characteristics can all influence teacher expectancies. As cited previously, the Willis and Brophy (1974) study showed student behavior or misbehavior to be related to teacher expectancies and teacher behavior. In addition there has been concern about the potentially negative effects that a handicapping condition might have on teacher expectancies.

Because students with handicapping conditions generally arrive pre-certified and pre-labeled as having some sort of deficiency, there has been concern that their teachers would have inappropriately low expectations. Several studies have been designed to examine the specific effect of a handicapped label on teacher expectancies. In two related studies, videotapes of normal children who were either described as normal, gifted, mentally retarded (Salvia, Clark, & Ysseldyke, 1973), or emotionally disturbed (Foster, Ysseldyke, & Reese, 1975) were shown to teacher education students. It was found that teachers rated the same children significantly lower when they were labeled handicapped than when they were described as normal or gifted. Teachers did tend to revise their expectancies for the "handicapped" students upward after actually watching the children engaged in various tasks, but the children described as nonhandicapped were still rated significantly more favorably. Yoshida and Meyers (1975), on the other hand, found no differences in predictions that teachers made for the future achievement of an elementary school child in concept formation after viewing a videotape of the child presented sometimes as a sixth grader and sometimes as an educable mentally retarded (EMR) student. In both conditions teachers revised their predictions upward during a sequence of trials in which the student's correct responses increased, indicating a sensitivity to changes in student behavior. Yoshida (1976) suggested that the results from this study, as well as the Foster et al. (1975) study, indicate that teachers do not allow the negative expectancies they may have for labeled handicapped children to block their ability to perceive the progress and achievement those children make, as some special educators have feared. It must be recalled, however, that the Foster et al. (1975) and the Salvia et al. (1973) studies still found the same child rated lower when labeled handicapped, even after the child's performance was viewed for a period of time. Thus, it may be that while teachers do perceive the progress and gains made by labeled handicapped children, their initial expectancies are sometimes biased and lower than warranted by the child's capability as a function of the label. Furthermore, subsequent performance may not eliminate this discrepancy entirely, although it may close the gap somewhat. Thus, although the teacher may expect the handicapped child to achieve and learn, he/she may not expect the child to achieve at the level or rate at which the child is actually capable of achieving.

A series of curriculum studies support the contention that the general expectancies teachers hold for the academic achievement of handicapped students may be more negative than the expectancies they hold for normal students and lower than is warranted by their ability level. Fine (1967) found that elementary special education teachers placed greater emphasis on personal and social adjustment and less emphasis on academic achievement than did regular elementary teachers. This would be consistent with a belief that handicapped students can make only limited academic progress, although in actuality most handicapped students could be expected to achieve some level of success in most academic areas. Schmidt and Nelson (1969) found the emphasis on affective rather than cognitive goals among secondary special education teachers as well.

Meyen and Hieronymus (1970) investigated the relative importance of certain academic skills in the curriculum for EMR students and the age at which students should be expected to achieve those skills. They presented a group of special class teachers with lists of operationally defined skills. The teachers were asked to estimate the age at which instruction in each skill should be initiated as well as its importance in the curriculum for the EMR child. EMR and normal children were also tested to determine the age at which these skills were actually attained.

The results showed that the EMR group performed within 5 years of the normal students on only 42 of 204 items. The judges suggested the initiation of instruction for most of the skills in the 11- to 14-year-old category, and EMR students achieved these skills between the ages of 12 and 15. The normal students, on the other hand, demonstrated success on most of the skills by the age of 8. Meyen and Hieronymus wrote that the lateness of the ages suggested for initiating instruction in these skills with EMR pupils reflects the typical special education philosophy that academic skills should be taught later to EMR students than to normal students. While this practice makes sense in terms of the slower rate of cognitive growth of retarded students, the observed developmental lag between the performance of EMR and normal students was too great to be explained solely by intellectual ability. These authors argued that if 80% of normal 8-year-olds demonstrate mastery of a skill, the same skill should be able to be learned by the EMR child at age 10 or 11. Thus, the late age recommended for initiating instruction with EMR students may be a determining factor in the greater than expected developmental lag.

Heintz (1974) asked special class teachers to estimate the ultimate reading level for described EMR students. He found that 20% of the teachers estimated that EMR pupils would reach no higher than a second grade level, and only one-third of the teachers expected EMR students to reach a fifth grade reading level or higher. He pointed out that the average EMR child would have a mental age between 10 and 12 years around the age of 16. Few teachers, however, expected the EMR pupils to be reading at a level commensurate with their mental age.

The studies reviewed in this section provide some evidence that a handicapped label, especially the label of mentally retarded, may cause teachers to form expectancies that are lower than either the observed performance (in the videotape studies) or the theoretical mental ages (in several of the curriculum studies) would warrant. The curriculum studies also suggest that the negative expectancies for retarded students may be generalized expectancies, related to all retarded students, rather than specific expectancies for single students. These generalized expectancies would appear to result in an emphasis on affective rather than cognitive goals in programs for the retarded, as well as in skills and concepts being introduced in the curriculum at a later cognitive stage for retarded rather than normal students. Thus, it would seem that teacher expectancies for the handicapped, particularly the retarded, may be said to be biased in the sense that they are inappropriately low. There is no evidence, however, that teacher expectancies for handicapped students are so biased that they preclude the teacher's perceiving the progress or achievement the child does make.

CAN BIASED TEACHER BEHAVIOR BE CHANGED?

Before considering whether biased teacher behavior can be changed, it is necessary to consider reasons why teachers treat students differently on the basis of their expectancies.

Brophy and Good (1974) suggest that teachers are unconsciously treating students for whom they hold different expectancies differently. They point out that the classroom is a busy place with such a rapidly paced sequence of action that teachers find it difficult to keep up, much less monitor, their teaching behaviors. This has been confirmed in a study by Martin and Keller (1976) in which teacher interactions with students were observed and recorded. Teachers were then asked to estimate the frequency with which various types of interactions occurred. This study found significant discrepancies between observed behaviors and teacher estimates concerning their interactions with students. Martin and Keller attributed the lack of teacher awareness to the bustling classroom environment, to the lack of good classroom feedback procedures, and to the fact that teachers do not have a conceptual framework to facilitate consideration of teacher-student interaction patterns.

Brophy and Good (1974) also raise the possibility that teachers are not conscious of treating students differently because they attribute student learning, or at least failure to learn, to characteristics of the student rather than to their own teaching behavior. The research related to this point is somewhat mixed. Some of the studies cited by Brophy and Good show that teachers attribute successful learning to teaching performance, but attribute failure to learn to student characteristics. This finding has been related to ego defensiveness on the part of the teachers, or a desire to rationalize learning failure. Other studies (Ames & Ames, 1973; Beckman, 1972) have shown teachers to explain both success and failure in terms of student variables. In either case, it seems clear that teachers who do not feel teaching behavior is related to the failure of students to learn would not particularly monitor that behavior or focus upon it as a potential cause of low student achievement.

Teacher expectancies for handicapped students that are lower than the level at which the students are actually capable of performing may stem from the knowledge that the student has been labeled handicapped, and thus judged deficient in some way, and from the lack of norms by which to judge the progress of handicapped students. Regarding the first point, the fact that handicapped students, particularly retarded students, have been referred, presumably because of learning problems, for special education screening and have been tested, diagnosed, and labeled, may lead to teacher uncertainty as to whether those students can learn at all, what they are capable of learning, and what rate of progress to expect. This may be especially true of regular class teachers, most of whom do not feel equipped to teach retarded students, even with special education assistance (Shotel, Iano, & McGettigan, 1972). Johnson (1962), however, suggested that special education teachers also tend to assume that retarded students fail to perform at expected levels "because" they are retarded, even though expectancies for achievement have already been lowered to account for slower mental development.

Even when teachers do expect the handicapped to learn, developing accurate expectancies in relation to the child's capabilities may prove to be a problem. Regular class teachers dealing with nonhandicapped students generally have grade level norms that guide them in forming expectancies for students. Thus, when a child seems to learn at an average rate, they can predict fairly accurately where that child will be at given points during the year. When children learn slightly faster, or more slowly than average, the teacher still simply has to revise the grade norms slightly upward or downward. When a child's rate of learning is highly discrepant, however, teachers may be less able to predict what skills the child will be learning at any point in time, or the rate at which those skills will be acquired. In a recent study, experienced special education teachers reported learning to project accurate annual goals and short-term objectives for handicapped students to be the most difficult aspect of program planning for those students (Safer, Lewis, Morrissey, & Kaufman, 1978). Furthermore, they stated that those skills could not really be taught, but had to develop from experience. Until the teacher has developed those skills, he/she may well be setting goals that are too low for a child, but failing to realize it, or he/she is setting goals that are too high and is attributing the child's failure to reach those goals to the handicapping condition.

One guide that has often been suggested, particularly in setting goals and assessing progress of retarded students, has been the mental age of the student. The assumption is that retarded students can be expected to achieve the same skills and concepts as normal students of the same mental age. Although Heintz (1974) cites studies that have found most mentally retarded students able to achieve the same level of success in academic areas as normal students of the same mental age, there is other evidence that suggests mental age is at best a rough guide to forming appropriate expectancies for retarded students.

First, as Heintz points out, a number of other studies have found retarded students not achieving at a level equal to that of nonhandicapped peers of the same mental age. Furthermore, because the mental age is generally derived using an IQ plus the child's chronological age, the mental age estimate can only be as accurate as the intelligence test itself. In recent years there has been considerable controversy as to how appropriate standard intelligence tests are for minority group students and students from low socioeconomic groups. To the degree that the IQ underestimates the ability of children from these groups, so too will the mental age. Thus, a teacher who uses the mental age as a basis for forming expectancies for minority group students may be underestimating the capabilities of those students.

Mental age can also be an overestimate of a student's capabilities at a particular point in time when other factors interfere. In recent years Zigler (1966, 1969) and MacMillan (1971, 1977) have suggested that certain social-emotional and motivational factors, which stem from the retarded child's history of failure, can prevent that child from achieving at a level he/she is theoretically capable of achieving. These factors include: a generalized expectancy for failure, and resultant behavior designed to avoid failure rather than to achieve success; "settling for" a lower degree of success; feelings of chronic ineffectiveness (from the theory of White, 1959) and a reduced level of motivation to explore and master the environment; and an outer-directed problem-solving style in which the child relies on external and often irrelevant cues in problem solving situations rather than on his/her own cognitive resources. Teachers not cognizant of such factors may form expectancies for retarded students consistent with their theoretical mental ages and attempt to teach at that level; then, when student learning does not match the expected learning, teachers permanently reduce their expectancies for those students. The reduced expectancies may match the level at which those students are operating but may be lower than the level that the students are capable of attaining if the teacher deals with the social-emotional, motivational factors. In any case, it seems clear that there are times when mental age is an overestimate of the retarded child's current capabilities, and thus fails to provide teachers with an estimate of what skills the child will learn and when he/she will learn them.

Without even a rough guide such as mental age, teachers, particularly inexperienced teachers, may tend to form expectancies for retarded students that are inadvertently inappropriate or biased. Furthermore, the same factors that led to the initial inappropriate expectancies may prevent teachers from perceiving that those expectancies are inappropriate and from revising them sufficiently. Thus, the lack of appropriate norms for handicapped students may result in inappropriate expectancies for those students which are difficult to detect and which thus become perpetuated.

At this writing, only a little work has been done that has attempted to change biased teacher behavior or expectancies. Good and Brophy (1972b) observed teacher-student interactions, then in a single interview, provided teachers with specific information showing students with whom they had very low rates of interaction, and students with whom they tended not to persist and provide a second response opportunity following failure on a first attempt. The researchers made recommendations as to how teachers might change their interaction patterns, then continued to observe in the classrooms of those teachers. The results showed significant changes in teacher behavior following the interview. Teachers "stayed with" the target students following failure and increased their interactions with low participation students. In both instances, following very specific feedback regarding their interaction with specific students, teachers were able to achieve parity among their high and low participation students, at least in terms of these types of teacher-student interactions. Good and Brophy (1972b) concluded that when provided specific feedback, teachers were able and eager to change their interaction pattern.

Although concern has been expressed regarding biased teacher expectations and behaviors related to handicapped students (Larsen, 1975), to date no study has been carried out that has attempted to change those expectancies and behaviors. The section that follows, however, considers the implications of the work that has been presented and makes suggestions for teachers of the retarded.

IMPLICATIONS FOR TEACHERS OF THE MENTALLY RETARDED

The work that has been presented would seem to have several implications for teachers of the mentally retarded.

First, the work of Brophy and Good (1974) suggests that some teachers have accurate expectancies for their students and use those expectancies to create a more appropriate environment for low achievers. It might be well for placement committees to consider placing retarded students with such proactive teachers. Other teachers, those Brophy and Good described as reactive, may unconsciously create classroom environments that are inappropriate for low achievers or retarded students. It may be necessary to work with those teachers to help them become proactive. This can be done in several ways. Observers, possibly resource or diagnostic/prescriptive teachers, could observe teachers using an objective observation schedule. They could then help those teachers become aware of any inappropriate behaviors they may have. Brophy and Good reported that teachers are generally willing and anxious to change inappropriate teaching behavior once they are made aware of it. They also suggested a deliberate and tactful strategy for working with teachers in this area. This includes collecting data, identifying explicit problems from the data, locating contrast children with whom the teacher is already interacting appropriately, allowing teachers to explain differences in behavior, suggesting changes in behavior, agreeing on explicit treatment behaviors, and reobserving in the classroom.

For those teachers who overtly exacerbate differences among students by treating high expectancy students preferentially, or for those who tend to have inaccurate or inflexible expectancies regarding low achieving students, a more direct approach may be necessary. For example, it may be necessary to point out to the teacher the potential effects of overt biased comments and to explore with the teacher underlying assumptions and feelings related to low achievers. Does the teacher feel the inability of low achievers to meet certain criteria calls into question the teacher's competency? Does the teacher simply assume that some students, such as mentally retarded students or minority group students cannot learn much anyway and therefore focus on the students he/she feels to be more able? Are there characteristics of certain students that have unpleasant associations for the teacher? In some instances talking about the feelings or assumptions may help the teacher deal more appropriately with the student. In other instances it may be better to place low achieving or retarded students in a more responsive classroom.

The work by Ysseldyke and associates (Foster et al., 1975; Salvia et al., 1973) and the curriculum studies show that teachers may have a generalized expectancy for retarded students that is lower than would be expected on the basis of mental age. It was suggested that the fact that the child was retarded, whether because of the connotative image of the label or because of past experiences with retarded students, may serve as an explanation for poor performance and cause teachers to accept a lower level of achievement than might seem appropriate or even to accept no achievement at all. Zigler (1969) has suggested that sometimes we become so overwhelmed by the cognitive inadequacies of the retarded child that we assert the child is retarded because he/she is retarded. That is, we use slower mental development as a basis for labeling a child retarded and reducing our expectancies for him/her somewhat, then turn around and explain the child's failure to progress at even the slower and presumably appropriate rate on the basis that he/she is retarded.

A simplistic solution to this quandary is to state that teachers should expect more of retarded students. However, as was pointed out above, there may be numerous reasons why a retarded student fails to progress at a reasonable rate. What may be a better approach is to never reduce expectancies for a nonprogressing retarded student below those that can be expected from his/her rate of mental development simply because the student is retarded. The fact that the child is retarded has already been accounted for by projecting a slower rate of mental development and labeling the child. Thus, teachers should only further lower their expectancies as part of a deliberate hypothesis-testing, decision-making process. Perhaps the child failed to pick up certain prerequisite skills and the teacher needs to drop back a few levels and teach these skills. Perhaps the child's past failure experiences have led him/her to settle for lower levels of success in order to avoid failure or to rely on an outer-directed problem-solving style. The teacher may wish to lower expectancies for progress in order to deal directly with these factors. For example, the teacher may present the student with somewhat easier tasks than he/she is capable of or may present new skills and concepts at a slower pace to provide the child with more success experiences and to reduce his/her expectancy for failure. However, the decision to reduce expectancies should be deliberate and the level of expectancies should again be raised as soon as gains in performance are observed.

An additional problem discussed in the previous section was one of determining appropriate goals and objectives for low achieving and retarded students. Although teachers report that they become more accurate in determining appropriate expectancies with experience, the lack of norms still makes this task difficult. There are problems in using mental age as a guide for planning instruction. Still, mental age may be the best guide currently available. Using the mental age, the teacher can at least consider the skills and concepts nonhandicapped students learn at that same cognitive level. If the child is achieving at a lower level, that can serve as a clue that too little is being expected of the child, and a deliberative search for factors that may be causing the lower level of achievement can be commenced. Should the child be achieving at the expected mental age level, however, it cannot be assumed that the level of expectancy is appropriate. Several reasons are given as to why mental age can be an underestimate of the child's ability. The teacher should still be constantly probing to determine whether the child can do more.

Teachers can also use sequences of objectives that are commercially available for various skills to help determine appropriate expectancies for a child. Once it is determined where a child is in a sequence, it can be determined what skills should be presented next, although in some instances the teacher may need to break skills into more discrete components. Although sequences of objectives may not provide much guidance in determining the rate at which to expect the child to progress, there are some indications that experience with different children over a period of time ultimately leads to a better accuracy in determining rate of progress.

Special problems related to appropriate expectancies can arise when the retarded child is placed in a regular classroom. The regular teacher may assume, through lack of experience, that retarded students can learn very little, or that the curriculum and teaching methods for handicapped students are drastically different from those of the regular classroom. It is important for special educators to work with these teachers to help them develop an accurate sense of what and how quickly the retarded child can be expected to learn, as well as how they can use the knowledge they already have concerning the development of various academic skills to teach these skills to retarded students.

SUMMARY

The studies that are reviewed in this chapter attest to the great amount of interest, in recent years, in teacher expectancy effects. Despite this high level of interest, sensitive reviews by MacMillan, Jones, and Aloia (1974) and Yoshida (1976) have pointed out that there is much more that needs to be learned, particularly in terms of the interaction between teacher expectancy effects and the label *mentally retarded*.

At the same time, the research that has been carried out suggests that teachers do have different expectancies for different students, that at least some teachers behave differently toward students on the basis of those expectancies, and that there is reason to believe that those differences in teacher behavior can affect student outcomes (both positively and negatively). Whether or not the retarded child is labeled, it seems reasonable to assume he/she will be low achieving in relation to his/her nonhandicapped peers. After all, it is generally the child's low achievement that leads to initial referral for diagnosis. Thus, it does not seem necessary to await further research results to at least sensitize teachers of retarded students to the potential effects that expectancy can have on teacher behavior and presumably on student outcomes or to suggest the adoption of some of the deliberate strategies that have been offered in this chapter.

REFERENCES

Ames, C., & Ames, R. Teachers' attributions of responsibility for student success and failure following informational feedback: A field verification. Paper presented at the annual meeting of the American Educational Research Association, New Orleans, 1973.

Bartel, N., & Guskin, S. A handicap as a social phenomenon. In W. M. Cruickshank (Ed.), *Psychology of exceptional children and youth*. Englewood Cliffs, N.J.: Prentice-Hall, 1971.

Beckman, L. Teachers' and observers' perception of causality for a child's performance. Final report, Grant No. OEG-9-70-0065-0-I-031, HEW, Office of Education, 1972.

Beez, W. Influence of biased psychological reports on teacher behavior and pupil performance. In M. Miles & W. Charters, Jr. (Eds.), *Learning and social settings: New readings in the social psychology of education*. Boston: Allyn and Bacon, 1970.

Bloom, B. Learning for mastery. In B. Bloom, J. Hastings, & G. Madaus (Eds.), *Handbook on formative and summative evaluation of student learning*. New York: McGraw-Hill, 1971.

Brookover, W., Patterson, A., & Thomas, S. *The relationship of self image to achievement in junior high school students*. (U.S. Office of Education, Cooperative Research Project No. 845.) East Lansing: Michigan State University, College of Education, 1962.

Brophy, J., & Good, T. Teacher's communication of differential expectations for children's classroom performance: Some behavioral data. *Journal of Educational Psychology*, 1970, *61*, 365–374.

Brophy, J., & Good, T. *Teacher-student relationships: Causes and consequences*. New York: Holt, 1974.

Brown, W. The influence of student information on the formulation of teacher expectancy. (Doctoral dissertation, Indiana University, 1969.) *Dissertation Abstracts International*, 1969.

Carroll, J. The prediction of success in intensive foreign language training. In R. Glaser (Ed.), *Training research and education*. Pittsburgh: University of Pittsburgh Press, 1962.

Carroll, J. A model for school learning. *Teachers College Record*, 1963, *64*, 723–733.

Claiborn, W. Expectancy effects in the classroom: A failure to replicate. *Journal of Educational Psychology*, 1969, *60*, 377–383.

Dennerell, D. *Dimensions of self-concept of later elementary children in relationship to reading performance, sex role, and socioeconomic status*. Unpublished doctoral dissertation, University of Michigan, 1971.

Dexter, L. A social theory of mental deficiency. *American Journal of Mental Deficiency,* 1958, *62,* 920-928.

Dusek, J. Do teachers bias children's learning? *Review of Educational Research,* 1975, *45,* 661-684.

Dusek, J., & O'Connell, E. Teacher expectancy effects on the achievement test performance of elementary school children. *Journal of Educational Psychology,* 1973, *65,* 371-377.

Fine, M. Attitudes of regular and special class teachers toward the educable mentally retarded child. *Exceptional Children,* 1967, *33,* 429-430.

Finn, J. Expectations and the educational environment. *Review of Educational Research,* 1972, *42,* 387-410.

Fleming, E., & Anttonen, R. Teacher expectancy as related to the academic and personal growth of primary-age children. *Monographs of the Society for Research in Child Development,* 1971, *36,* (5, No. 145).

Foster, G., Ysseldyke, J., & Reese, J. "I wouldn't have seen it if I hadn't believed." *Exceptional Children,* 1975, *41,* 469-473.

Good, T., & Brophy, J. Behavioral expression of teacher attitudes. *Journal of Educational Psychology,* 1972, *63,* 617-624.(a)

Good, T., & Brophy, J. *Changing teacher and student behavior: An empirical investigation* (Tech. Rep. 58). Columbia: Center for Research in Social Behavior, University of Missouri at Columbia, 1972.(b)

Harnischfeger, A., & Wiley, D. The teaching learning process in elementary schools: A synoptic view. *Curriculum Inquiry,* 1976, *6,* 5-43.

Heintz, P. Teacher expectancy for academic achievement. *Mental Retardation,* 1974, *12,* 24-27.

Johnson, G. Special education for the handicapped—A paradox. *Exceptional Children,* 1962, *29,* 62-69.

Jose, J., & Cody, J. Teacher-pupil interaction as it relates to attempted changes in teacher expectancy of academic ability and achievement. *American Educational Research Journal,* 1971, *8,* 39-49.

Kester, S., & Letchworth, G. Communication of teacher expectations and their effects on achievement and attitudes of secondary school students. *Journal of Educational Research,* 1972, *66,* 51-55.

Larsen, S. The influence of teacher expectations on the school performance of handicapped children. *Focus on Exceptional Children,* 1975, *8,* 1-16.

MacMillan, D. The problem of motivation in the education of the retarded. *Exceptional Children,* 1971, *37,* 579-585.

MacMillan, D. *Mental retardation in school and society.* Boston: Little, Brown, 1977.

MacMillan, D., Jones, R., & Aloia, G. The mentally retarded label: A theoretical analysis and review of research. *American Journal of Mental Deficiency,* 1974, *79,* 241-261.

Martin, R., & Keller, A. Teacher awareness of classroom dyadic interactions. *Journal of School Psychology,* 1976, *14,* 47-55.

McCandless, B. *Children and youth: Behavior and development.* New York: Dryden Press, 1973.

Mendels, G., & Flanders, J. Teacher expectations and pupil performance. *American Educational Research Journal,* 1973, *10,* 203-212.

Merton, R. *Social theory and social structure.* Glencoe, Ill.: Free Press, 1957.

Meyen, E., & Hieronymus, A. The age placement of academic skills in curriculum for the EMR. *Exceptional Children,* 1970, *36,* 333-339.

Rosenshine, B., & Furst, N. Research on teacher performance criteria. In B. O. Smith (Ed.), *Research in teacher education: A symposium.* Englewood Cliffs, N.J.: Prentice-Hall, 1971.

Rosenthal, R., & Jacobson, L. *Pygmalion in the classroom: Teacher expectancy and pupil's intellectual development.* New York: Holt, 1968.

Rubovits, P., & Maehr, M. Pygmalion analyzed: Toward an explanation of the Rosenthal-Jacobson findings. *Journal of Personality and Social Psychology,* 1971, *19,* 197-203.

Ruckhaber, C. Differences and patterns of performance of low achieving and high achieving intellectually able fourth-grade boys. (Unpublished doctoral dissertation, University of Michigan), *Dissertation Abstracts International,* 1966.

Safer, N., Lewis, L., Morrissey, P., & Kaufman, M. Implementation of IEP's: New teacher roles and requisite support systems. *Focus on Exceptional Children,* 1978, *10,* 1-20.

Salvia, J., Clark, G., & Ysseldyke, J. Teacher retention of stereotypes of exceptionality. *Exceptional Children,* 1973, *39,* 651-652.

Schmidt, L., & Nelson, C. The affective/cognitive attitude dimension of teachers of EMR minors. *Exceptional Children,* 1969, *35,* 695-701.

Shotel, J., Iano, R., & McGettigan, J. Teacher attitudes associated with the integration of handicapped children. *Exceptional Children,* 1972, *38,* 677-683.

Silberman, M. Behavioral expression of teacher's attitudes toward elementary school students. *Journal of Educational Psychology,* 1969, *60,* 402-407.

Sullivan, H. *The interpersonal theory of psychiatry.* New York: Norton, 1953.

Thorndike, R. Review of Robert Rosenthal and Lenore Jacobson, Pygmalion in the classroom. *American Educational Research Journal,* 1968, *5,* 708-711.

White, R. Motivation reconsidered: The concept of competence. *Psychological Review,* 1959, *66,* 293-333.

Willis, S., & Brophy, J. The origins of teachers' attitudes towards young children. *Journal of Educational Psychology,* 1974, *66,* 520-529.

Yoshida, R. Point, counterpoint: An evaluation of the teacher expectancy variable for the mildly retarded. Unpublished manuscript, 1976. Available from R. Yoshida, Program Support Branch, Bureau of Education for the Handicapped, 400 Maryland Ave., S.W., Washington, D.C., 20202.

Yoshida, R., & Meyers, C. Effects of labeling as EMR on teachers' expectancies for change in a student's performance. *Journal of Educational Psychology,* 1975, *67,* 521-527.

Zigler, E. Personality structure in the retardate. In N. Ellis (Ed.), *International review of research in mental retardation* (Vol. I). New York: Academic Press, 1966.

Zigler, E. Developmental vs. difference theories of mental retardation and the problem of motivation. *American Journal of Mental Deficiency,* 1969, *73,* 536-555.

II

Methodological Considerations in Evaluating Mainstream Programs

CHAPTER 3

Evaluating Programs for Educating Mentally Retarded Persons
Changing Paradigms

Fred A. Crowell

PROBLEMS AND PARADIGMS

> When it is demanded that problems be forced to fit methods, rather than vice versa, then the need for a paradigm shift is patently clear.
>
> Marcia Guttentag
"Evaluation and Society"

During the past decade, there have been dramatic changes in approaches to providing services and residential care for retarded persons as a consequence of applying the principle of normalization. This trend from institutional care to community-based care and the least restrictive alternative is the first stage in an effort to improve the quality of life of retarded persons. The second stage in this effort is the design, implementation, and evaluation of mainstreaming programs for educating handicapped persons.

The evaluation of these programs is perhaps more critical than most professionals would admit. Their concept of what evaluation activities entail, or could entail, has been shaped by a traditional set of assumptions that limits the scope of evaluation activities. These constraining assumptions are a potential source of political, methodological, and communication problems in an organization's attempt to provide educational and training services for handicapped persons.

The set of constraining assumptions constitutes a *paradigm*. Paradigms usually simplify and make things more manageable for those who adopt and use them. The concept of a paradigm has been used in at least 27 different ways by writers in a number of disciplines (Masterman, 1970). Thomas Kuhn (1962), perhaps the most widely quoted of this group, used paradigm to refer to the set of assumptions, exemplars, and techniques common to a community of scientists. A similar but more general usage is proposed by Maruyama (1974) to refer to the logic and the set of epistemological assumptions that may vary across cultures, professions, and individuals.

This chapter examines the problems and paradigms of evaluations within human services and provides a rationale for a needed shift from a dominant epistomology or paradigm to a multiple perspective paradigm. The arguments presented are designed to broaden the reader's conceptions to accept the view that there are:

1. Other ways of evaluating programs than those methods that are now being used
2. Alternative means to represent problems to give rise to the need for evaluation
3. Alternative sets of assumptions, each of which may identify potentially different problems
4. Limits to the number or kinds of problems one can solve, to the patterns one can detect, and, in short, to what one can know

Epistemological assumptions place limits upon what can be known and how to go about generating data. Persons, whether they are parents, teachers, service providers, researchers, or program evaluators, operating with these assumptions are bound to solve some problems while creating others. Even the boundaries of what constitutes a problem are defined by paradigmatic assumptions.

In other words, our images of the world are limited. We cannot solve all the problems. We may choose to solve a certain class of problems by generating specialists, such as evaluators, or we may choose to focus upon other problems and produce solutions in which evaluators are no longer necessary. I believe that we have already made our choice for the former condition. This chapter explores the direction in which this choice is leading us within the dominant paradigm, as opposed to the alternative directions that might emerge as a consequence of a major paradigm shift.

PROGRAM EVALUATION: THE DOMINANT PARADIGM

> ...I would like to reiterate a commitment to randomized experiments wherever possible as the most appropriate means for program evaluation.
>
> Paul Wortman
> *The Evaluation of Social Programs*

What is the dominant paradigm, and why is it dominant? A complete response to this question lies beyond the scope of this chapter. It is necessary, however, to construct an image sufficient for the reader to appreciate the problem posed and some of the major implications of the argument for a paradigm shift. The assumptions and logical structures that characterize evaluators or researchers operating within the dominant paradigm can best be viewed from the perspective of the individuals themselves:

> ...evaluation is always undertaken with reference to some intentional action that is designed to influence one or more people, change personal/social relationships, or alter a material situation.... *Evaluation* is the measurement of desirable and undesirable consequences of the action *designed to achieve some objective that the actor values* (Riecken, 1977, p. 394, italics mine).

The perspective of the actor (service provider) is seen as superior and dominant over the perspectives of the target audience for whom the program is designed.

Also within the framework of the dominant paradigm:

> A key issue is whether social programs must necessarily undergo continual change while an evaluation is being conducted. Program administrators who desire an effective evaluation of their program must learn to consider the needs or requirements for effective evaluation research as well as the needs or pressures for changing their program (Apsler, 1977, p. 15).

The assumption, in other words, is that the evaluator can only make sense out of a world that fits his/her model and procedures, i.e., a world that is simplified and stands still long enough to pinpoint "reasons for any observed changes in outcome" (Apsler, 1977, p. 15). The program administrator in this situation obviously must accommodate the needs of the evaluator and in the process relinquish control over program changes that might otherwise occur as a result of evaluative data.

The source of such assumptions in evaluation can be traced to numerous claims within the research context. One statement may be used to illustrate: "...A scientific analysis of retardation demands tightly controlled experiments, artificial unconfounding of variables, and simplified situations to allow study of isolated processes" (House, 1977, p. 541).

In their quest to gain scientific respectability, educational researchers and evaluators have emulated researchers in the physical sciences. The quantitative, experimental methodology of the physical scientist provided an appealing model for the social sciences, adopted first by psychologists and then by educational researchers. In describing this emulating process, Patton (1975) has referred to the dominance of the scientific paradigm.

> The paradigm, which I refer to in this paper as *The* Scientific Method derives from and is based on the natural science model. Over time it has emerged and has been legimated as the only path to cumulative knowledge (p. 1).

The power of a paradigm to dominate current thought and practice is illustrated succinctly in the title of the recently formed professional group for evaluators, the Evaluation Research Society, founded October 16, 1976. In the organization's initial newsletter, Lee Cronbach (1977) has pointed out this dominance to the new members:

> Evaluation, in the most prestigious writings, is defined as a scientific activity. The fashionable synecdoche has everyone referring to "evaluation research." This has unfortunate consequences; it leads us to ignore significant aspects of our job and to adopt false criteria of excellence.
> ...if evaluation is not primarily a scientific activity, what is it? It is first and foremost a political activity, a function performed within a social system (p. 1).

This distinction between evaluation and research is reinforced by Guttentag (1977a) who points out the strength and weakness of the experimental paradigm in evaluation contexts:

> A paradigm is an overall model that encompasses all evaluations, and is a way of structuring the conceptual and methodological steps in any evaluation (p. 18). ...if one takes the experimental method as an overall method for evaluation, then the consequences are that a great many programs cannot be evaluated because they do not conform to the essential requirements for the use of the experimental method (p. 19).

In summary, the dominant paradigm can be characterized as an inquiry approach shared by a community of inquirers who advocate *experimental* methods, *cause-effect* relationships, *intersubjectivity* of data, *quantitative* rather than qualitative data, and an emphasis upon *data quality* within a *single* perspective.

However, the dominant paradigm does have its critics and opponents, who focus upon the needs of multiple data users. Their advocacy for a stress upon multiple perspectives, discussed further in the next section, has been expressed in the following:

> Evaluations of programs should not be restricted to measuring only program or client outcomes, with or without control group comparisons. Measures of program accessibility, continuity, and comprehensiveness are also

critical. That is to say, evaluating a program is more than merely evaluating the outcomes for the program's clients. The need to go beyond simple outcomes is due to the fact that there are many different perspectives on what constitutes a good or effective children's program. These perspectives include those of professional service providers, managers, legislators, funding sources, the general public, a child's family, and the child. A useful evaluation approach must be able to measure multiple criteria that address more than one perspective...(Koocher & Broskowski, 1977, p. 584).

MULTIPLE PERSPECTIVE EVALUATION (MPE): TOWARD A PARADIGM SHIFT

Developing and disseminating a sound common perception is what the institution of evaluation most needs today.

Lee J. Cronbach
"Remarks to the New Society"

For those professionals who are trained and immersed within the dominant paradigmatic framework, there are no alternative ways of conceptualizing the evaluation process. In order to collect valid and useful data for evaluation, one must use randomized experiments (Wortman, 1976). One could also use a *quantitative, observational* procedure to collect data:

> To state one of our own biases, we suggest that direct observation under everyday living conditions is the only measurement method that can yield valid information concerning the ethical, political, and economic decisions made by governmental and other institutions that affect the lives of retarded people (Sackett & Landesman-Dwyer, 1977, p. 28).

The well-trained single perspective evaluator must use procedures that yield cause-effect relationships. Moursund (1973) has stated that: "Evaluation must be fundamentally concerned with causality, since the main function of evaluation is to determine the effects of (that is, those things that are caused by) some program or situation or set of circumstances" (p. 62).

Reactions to this epistemological blindness to other epistemological points of view are receiving increasing attention from both researchers and evaluators. Some of the problems generated by attempts to force a fit between the methods of the dominant paradigm, stressing generalizable, objective, quantitative data, and the demands of participant problem solvers operating under changing conditions, i.e., dynamic, interactive systems, have been documented by several authors, including Cronbach (1977), Edwards and Guttentag (1975), Guttentag (1977a, 1977b), Patton (1975), and Stake (1973). A rejection of the exclusive reliance upon experimental procedures and a focus upon the failure of evaluators (constrained by the dominant paradigm) to obtain and use data from multiple sources and multiple perspectives are a common theme of these authors. The paradigm shift, according to Guttentag (1977b), is necessitated by our societal transition from an industrial to a post-industrial society. The transition is from a society that emphasizes domination over nature to a society that emphasizes the creation of social settings, human services, and participatory design. Guttentag stresses the need for a paradigm that is decision-oriented, not consequence-oriented.

Also rejecting the experimental techniques and assumptions, House (1977) has proposed a naturalistic inquiry approach for evaluators:

> The class of arguments that try to *establish* a structure of reality and assume the least agreement in advance between the author and audience are those most used in "naturalistic" evaluation.
> ...The focus is upon the *complexity* of everyday life, and naturalism tries to understand the everyday world in the experience of those who live it. The naturalist shows profound respect for the empirical world. *Participants* serve as constant sources of ideas and as checks on the developing ideas of the naturalist. *Multiple perspectives* are essential to portray the whole picture (p. 37, italics mine).

In other words, the new paradigm should provide the evaluator with the degrees of freedom to deal with complex processes, participative problem solving or designing, and multiple perspectives.

The Multiple Perspective Evaluator

What would the new paradigm look like or, more specifically, what would be the behavior of an evaluator who functioned on the basis of such a paradigm? First of all, he/she would have a high tolerance for uncertainty and ambiguity. Instead of insisting upon a universal audience, he/she could work comfortably with multiple audiences. Instead of giving preference to quantitative techniques, he/she would treat quantitative and qualitative procedures as complementary. In all cases, ambiguity and differences are not only accepted but are regarded as essential ingredients in every evaluative task.

Evaluators operating within the dominant paradigm, analogous to color-blind and stereopsis-blind individuals who fail to respond to the richness of a world of colors and depths, evaluate within a dimensionally impoverished world, totally unaware of impoverishment:

> Note that color-blindness and stereopsis-blindness went undiscovered through thousands of years of interpersonal communications, communications that would seem to have made them obvious. Discovering these differences in how people perceive and know takes more effort than might be expected: we tend to feel that everyone knows in the same way. Our way (Pennington, 1977, p. 7).

The evaluator whose actions are constrained by the dominant paradigm seeks to minimize differences between observers and to treat any variations from a true score or observation agreement as error variance. According to this epistemological position, to be objective is to reduce errors, i.e., observational differences, to zero.

The multiple perspective evaluator recognizes that two or more perceptions of a given process may be different, yet equally valid. To assume otherwise is to fall into the epistemological trap that presumes there is only one way of knowing, a failure to cope with the complexity of the world of human services and evaluations:

> Homogenistic thinking attributes the differences in interpretation or opinion to errors or lack of information...hierarchial and competitive thinking sees differences as conflicts...polyocular thinking regards differences as complementary (Maruyama, 1974, p. 23).

MPE and the Concept of Validity

The new paradigm label multiple perspective evaluation seems to capture the essential aspect of an approach that is required to tap multiple sources of data in order to provide valid evaluation products. "Validity" within this new framework takes on a different interpretation than that accorded to the concept within the dominant paradigm. In the latter context, validity refers to intraperspective agreement, whereas in the MPE case it refers to *both* intraperspective agreement and to interperspective *disagreement*. The idea that disagreement can cause valid results jars the conceptual underpinnings of validity because the epistemological assumptions that the structure of reality is a given and that the task is to achieve as high a degree of observer agreement as possible in representing that structure still hold.

An alternative assumption is possible: the structure of social reality is continually changing and is deeply dependent upon observers of the system for a valid description. When two or more observers *disagree* in their descriptions there are three possible outcomes: 1) the observers are describing the same system in the same perspective, and the disagreement is seen as measurement error; 2) the observers are describing the same system from different perspectives, and the disagreement is seen as complementary validity; and 3) the observers are describing different systems, and the disagreement is an accurate indicator of different systems of interest.

Problems arise in evaluation when all observer differences are assumed to result in outcomes 1 and 3. In such cases observer differences are always minimized as errors, or "noise." Differences arising out of the second outcome are rarely attended to and therefore do not enter into questions of validity. The reasons for this failure to regard different descriptions of the same process as complementary and valid descriptions can be traced to the "Lockean" (Churchman, 1962, 1971) influence within the dominant paradigm.

This single perspective (Lockean) evaluator's over-concern with hard data or high quality data is often made at the expense of audience relevance:

> To concentrate on "the quality of data" is too narrow; our concern should be with the *utility* of data. Data are no good if the report on them is ready too late. They are precious little good if the relevant audience does not comprehend them...the whole concept of formal research designs has to be reconsidered in the evaluation context. A design that promotes internal validity does not necessarily improve external validity, and it generally is achieved at some sacrifice of relevance to decisions (Cronbach, 1977, p. 2).

A multiple perspective evaluator must be sensitive to the data needs of different program participants and to the type of persuasive argument that best matches a particular audience's perspective. House (1977) has stated that

> An evaluation can also be invalid in this secondary sense if the argument forms employed are wrong. For example, in this society, "means-ends" arguments, particularly cost-effectiveness arguments, are particularly potent. If one were to employ an argument based on maximizing excellence instead of choosing the best available alternative, it might carry little weight although being equally true and valid from the perspective of the universal audience (p. 44).

Concepts function as controllers by selecting certain behaviors and rejecting others. The single perspective (dominant) paradigm concept of validity selects consensual, objective (bias-free) behaviors and rejects methodological behaviors that fail to match the conceptual criteria of consensus, objectivity, etc. A shift in paradigms entails new criteria and new controlling relationships. Within the new paradigmatic context, validity as a controller is a richer, variety-expanding concept that contains the former concept of validity as a special limiting case. Most program evaluation situations involve more than one perspective among multiple data users.

The problems generated by the emergence of new conceptual controllers, such as "validity," are addressed in the next section, which focuses on the implications of demythologizing the single perspective myths of objectivity and the universal audience.

PROFESSIONAL AND
METHODOLOGICAL IMPLICATIONS OF A PARADIGM SHIFT

> ...we must realize that we evaluators live in two worlds, the outer world of practice and the inner world of self, and that both worlds are real. But they contradict each other, do they not? The reply may be that the two worlds are dialectical, by which is meant that through contrast we can learn a great deal about each of them.
>
> C. West Churchman
> "Philosophical Speculation on Systems Design"

A shift from one major paradigm to another should entail discriminable differences in the assumptions (and in the behavior that is constrained by the assumptions) of those whose task is to design and conduct evaluations of programs. These behavior differences should be observable in such areas as interactions with program staff, instrument design and selection, responsiveness to needs of data users, and professional publications.

MPE and Publications

Over the past 4 years, only 18 articles out of a total of 822 articles in journals that are dedicated to the education and training of mentally retarded persons *(Mental Retardation, American Journal of Mental Deficiency,* and *Education and Training of the Mentally Retarded)* are concerned with evaluation, program evaluation, or accountability. Of these 18 articles, only 5 articles are reports about program evaluations or the development of evaluation instruments. Four assumptions have a role in the resulting scarcity of publications:

1. Education and training programs for retarded persons are not evaluated
2. Education and training programs are evaluated but not reported
3. Program evaluations are reported, but labeled as something else, e.g., "research"
4. Program evaluations are reported, but edited out of the dissemination pool of ideas by journal editors who reject evaluation studies because they are not "research" or do not use accepted (dominant paradigm) methodological techniques. (Most, if not all, journal editors are highly skilled researchers trained in the techniques and assumptions of the dominant paradigm tradition.)

MPE and Staff-Evaluator Interactions

Perhaps the most obtrusive difference that is observable as a consequence of the paradigm shift is of most concern to the project decision makers and to the evaluator, i.e., the communication failure between the evaluator and the program staff. Program administrators, especially those trained in a strong research tradition, have an image of evaluation that generates expectations and defines evaluator competencies that may not match the behaviors exhibited by the MPE evaluator. The methodological competencies of a multiple perspective evaluator may even be seen as *incompetencies* by an advocate of a single perspective evaluation (SPE) or the decision maker. To the extent that the evaluation design and implementation are shaped by the image of the SPE administrator, the multiple perspective evaluator is constrained to operate as a single perspective evaluator, often frustrated in the continuous interplay of mismatched images. The multiple perspective evaluator attempts to seek out yet another perspective to give the evaluation "polyocular" vision, only to be discouraged by the administrator who views additional data sources as either too costly, redundant data, soft data, or noise in the system.

MPE and Instrument Design/Selection

The first step toward achieving multiple perspective evaluation is already in process. The development and use of multiple instruments within a single perspective are gaining wider acceptance as a means of achieving *both* higher quality data and meeting the needs of several data users sharing the same perspective (Irvin, Crowell, & Bellamy, in press).

The second step is conceptually and methodologically more difficult: the design and use of multiple instruments within multiple perspectives. In cases where a service provider uses several instruments of evaluation, such as a rating device, an observation code and a standardized test, the concepts and structures of these instruments, which yield a "raw data set," are selected by the evaluator or by the entire program staff. Alternatively, the evaluator can function as a participant-observer; can obtain data on objectives from staff, clients, parents, and teachers; or can train parents, supervisors, and trainers to design and use an observation code. In these situations, either single or multiple instruments for generating data are used in a multiple perspective context.

MPE and Responsiveness to Data Users

The evaluator who is sensitive only to the data needs of the program staff tends to design and use one or several instruments, such as a rating scale and a questionnaire, that function as *single perspective filters*. Thus far we have used perspective to denote a mode of inquiry (e.g., Lockean). It also may be used to distinguish the ways of describing and prescribing systems (i.e., modeling). Pask (1973) has described four such modeling perspectives that professionals in human services might use to generate

Table 1. Users and generators of four types of program data

Data generator	Data user				
	Service recipient	Significant others	Service provider	Community participants	Program evaluator
Service recipient	Ld	Lp	Lp	Lp	Lp, Ld
Significant others	Lp	Ld	Lp	Lp	Lp, Ld
Service provider	Lo, Lp	Lo, Lp	Ld	Lo, Lp	Lo, Lp, Ld
Community participants	Lp	Lp	Lp	Ld	Ld, Ld
Program evaluator	Lm, Lp	Lm, Lp	Lm, Lp	Lm, Lp	Lp, Ld, Lm

Lo = observer language
Ld = design language
Lp = participant language
Lm = metasystematic, multiperspective language

and interpret data: statistical, functional, normative, and organizational. The most widely used modeling perspectives in these human service areas are the statistical and functional (causal) perspectives, resulting in Lo data.

Data can be classified within a multiple perspective evaluation context in several ways as shown in Table 1. Lo data, observer language, is generated by "expert" *observers* of system behavior (usually by program staff or significant others trained by program staff). Naturalistic observation, rating scales, and checklists designed by program staff are types of Lo data instruments. The "expert" data producer is very pervasive in the conception and delivery of human services. Maruyama (1974) has stated that:

> ...persons in a specialized field tend to see its specialized focus as valid and applicable to any situation *regardless of context*. For example, a civil engineer may consider his highway design as desirable in any society, an educationalist may consider his philosophy of education as applicable to any culture,...a city planner may disregard the opinions of grassroots people on the assumption that he is the "expert" (p. 18).

In designing the instruments used to generate data used to solve problems by participants in the service program, the service provider effectively defines the problems from his/her perspective. In so doing, the service provider also defines the set of acceptable program solutions.

Another type of data that can be generated in a service delivery context, Ld data, refers to any data that result from the *design* selections made by any participant-designer in the program and used primarily by that participant and secondarily by the program evaluator. Record-keeping, diaries, and other personalistic data produced for the participant's own use are examples of Ld data. The Kelly grid technique (Slater, 1976) is another type of Ld generating instrument. Using this instrument, a retarded person acts as his/her own evaluator by structuring the constructs and elements that yield a view of his/her world. Although the Kelly grid has not been used with severely retarded persons, it has been used successfully with moderately retarded persons (Barton, Walton, & Rowe, 1976).

Lp data are *participant*-generated data used primarily by other participants and by the evaluator. Lp data requires two or more participants interacting within the participants' object language for any data to be generated. Participants interact by means of an object language that is described by the model builder or inquirer in a higher order meta-language (Pask, 1973). For multiple perspective evaluators, there is an important distinction between an object language and a meta-language. Using ethnographic techniques, the evaluator is able to discover, for example, the prescriptive rules that participants use to communicate and interact in their object language. An ethnographic technique that describes interactions in terms of participant-generated categories, *not* observer-defined categories, yield Lp data.

Lm data are evaluator-generated data that translate single perspective data types Lo, Ld, and Lp into metasystemic data to be used by all program participants. Beer (1970) described the concept of metasystem as:

> a system which stands over and beyond a logically inferior system, and one which is competent to handle that lower system's logic. Metasystems are logically superior and not necessarily more senior or more highly endowed with status or privilege; also, in an hierarchy of systems there will be several orders of "meta" (p. 119).

Multiple perspective evaluation could not occur without all four data types. Ld and Lp data are roughly what anthropologists refer to as "emic" descriptions (the insider's view), and Lo data corresponds to "etic" descriptions (the expert outsider's view).

The multiple perspective evaluator-generated data, Lm data, are a synthesis of the etic aspects of Lo data and the emic aspects of Ld and Lp data, preserving the differences between the perspectives, viewed by the evaluator as complementary. Participant images could be generated and compared by Lm type procedures similar to multi-attribute utilities (Edwards & Guttentag, 1975) as a basis for providing polyocular vision to program participants. The use of Lm data might result in quite different evaluations than those now conducted and reported. Of the 18 evaluation articles identified earlier spanning the period 1974-1977, 5 of the articles described a data generating procedure. All five procedures were Lo data types. That is, in each case the data generating instrument or instruments were designed and used by program staff or a researcher to *observe,* i.e., describe client behavior or client-material interactions. A conception of evaluation as consequence-oriented research or as an impact analysis activity (Maruyama, 1974) constrains program decision makers to generate and use only Lo data. The hidden assumption is revealed when the question is restated to read: What is the impact of program "X" on outcome "Y," according to *my* problem definition? Lo data might meet the information needs of one program data user, but it fails to meet the needs of other users.

"Impact" Evaluation: An Example

In a recent study evaluating staff training in group homes for retarded persons (Schinke & Wong, 1977), experimental and control groups (assumption: all other factors must be equal) were used to assess the impact and effectiveness of training staff in operant techniques (assumption: the purpose of all inquiry is to produce causal, functional descriptions of the object of inquiry). Schinke and Wong selected four Lo data evaluation instruments: a 25-item knowledge test, a 47-item attitude checklist, an 18-item job satisfaction rating, and a 29-category observation code. Although this multiple instrument evaluation design resulted in data on the behaviors of both staff and residents, the data generator and the data user in each case was the researcher-evaluator who, by designing and selecting instrument categories, precluded any other perspective from entering into the data pool. The researchers defined the evaluation problem: to test the hypothesis that there would be beneficial changes as a result of training. There is no mention of training objectives or problem definitions from the point of view of the staff, of the designers of the training program, or of the program participants.

By not examining their evaluation assumptions, Schinke and Wong failed to generate several different problem representations and thereby opened themselves to committing an error of the "third kind," i.e., the "probability of having solved the 'wrong' problem when one should have solved the 'right' problem" (Mitroff & Turoff, 1974). Solving a *research* problem when one should have solved an *evaluation* problem is an example of committing an error of the third kind.

IMPLICATIONS OF A PARADIGM SHIFT
FOR EVALUATING MAINSTREAMING PROGRAMS

> Today the battle cry in special education is for *mainstreaming;* and although there may be some serious impediments, the question clearly is no longer *whether* to mainstream but rather *how* most effectively to mainstream.
>
> D. L. MacMillan and M. I. Semmel
> "Evaluation of Mainstreaming Programs"

As we move rapidly into a post-industrial world, can we shift our epistemological filters from the dominant paradigm appropriate to an industrialized society to the polyocular images of interacting systems with nonseparable components? It will not be an easy task because it will require a major effort in self-reflection on the part of evaluators already trained in the dominant tradition.

A paradigm shift should open up new problem areas: it should encourage evaluators to ask different kinds of questions and to use different methodologies. These new questions and methods should be appropriate for the "change" phase of a "stability-change" cycle of evolving knowledge processes. If, as Guttentag (1977b) and others suggest, we are culturally now in a change phase of the cycle, then the SPE assumptions and methods for evaluating programs, such as mainstreaming are too limiting and restrictive. Mainstreaming evaluation questions are being asked within an SPE paradigm that is only appropriate for simple stable systems in which all participants share the same perspective. If these conditions do not exist, there is a gross mismatch between our paradigmatic tools and the evaluation task to be accomplished.

Mainstreaming: Stability or Change?

The evaluation questions being asked in the context of mainstreaming program evaluations demonstrate the weakness of an SPE approach. If the variety of questions being asked are examined, two major concerns are found: what is the *cost* of mainstreaming program "X" and what are the *problems* it generates (for teachers and administrators)? Alternatively, the focus is upon the effectiveness of program "X" in integrating handicapped students into regular classes. The assumption in each case is that the regular class structure and the administrative structure supporting it do not require any changes. The prevailing attitude is one of mainstreaming students in special classes, regardless of problems created by such attempts for both regular teachers and students. The SPE assumption of separability of system components prevents alternative conceptions of the mainstreaming problem from surfacing. For example, can one mainstream handicapped students without mainstreaming teachers, curricula, instructional resources, counselors, school psychologists, and other components of a school system? The single perspective evaluator would respond in the affirmative. The multiple perspective evaluator would say no: each system component's effectiveness is a function of the effectiveness of each of the other components in the system. From an MPE perspective, we are not engaged in a process of normalizing education for the handicapped student. We are, instead, attempting to cope with educational changes that are a function of contemporary societal pressures to ensure equal opportunity and rights for *all* members of the societal system, not just the handicapped. In this respect, mainstreaming is an unfortunate label. It stresses the stability and appropriateness of general educational programs during a cultural period when change is the name of the game. According to an MPE assumption of nonseparability of system components, one cannot mainstream only handicapped students. If mainstreaming means an individualized plan for maximizing educational benefits for the student, then it must apply to all students and all program components: teachers, administrators, parents, paraprofessionals, and other program participants. The *system* must be mainstreamed and each participant has an evaluative role in bringing about such changes.

Evaluative Roles in Mainstreaming Programs

To paraphrase MacMillan and Semmel (1977), the question is no longer *whether* to change but rather *how* most effectively to change the system. Single perspective evaluation efforts are not change-oriented. The dominant paradigm inherited from the physical sciences imposes a framework of stability upon the component that is to be evaluated. Multiple perspective evaluators take "change" as a given and attempt to promote continued change that is necessary for system survival and evolution into a more complex and adaptable system.

In the case of education, MPEs would seek to facilitate the widest distribution possible of evaluation functions among program participants. This could take several forms, including extensive inservice training for teachers, parents, administrators, and school psychologists. Not only would the training sessions be concerned with questions of *who* would perform *what* kinds of evaluation functions, they would also attend to the problems of *how* participants cope with the uncertainties generated by role modifications. The use of such inservice programs with a variety of perspectives involved in the decision-making process has already achieved some degree of success as evidenced by Project I.E.P.: "Those interviewed agreed that consideration of multiple perspectives resulted in development of a system responsive to the concerns of all who would be involved in its implementation" (Safer, Morrissey, Kaufman, & Lewis, 1978, p. 14).

SPE versus MPE Concerns and Issues

The SPE approach to evaluating mainstreaming programs is dominated not only by the myth of separability, but also by the myths of objectivity (hard data), universal audience (the data speak for themselves), and control (all other factors are equal). These myths combine to restrict the question-asking and data-collecting procedures of the evaluator to an oversimplified approach to the problem:

> To conclude, one of the greatest needs in future approaches to the evaluation of mainstreaming programs is to provide an adequate conceptualization of the processes involved. Both theory and methodology need to avoid the oversimplification of traditional educational research (Jones, Gottlieb, Guskin, & Yoshida, 1978, p. 592).

The increased variety of questions posed, the added dimensionality of participatory evaluation, and the demythologizing assumptions of an MPE approach should all contribute toward a more adequate conceptualization of the processes involved in mainstreaming.

A shift from SPE to MPE conceptualizations and methodologies, however, will generate a new set of training and funding problems that inevitably accompany changes in roles and representations of organizational participants and professional service providers.

Training Problems

The MPE evaluator would receive training in a multiple instrument, multiple audience technology. The development of such technology would be contingent upon a general acceptance of the new paradigm, especially by the state and federal granting agencies. Evaluators would also be trained to be self-reflective and to design this self-referencing characteristic into each program evaluation. Ambiguity and paradox inevitably accompany self-reference (Gorn, 1967). The selection and training of MPE evaluators would, therefore, result in individuals with a high tolerance for uncertainty and ambiguity. A sensitivity to different audiences and capturing different perspectives through participatory instrument design will also be important skills. The MPE evaluator will require instrument development skills that go beyond single perspective data generation and analysis skills.

There are currently few graduate programs for training educational evaluators. This lack of programs should, in principle, increase the opportunity to design multiple perspective training programs. Certain prescriptive elements of a MPE training program are identified:

1. Training should include instruction *about* and *from* a variety of epistemological views

2. Trainees should have or should acquire a systemic world view (a systems world view acknowledges that there are alternative world views [Churchman, 1971])
3. Training should include instruction in both quantitative and qualitative methodologies with a balance in emphasis between the two (neither having priority over the other)
4. Trainees should acquire a repertoire of evaluative arguments based upon a variety of inquiry and modeling perspectives so that arguments can be matched to a data user's perspective (House [1977] identified 23 kinds of evaluative arguments for use by an evaluator to persuade an audience)
5. Trainees should have or should acquire communication, formal operations, and organizational development skills in order to cope with the complexity of multiple interactions and multiple problem representations (avoiding and assisting others to avoid errors of the third kind are useful skills)
6. Emphasis upon instrument design skills should strike a balance between data quality and data utility in relation to multiple users (multiple users translates to multiple problem definers)
7. Trainees should be exposed to a diversity of cross-discipline views ("any two points of view are complementary" [Weinberg, 1975])

Inservice training within each organization will also achieve high priority. The distribution of evaluation functions among school personnel, students, parents, and paraprofessionals will generate situations of actual and potential conflict even under the best of circumstances. Inservice training programs are one means of sharing modified role expectations and resolving conflicts in addition to providing the evaluation competencies necessary for participant involvement. Current efforts at providing inservice assistance for teachers involved in implementing mainstreaming programs (MacMillan & Semmel, 1977; Safer et al., 1978) and efforts to increase parent participation in planning-evaluation activities (Yoshida & Gottlieb, 1977) could be extended to achieve MPE design goals of participatory evaluation in all phases of program evaluation.

Funding Problems

Project proposals are usually written by a research-trained administrator to obtain funding to answer a research question. The summative design of the proposal is a means of satisfying the funding agency's requirements for evaluation. The summative or final judgment of the worth of the program is documented in terms of program evaluation data (collected and analyzed with quantitive, experimental methods whenever possible). The validity of the program data is determined by the data themselves.

In contrast to the above situation, project proposals incorporating a multiple perspective design would require collaboration by an administrator and an MPE evaluator in planning the whole program's structure and in identifying the potential data users as participant-designers of that structure. The evaluation design would specify the number and kinds of data instruments—Lo, Ld, Lp, and Lm—only after user problems have been specified. In order to keep the "expert" data user from dominating the problem definition from which all program objectives, operations, and evaluation evolve, a variety of problem definitions are obtained and used to provide a beginning program structure. For example, a proposal for funding curriculum design and inservice training for mainstreaming handicapped students into regular classes would involve both special and regular class teachers, curriculum specialists, a school administrator, parents, and a representative sample of the students themselves, in addition to the project administrator and an evaluator. Such a procedure is more than the typical needs assessment referred to in many project proposals, and it guarantees participant planning that a paradigm shift seeks to provide.

The shift away from "expert" single perspective designs will also ensure a greater emphasis upon *formative* and *process-oriented* evaluation where the program does not have to stand still to accommodate single perspective constraints, e.g., the internal validity requirements of a research-trained administrator. The use of multiple program designers throughout the developing program ensures program changes, and each change increases the effectiveness of the whole program.

The cost of developing multiple instruments is only a partial, contributory factor to the preponderance of Lo data. Even if MPE designs are perceived as more costly than SPE designs, the costs are surely justified in terms of the overall reduction in social costs. Estimates based upon 1970 data and prices (Conley, 1973) indicated that every vocational rehabilitative dollar spent on a retarded person would generate between 2 and 14 dollars in future earnings, depending upon the severity of retardation. When one considers that lifetime institutional costs are estimated at $400,000 for each retarded individual, then the added program costs for multiple perspective, multiple instrument evaluation shrink to insignificant amounts. According to Scriven (1976), such evaluations are truly "cost-free" and can be achieved at any level of evaluation design complexity in terms of increased efficiency or benefits that accrue to program participants and consumers. The failure of program evaluations to generate Ld, Lp, and Lm data is related more to the presence of constraining assumptions than to the absence of program funds.

Programs for training mentally retarded persons depend to a large degree upon state and federal funding. If those individuals responsible for granting funds for such programs do not recognize the need for multiple perspective evaluation, then the paradigm shift is less likely to take place.

If the shift does not occur, then single perspective evaluation based upon type Lo data will continue to dominate evaluation designs. Data quality will remain the center of our attention at the expense of data utility. Project grants will be assured funding if "rigorous" data collection methods are described in the grant proposal, e.g., an experimental procedure.

Granting agencies may heed other voices, however, and agree with Mitroff and Bonoma (1978) that:

> In both the real world of evaluation and the more tightly controlled one of the laboratory, we believe that "validity" cannot be even approached until one learns to question his or her assumptions as closely as he or she questions the rigor with which data was generated. Such an ability to question requires an openness and flexibility that is not found in many individuals, scientists or otherwise (p. 256).

It is hoped that grant reviewers will be part of that small group of flexible and open individuals when it comes time to pass judgment on proposals that incorporate an MPE design. The final section of this chapter proposes that such designs will enhance the quality of life of program clients.

MULTIPLE PERSPECTIVE EVALUATION AND THE ASSESSMENT OF QUALITY OF LIFE OF MENTALLY RETARDED PERSONS

> ...the key to improved quality of life is not planning for or measurement of others, but enabling them to plan and measure for themselves.
>
> Russell Ackoff
> "Does Quality of Life Have to be Quantified"

We have arrived full circle back to our two-stage effort at coping with the quality of life problems. It has been assumed that the quality of life of an individual suffers as the person is labeled deviant and is isolated from the mainstream of society. The corrective solution presumably, according to the principle of normalization, is to integrate retarded persons into the community by providing community-based care facilities (stage one) and to provide integrated learning experiences in normal, nonspecial classrooms or by vocational training and job placement in integrated work settings (stage two). When these two stages of program solutions have been fully implemented and the objectives of mainstreaming have been accomplished, then the quality of life of our mentally retarded population will have been improved to the fullest extent of our capabilities. Or will it? There are those who would, in the spirit of multiple perspectives, have us examine alternatives:

> The foregoing analysis suggests that although the normalization principle has played a crucial role in the development of community services for mentally retarded citizens to date, there are some serious shortcomings that call into question the efficacy of continued adherence to normalization's recommended guidelines. Specifically, the principle is not verifiable and is geared to organizational instead of individual needs. Furthermore, those aspects of the principle that appear to be testable have not been supported and the practices of using "normal" as a criterion and denying that retarded individuals are indeed different are highly questionable. There appears to be a need for alternative guidelines and/or strategies to guide future efforts in this area (Mesibov, 1976, p. 31).

Other dissenting voices, including Rhoades and Browning (1977), Stephens (1975), and Kolstoe (1972), find fault with the assumptions underlying the principle of normalization. Framed within the context of contrasting paradigms and the language of this chapter, they appear to be questioning the wisdom of developing and implementing educational and community-based programs that have emerged from a homogenistic epistemological perspective (Maruyama, 1978). The major assumption is that we must all be alike and that differences are to be treated as an undesirable state of affairs. The modeling perspective is functionalistic: find the causal relationship between "X" (cause) and social incompetence (effect). The answer is clearly deviance. Eliminate deviance by mainstreaming and normalizing (prescription: apply homogenistic thinking).

Is the quality of life of a retarded person increased as he/she is remade in the image of the so-called "normal" person? It may not be the case as when the single perspective of predominantly middle class personnel provide care and design instructional materials:

> ...there is still a strong tendency among persons who guide the welfare of retarded people to behave as if there were but one culture, and that normalization should therefore be judged by middle class standards of speech, dress, hygiene, nutrition, and even recreation.... When these personnel set goals for more normalized community living and when they evaluate progress toward these goals, they often reveal a marked "middle class" cultural bias (Edgerton, 1975, p. 137).

What, then, is the solution? What does a paradigm shift toward multiple perspective evaluation offer the educator or the service provider in the way of resolving the quality of life issue? The answer proposed within an MPE context is the acceptance and promotion of diversity and participation.

The diversity viewpoint has support from the diversity-stability hypothesis of ecosystemic descriptions and from the participative designing perspective provided by Ackoff (1975):

> ...We simply do not now have the capability of producing the kind and number of measurements of quality of life that are needed for a rational design of an effort to improve it.... An alternative to measuring the quality of life is participative planning.
> ...the planning problem of social planners should be, not how to improve the quality of life of others, but how to enable them to improve their own quality of life (p. 217).

If we, as educators and program service staff, plan our programs so that there are no variety in lifestyles (the retarded person must fit into a "normal" lifestyle) and no choices about vocational, living, and recreational environments, are we not attempting to solve "our" problem as defined by our single, limited perspective? The use of participatory planning and designing ensures that multiple perspectives enter into the representation of problems and into the search for effective systems design solutions. In the Leibnizian language of the operations researcher, the goal is to prevent sub-optimizing.

That the retarded person, especially the severely and profoundly retarded person, has a perspective that is different and that can be shared with others is no doubt dismissed by many parents, program staff, and teachers. This automatic rejection of a client's input into planning and evaluation decisions has its roots partly in the verbal expression of an epistemological position: there is only one way to represent a problem—my way.

If we are to heed Ackoff's advice and involve the retarded individual in choices that will affect his/her quality of life, due in large part to that involvement, then we must provide opportunities for participation wherever possible, especially within the evaluation process. Bogdan and Taylor (1976) remind us that we too often fail to listen to the perspective of the retarded person. In addition to our observation codes and ratings by significant others, we need to conceptualize data-generating procedures, such as the Kelly grid technique (Barton et al., 1976), for producing data that are structured by the retarded individual. Changes in that structure (elements and constructs and relationships between them) can then be identified and related to other descriptions by program participants and to actions taken to increase the quality of life of the client. Allowing the clients to participate in the evaluation process automatically increases their quality of life.

The Retarded Person as Designer

The image of human individuals is one of complex co-designers of systems in which they are also participants. Should we then accord the status of designer to retarded individuals and, in so doing, take the full step in declaring their humanness as co-designers? They too can make choices, given the opportunity; they too can set goals and achieve them. Retarded persons also function as inquiring systems. Perhaps the simplicity of our images of retarded persons is in large measure a consequence of the simplicity of our functional models, as well as the need to generate jobs for care and training specialists (i.e., systems have non-separable components: perceived incompetence in one part generates perceived need for added competencies in other parts of the system).

Images of retarded persons by the public, peers, and professionals affect the way they respond to the retarded person and these images, in turn, affect the behavior of the latter. Gottlieb (1975, 1977), who has reviewed studies of attitudes toward retarded students and toward mainstreaming, concluded:

> As the mainstreaming of handicapped children becomes an accepted aspect of school programming, one of the critical needs will be the development of curriculum units that emphasize the individuality of people, that people are different in ability and appearance, and that they should be valued for what they are. Mainstreaming does not involve retarded children exclusively. Just as the curriculum for retarded children will have to be modified, so, too, will the curriculum for the nonhandicapped children (Gottlieb, 1977, p. 40).

Gottlieb's statement calls our attention to the separability issue of systems design and argues that the design solution of mainstreaming involves non-separable components. As the view that differences are necessary and complementary is internalized in the educational process through curriculum design and inservice training programs, a new image of the retarded person as co-designer will emerge.

The thesis of this chapter is that our images are controlled by our assumptions. If those images are too simplistic, we are in danger of asking the wrong kind of questions, or, in some cases, not asking enough questions. Too often the functional model user or the Lo data user mistakes "necessity for sufficiency" (Pennington, 1977). Functional descriptions may be necessary for us to generate our image of the retarded person as a co-designer, but they are not sufficient.

Quality of Life as Systems Design

Whether we are engaged in the process of designing an instructional system for integrating retarded and regular students or designing a vocational training program for severely retarded adults, we are faced with defining a "systems design problem." How we proceed to define that problem depends crucially upon our epistemological assumptions. The task established at the beginning of this chapter was to identify a matrix of assumptions and methods that dominate thinking in research and evaluation of programs for retarded persons and to articulate the images of those who would strive to live in a world of multiple world views. The shift toward this multiple perspective position entails a new image of ourselves and of retarded persons as co-designers of a social system where the quality of life is directly proportional to our participation in that design process.

Our concepts of quality of life, normalization, and mental retardation are products of a single world view in which our way of "seeing" has been the only way, our way of defining the problems of retardation and providing solutions has been the only way. The message proposed in these pages is that there are multiple ways and each contributes to the "requisite variety" (Ashby, 1963) that enhances the quality of life of the participant designers. The complementarity of different perspectives is brought into focus by Rist (1977) in his examination of quantitative and qualitative paradigms:

> ...the fact that these two paradigms are in tension over the very most basic assumptions upon which they base their research efforts opens up the potential for a dialectic where the resolution is not an "either-or" but each answering a part of the question at hand. If each approach does provide a perspective which tends to be the mirror opposite of the other, the creative effort becomes one of finding ways to take these partial images of reality and piece them into a new orientation or perspective (p. 48).

It is the task of multiple perspective evaluators to accomplish that task of fitting the partial images together and to assist each of us, regardless of labels, in co-designing a higher quality of life.

ACKNOWLEDGMENTS

I would like to express my appreciation to Charles Traynor, Nancy Weissman Frisch, Newt Rumble, Jim Medford, and Marshall Pallett for their comments, suggestions, and editorial assistance. I would also like to thank Tom Bellamy for providing the opportunity and time to produce this manuscript and Jay Gottlieb for his constructive editorial comments.

REFERENCES

Ackoff, R. Does quality of life have to be quantified? *General Systems Yearbook,* 1975, *20,* 213–219.
Apsler, R. In defense of the experimental paradigm. *Evaluation,* 1977, *4,* 14–18.
Ashby, W. R. *Introduction to cybernetics.* New York: Wiley, 1963.

Barton, E. S., Walton, T., & Rowe, D. Using grid technique with the mentally handicapped. In P. Slater (Ed.), *The measurement of intrapersonal space by grid technique, Volume 1: Exploration of intrapersonal space.* New York: Wiley, 1976.

Beer, S. Managing modern complexity. *Futures,* 1970, *2,* 114–122.

Bogdan, R., & Taylor, S. The judged, not the judges: An insider's view of mental retardation. *American Psychologist,* 1976, *31,* 47–52.

Churchman, C. W. *On Inquiring Systems* (Monograph No. SP-877). Santa Monica, Cal.: System Development Corporation, 1962.

Churchman, C. W. *The design of inquiring systems.* New York: Basic Books, 1971.

Churchman, C. W. Philosophical speculation on systems design. *Omega, The International Journal of Management Sciences,* 1974, *2,* 451–465.

Conley, R. W. *The economics of mental retardation.* Baltimore: Johns Hopkins Press, 1973.

Cronbach, L. J. Remarks to the new society. *Evaluation Research Society Newsletter,* 1977, *1*(1), 1–3.

Edgerton, R. Issues relating to the quality of life among mentally retarded persons. In M. J. Begab & S. A. Richardson (Eds.), *The mentally retarded and society: A social science perspective.* Baltimore: University Park Press, 1975.

Edwards, W., & Guttentag, M. Experiments and evaluations: A reexamination. In C. Bennett & A. Lumsdaine (Eds.), *Evaluation and experiment: Some critical issues in assessing social programs.* New York: Academic Press, 1975.

Gorn, S. The computer and information sciences and the community of disciplines. *Behavioral Science,* 1967, *12,* 433–452.

Gottlieb, J. Public, peer, and professional attitude toward mentally retarded persons. In M. J. Begab & S. A. Richardson (Eds.), *The mentally retarded and society: A social science perspective.* Baltimore: University Park Press, 1975.

Gottlieb, J. Attitudes toward mainstreaming retarded children and some possible effects on educational practices. In P. Mittler (Ed.), *Research to practice in mental retardation, Volume I: Care and intervention.* Baltimore: University Park Press, 1977.

Guttentag, M. On quantified sachel: A reply to Apsler. *Evaluation,* 1977, *4,* 18–20.(a)

Guttentag, M. Evaluation and society. *Personality and Social Psychology Bulletin,* 1977, *3,* 31–40.(b)

House, E. *The logic of evaluative argument* (CSE Monograph No. 7). Los Angeles: UCLA, Center for the Study of Evaluation, 1977.

Irvin, L., Crowell, F. A., & Bellamy, G. T. Multiple assessment evaluation of programs for severely retarded adults. *Mental Retardation.* (In press)

Jones, R. L., Gottlieb, J., Guskin, S., & Yoshida, R. K. Evaluating mainstreaming programs: Models, caveats, considerations and guidelines. *Exceptional Children,* 1978, *44,* 588–601.

Kolstoe, O. D. Programs for the mildly retarded: A reply to the critics. *Exceptional Children,* 1972, *37,* 475–479.

Koocher, G. P., & Broskowski, A. Issues in the evaluation of mental health services for children. *Professional Psychology,* 1977, *8,* 583–592.

Kuhn, T. S. *The structure of scientific revolutions.* Chicago: The University of Chicago Press, 1962.

MacMillan, D. L., & Semmel, M. I. Evaluation of mainstreaming programs. *Focus on Exceptional Children,* 1977, *9*(4), 1-14.

Maruyama, M. Paradigms and communication. *Technological Forecasting and Social Change.* 1974, *6,* 3-32.

Maruyama, M. Heterogenistics and morphogenetics: Toward a new concept of the scientific. *Theory and Society,* 1978, *5,* 75-96.

Masterman, M. The nature of a paradigm. In I. Lakatos & A. Musgrave (Eds.), *Criticism and the growth of knowledge.* Cambridge: Cambridge University Press, 1970.

Mesibov, G. R. Alternatives to the principle of normalization. *Mental Retardation,* 1976, *14,* 30-32.

Mitroff, I. I., & Bonoma, T. V. Psychological assumptions, experimentation, and real world problems. *Evaluation Quarterly,* 1978, *2,* 235-260.

Mitroff, I. I., & Turoff, M. Technological forecasting and assessment: Science and/or mythology? *Technological Forecasting and Social Change,* 1973, *5,* 113-134.

Mitroff, I. I., & Turoff, M. On measuring the conceptual errors in large scale social experiments: The future as decision. *Technological Forecasting and Social Change,* 1974, *6,* 389-402.

Moursund, J. P. *Evaluation: An introduction to research design.* Monterey: Brooks/Cole, 1973.

Pask, G. Models for social systems and for their languages. *Instructional Science,* 1973, *1,* 395-445.

Patton, M. Q. *Alternative evaluation research paradigm.* Grand Forks: University of North Dakota, 1975.

Pennington, P. *Our perception of energy.* Unpublished manuscript, Portland, Oregon, 1977.

Rhoades, C., & Browning, P. Normalization at what price? *Mental Retardation,* 1977, *15,* 24.

Riecken, H. W. Principal components of the evaluation process. *Professional Psychology,* 1977, *8,* 392-410.

Rist, R. C. On the relations among educational research paradigms: From disdain to détente. *Anthropology and Education Quarterly,* 1977, *8,* 42-57.

Sackett, G. P., & Landesman-Dwyer, S. Toward an ethology of mental retardation. In P. Mittler (Ed.), *Research to practice in mental retardation, Volume 2: Education and training.* Baltimore: University Park Press, 1977.

Safer, N. D., Morrissey, P. A., Kaufman, M. J., & Lewis, L. Implementation of IEPs: New teacher roles and requisite support systems. *Focus on Exceptional Children,* 1978, *10,* 1-20.

Schinke, S. P., & Wong, S. E. Evaluation of staff training in group homes for retarded persons. *American Journal of Mental Deficiency,* 1977, *82,* 130-136.

Scriven, M. Payoffs from evaluation. In C. C. Abt (Ed.), *The evaluation of social programs.* Beverly Hills: Sage, 1976.

Slater, P. (Ed.). *The measurement of intrapersonal space by grid technique.* New York: Wiley, 1976.

Stake, R. *Program evaluation, particularly responsive evaluation.* Paper presented at a conference on New Trends in Evaluations, Goteborg, Sweden, October, 1973.

Stephens, W. E. Mainstreaming: Some natural limitations. *Mental Retardation,* 1975, *13,* 40–41.

Weinberg, G. M. *An introduction to general systems thinking.* New York: Wiley, 1975.

Wortman, P. Research versus decision requirements and best practices of evaluation. In C. C. Abt (Ed.), *The evaluation of social programs.* Beverly Hills: Sage, 1976.

Yoshida, R. K., & Gottlieb, J. A model of parental participation in the pupil planning process. *Mental Retardation,* 1977, *15,* 17–20.

CHAPTER 4

Evaluating Educational Changes with Single-Subject Designs

Alan C. Repp and John Lloyd

The history of mental retardation in the United States has been one of changing goals and objectives. In the early 1800s there were efforts by Seguin, Howe, and others to teach retarded persons to be self-sufficient. In the mid 1800s, with this goal not having been met and with residential institutions propagating, the objective became custodial care. In the late 1800s and early 1900s, the objective became the eradication of residential institutions and the key word was "eugenics." In the mid 1900s, a great social movement began and many minorities, including the mentally retarded, were affected. Today, there is a movement to provide humane care and educational opportunities for all retarded persons in all situations.

Mainstreaming embodies this movement. Mainstreaming is, in part, an attempt to educate individuals in the least restrictive environment possible. For some individuals, mainstreaming is a demeaning experience that provides no additional educational support, resulting in a failure of placement. For others, individualized programs are designed, resulting in

---

Preparation of this chapter was supported, in part, by Grants 300-77-0255 and G007700642 from the Bureau of Education of the Handicapped.

success for persons in their new sense. It is in this sense, in the effort toward *individualized programs,* that single-subject designs can contribute to the mainstreaming movement. Unlike traditional designs, which typically compare the behavior of one group of "treated" persons with one group of "untreated" persons, the single-subject design requires that a treatment condition be experienced by all individuals. Because it provides an evaluation of how well each individual has responded to his/her own treatment condition, the single-subject design fits quite nicely into traditional teaching procedures.

Although single-subject designs can be used by anyone, no matter his/her philosophy of psychology or education, the design has been made popular by behaviorists and has been traditionally associated with researchers in this field. The goals of applied behavior analysis are 1) to change behavior and 2) to determine whether specified environmental events or conditions have caused these changes in behavior. In spite of an increasing number of well-documented behavior change procedures, the first goal, behavior change, may not be reached in all cases. Similarly, in spite of the availability of procedures for determining whether certain events or conditions result in changed behavior, the second goal may not always be met.

Education shares the first goal of applied behavior analysis. Educators seek to bring about changes in students' behavior. Educators say that children have learned to multiply when they can say or write correct answers to multiplication problems; that they have learned to decode when they can say the speech equivalents of printed words; and that they have learned to spell when they can correctly write words or say the correct letters in the proper order for words. Saying or writing answers, words, or letters are behaviors that change when pupils learn. Usually, these changes are caused by some environmental events or conditions, i.e., by teaching. Teacher actions, instructional materials, observations of peers, and a host of other events and conditions go into the learning environment and may have effects on students' learning. Determining which one of these conditions, or combination of them, causes changes should be a goal of education, also. Knowing whether a specified teaching activity results in the mastery of an arithmetic skill allows us to use that activity with some assurance that pupils will learn.

In the following sections of this chapter procedures are discussed that allow one to try to determine whether behavior changes can be attributed to planned variations in the educational environment. In particular, the focus is on the use of four major designs—reversal, multiple baseline, multi-element, and changing criterion—for analyzing the behavior of individuals in order to determine the effects of changes that are made in the learning environment. First, however, the stage is set by describing dependent and independent variables and by providing the rationale for focusing on individual children's behavior.

DEPENDENT AND INDEPENDENT VARIABLES

In attempting to determine whether certain events or conditions alter behaviors, two types of variables must be considered: dependent and independent. The level of the dependent variable depends upon the quality or quantity of the independent variable. Numerous examples of this relationship can be found in education. Suppose that "number of correct answers to addition problems" is the dependent variable and "number of minutes allowed to work the problems" is the independent variable. If the level of the independent variable is changed from 1 minute to 5 minutes, the level of the dependent variable (number of correct answers) would probably get larger. Hence, the level of the dependent variable *depended* upon the level of the independent variable. Suppose that the frequency of counselors praising students was the dependent variable and that whether or not the counselors were trained to use praise was the independent variable. In this case, the level of the independent variable is either 0 (no training) or 1 (training). Would the level of the dependent variable (the use of praise) change if the level of the independent variable changed? Gladstone and Spencer (1977) found that when a simple modeling procedure in which counselors were shown how to praise was instituted, the frequency of the use of praise increased. Again, the level of the dependent variable depended on the level of the independent variable.

There are many more examples of this relationship. Cossairt, Hall, and Hopkins (1973) found that the levels of praise from the teachers for students' attending behaviors were dependent on an experimenter's instructions, feedback, and praise. Dalton, Rubino, and Hislop (1973) found that the number of test questions answered correctly by Down's syndrome children was improved when a token economy was used during teaching. Garcia and Trujillo (1977) reported that the number of imitative responses of three children classified as retarded was dependent on the experimenter's facial orientation. Simbert, Minor, and McCoy (1977) reported that when given an intensive self-feeding program, including manual guidance, praise, positive practice, and brief tray removal, the correct eating responses of six retarded children increased and their incorrect responses decreased. Kazdin and Erickson (1975) found that the number of instructions followed by students increased when they received praise and food for correct responding and when they were guided through the correct response after incorrect responding. In all of these cases there is a consistent similarity: each sought to determine whether the level of the dependent variable (the behavior to be changed) was altered as a function of the independent variable (the actions taken by teachers or experimenters).

There is a common feature in all applied behavior analysis work: behavior or its direct product is the dependent variable. The independent variable is not restricted to behavior, however. The independent variable may be behavior (e.g., teacher praise); environmental events, such as instructional materials (e.g., an arithmetic curriculum); access to activities (e.g., extra recess) or other rewards (e.g., an "A" grade); or environmental conditions, such as room temperature (e.g., 70° versus 75°) or seating arrangement (e.g., individual versus paired versus small group). In all cases, however, independent variables are changed in order to discover whether and/or to what extent their changes cause changes in a dependent variable.

A *functional relationship* exists when the level of a dependent variable depends upon the level of an independent variable. When increases in on-task behavior are dependent upon increases in teacher praise, on-task behavior is said to be a function of teacher praise. Conversely, when behavior is not dependent upon levels of an independent variable, a functional relationship does not exist.

Classes of Independent Variables

Independent variables in applied behavior analysis are environmental events or conditions. Traditional research often treats types of people (e.g., retarded versus nonretarded children) as independent variables, but for applied behavior analysts, subject differences are not considered fruitful areas of investigation. This is not to say that applied behavior analysts believe that subject differences do not exist, but rather that they are not fully open to being changed. No one would want to change a nonretarded child into a retarded child, so the differences between the behaviors of retarded and nonretarded persons are not of primary interest as *independent* variables. Instead, applied behavior analysts focus their attention on aspects of retarded children's environments that can be changed in order to improve their behavior. In this way, the differences in the behaviors of retarded and nonretarded persons are of interest as *dependent* variables.

One system for classifying independent variables relies on describing these variables in terms of their temporal relationship to the behavior of concern. When a teacher says, "Look, Janie. What color is this?" and points to a yellow flower, the teacher's behavior, including the verbal behavior, and the flower are all *antecedents* (events that occur before the behavior) to Janie's response, "Yellow." Other examples of antecedent events are commands, questions, models of how to do something (e.g., how to form the letter *m*), pictures which students are to name, part of instructional materials, and greetings (e.g., "Hello"). When the teacher then says, "Yes, it is yellow," and tossles Janie's hair, these events are all *consequences* (events that occur after the behavior) of the child's behavior. Other examples of subsequent events, consequences, are praise, token rewards, saying "thanks," and having to clean up spilled milk. A third class of independent variables refers to the environmental *conditions* that exist before, during, and after a behavior occurs. These conditions are called *setting events* and examples include the number of children in the room, air temperature, size of the room, furniture arrangements, and so forth. Whether or not antecedents, consequences, and setting events have effects on dependent variables is determined by systematically changing them and observing whether the behavior changes.

INDIVIDUAL ANALYSIS

Traditionally, the means for determining whether events or conditions control behavior has been to compare the average behavior of groups of children who are exposed to different teaching procedures: randomly selected groups exposed to certain levels or types of independent variables. There are many examples of this type of study. In teaching reading, young children who are given intensive training in phonic word attack skills perform better on tests of decoding than children taught by look-say approaches (Bliesmer & Yarborough, 1965; Carnine, 1977; Chall, 1967; Jeffrey & Samuels, 1967; Neville & Vandever, 1973; Potts & Savino, 1968). A group of institutionalized retarded children who lived on a unit using operant conditioning procedures were rated more socially well-adapted than similar children living on units emphasizing self-help, motor control, social skills, and communication or living on units emphasizing common recreational, self-help, and social skills (Roos & Oliver, 1969).

If one wished to assess the effects of contingent praise on correct responding using a group design, one could compare the average number of correct responses for a group of children receiving praise when correctly responding with the average number of correct responses for a group of children receiving praise at random times. In contrast, however, one could ask the same question (Is correct responding a function of contingent praise?) and seek to answer it by measuring the performance of an individual child. In this case one would measure correct responding several times under noncontingent (random) praise conditions and then, continuing to measure the same child's correct responding, change conditions so that praise would be given only when the child responded correctly. Hart,

Reynolds, Baer, Brawley, and Harris (1968) found that the cooperative play of a young girl was a function of contingent praise. The major difference between group and single-subject[1] studies is the type of observation. In the single-subject design each individual is observed under each condition, whereas, in the group design, individuals *may* be observed under each condition, but they usually are not—one group of individuals is observed under one condition, while another group is observed under a different condition. In single-subject studies, it is essential that each individual be considered separately. This does not mean, however, that the number of children studied must be limited to one. As long as each child is observed at each level of the independent variable and his/her performance at one level is compared only to his/her performance at another level, the design is a single-subject design.

Single-subject designs are not the end-all, and like all else, they have both advantages and disadvantages. A major advantage of single-subject designs is that the differences between individuals (between-subjects variability) do not cloud the evaluation of whether different levels of independent variables have different effects. Between-subjects variability is a major reason for group designs requiring the statistical evaluation of *average* differences. But, in single-subject designs, between-subject variability is controlled by having the same subject in each condition, there simply is no comparison *between* individuals. This leads to another advantage of the single-subject designs that allows one to draw conclusions about individuals. When well-designed and executed, single-subject designs make it possible for one to understand why an individual behaves in a certain way. Group designs do not allow this because they consider *averages* rather than *individuals*. Other advantages of single-subject designs are that they rule out, in large measure, contributions of other variables that may influence behavior changes, they are eminently useful in applied settings, and they do not require sophisticated statistical assumptions and analyses.

However, there are some disadvantages to these designs. One disadvantage is that the results of single-subject studies have somewhat limited generalizability to other subjects, groups of subjects, or settings. To some extent, this shortcoming can be circumvented by repeated demonstrations of a functional relationship using different individuals in different settings. A second disadvantage (although not limited to single-subject studies) is that simply conducting an experiment, any experiment, may contribute to behavior changes (Campbell & Stanley, 1963; Kazdin,

---

[1]*Single-subject* is only one of the many terms used to describe applied behavior analysis designs. Others include *intrasubject, within-subject, individual-subject,* and $N=1$.

1973). To some extent this problem can be avoided by unobtrusive measurement (Webb, Campbell, Schwartz, & Sechrest, 1966), but such measures are usually indirect indicators of behavior. Other disadvantages (Kazdin, 1973) are that 1) one cannot compare relative effectiveness of large programs, such as one curriculum versus another curriculum; 2) one cannot assess the initial effects of different programs because an individual goes through them sequentially, and the sequence may lead to additive effects; and 3) one cannot determine long-term effects because there is no provision for comparing the behavior of an untreated subject (whose behavior changes due to natural causes) with the behavior of a treated subject over the months or years involved.

In spite of these limitations, single-subject designs are quite useful in determining whether one's actions affect the behavior of others. This is particularly true in education where the major interest is to change the behavior of individuals as a result of teaching. Single-subject designs allow one to quickly determine whether the teaching activities have done what he/she had hoped they would do.

IDENTIFYING FUNCTIONAL RELATIONSHIPS WITH APPLIED BEHAVIOR ANALYSIS

Undoubtedly, there are many functional relationships in the educational environments of retarded children, and applied behavior analysis can be used to identify them. To do so, one must follow certain rules. The first rule is that *the dependent variable must be behavior*. The second rule is that *analysis must focus on the behavior of individuals* or on the direct product of their behavior (e.g., written arithmetic answers). The third rule is that *measures* of an individual's behavior *must be reliable*. The fourth rule is that the *design* of a study must include changes in the independent variable that *demonstrate a functional relationship*. After a brief discussion of the third rule, *reliability,* attention is shifted to the major single-subject designs that allow one to identify functional relationships.

Reliability

In most applied behavior analysis studies, measurement of the dependent variable is accomplished by frequent and direct observation of behavior. If, for example, the dependent variable is the number of times that a student answers correctly, then an observer would simply record, during a specified time period, each occurrence of correct and incorrect responding. If the behavior of concern is following teacher directions, then an observer would watch over a period of time and record each teacher command and note whether or not it was followed. In both of these examples the observer simply records the occurrence of events. In other forms of recording, observers might record 1) the duration of a behavior (e.g., the length of each tantrum), 2) whether or not a behavior occurred during a short interval of time (e.g., during the last 10 seconds, did the student smile?), or 3) whether or not the behavior was occurring when the observer looked at the student at prespecified time periods (e.g., every 10 seconds the observer looks at the student to see whether he/she is working on a task).[2]

There is likely to be some error in all observation systems. Observers may not see a behavior occur, may count another behavior as an occurrence of the target behavior, may lose track of time and record for too long or short a period, or in some other way make a mistake. Obviously, when inaccurate observations occur, the determination of functional relationships is jeopardized. In order to combat this problem, applied behavior analysts have devised procedures for checking on the reliability of observational data.

In general, observational reliability is assessed by having two observers record data simultaneously and then comparing the two records in order to find instances of agreement and disagreement. When the number of instances of agreement is high and the number of instances of disagreement is low, the observation is considered reliable. For example, Kazdin (1977b) recorded the number of 10-second intervals that a retarded child was attentive for the full 10 seconds. The observations of a second observer were then compared with those of the first observer by counting the number of intervals for which both observers recorded attentive behavior and the number of intervals for which both observers recorded inattentive behavior and labeling the total of these two counts as "agreements." Then the number of intervals when one observer recorded attentive behavior while the other recorded nonattentive behavior was counted and the total number of these intervals were called "disagreements." In order to determine the percentage of agreement, the total of the *agreements* was divided by the total of the *agreements plus disagreements* and multiplied by 100. When this was done for 37 separate sessions, Kazdin found that agreement between observers ranged from 86% to 100% with a median agreement of 95%, which means that observers were in agreement about whether the child was behaving attentively 95% of the time.

---

[2] Each of these observation techniques is known by a variety of names. The reader who is interested in descriptions and discussion of observation procedures is referred to Repp, Roberts, Slack, Repp, and Berkler (1976).

There are, of course, many ways to calculate observer reliability and there are many factors that affect reliability. These issues have been widely discussed (Baer, 1977; Hartmann, 1977; Hopkins & Hermann, 1977; Kazdin, 1977a; Kratochwill & Wetzel, 1977; Yelton, Wildman, & Erickson, 1977) and they go beyond the purpose of this chapter. The important point is that one must have reliable measurements of the variables in order to determine whether independent variables have functional effects on dependent variables.

Designs

The essential characteristics of single-subject designs are that 1) all levels of the independent variable that are to be studied are applied to the same subject and 2) the changes in the dependent variable are analyzed only with respect to that subject. In general, the purpose of single-subject designs is to meet the goals discussed at the beginning of this chapter: to change behavior and to find out why behavior changes. More specifically, there are five major purposes of the single-subject design (Bailey, 1978): 1) solving problems, 2) demonstrating the effectiveness of procedures, 3) comparing procedures, 4) conducting a parametric analysis, and 5) conducting an analysis of the components of procedures that have previously been shown to be effective.

Examples of these five goals should make them clear. *Solving problems* is an important objective: one needs to know how to change problematic behaviors, such as self-injury. *Demonstrating effectiveness* is also important because a procedure that has been shown to change certain behaviors can be used again when one faces the same behaviors. If one knows that certain procedures are effective in toilet training, one can rely on them when he/she has a student who is not trained. *Comparing procedures* allows one to determine whether one procedure is more effective than another: is social reinforcement more, less, or just as effective as token reinforcement? Conducting *parametric analyses* involves evaluating the effectiveness of several levels of the same independent variable as opposed to several different independent variables: which amount of free time—1 minute, 5 minutes, or 10 minutes—has the greatest effect on correct responding? Conducting a *components analysis* refers to investigating the contributions of parts of a procedure already known to be effective. For example, a token economy has many components—the tokens, social interactions during delivery of tokens, back-up reinforcers, and so forth—and one may be interested in determining the relative contribution of each part to the overall effectiveness of a token program.

Each of these objectives suggest a different type of single-subject design. The most common types—reversal, multiple baseline, multi-element, and changing criterion—are presented in some detail over the following pages. Many variations on these designs are also discussed, and there are other designs that may be of interest (see, e.g., Hersen & Barlow, 1976).

Reversal Design The reversal design—also known as the equivalent time samples (Campbell & Stanley, 1963), intrasubject replication (Sidman, 1960), or ABAB design (Kazdin, 1973)—consists of at least three phases during which the independent variable is either present or absent. During the phases where the independent variable is not present, the level of the dependent variable should be about the same. When the independent variable is present, the level of the dependent variable should change. In this design, behavior analysts seek to demonstrate the independent variable's control over the behavior by changing it at will. When the introduction of the independent variable leads to a change in behavior and its withdrawal leads to a return to previous levels, the investigator has demonstrated a functional relationship. When the same functional relationship has been shown with other students, the independent variable merits use as an instructional procedure. This is the essence of teaching: When the alteration of environmental events leads to a planned change in behavior, it can be said that the student has been taught that behavior.

The common characteristics of reversal designs are that 1) they all begin with a baseline period, 2) they all introduce an independent variable that changes the level of the behavior, and 3) they all change the level of the behavior back to or near the earlier baseline level. Often these successive steps are labeled *A* (baseline) and *B* (intervention). The simplest version of a reversal design, then, is ABA: baseline, intervention, baseline (Figure 1). Walker and Buckley (1968) were concerned with the attending behavior of a student and how it might be increased. During baseline (base operant rate in the figure) the child was observed to be attending during no more than 40% of the 10-second intervals; during the treatment, which involved earning points for attending, the child was observed to be attending during almost 80% or more of the intervals. When the independent variable was withdrawn (extinction), the child's attending behavior reversed to levels close to those observed during baseline. Clearly, the dependent variable changed as a function of the independent variable's application and removal.

The baseline phase in reversal designs (and in all of the designs to be discussed with the exception of the multi-element design) provides a standard against which the onset of treatment may be compared. Often, the length of the baseline period is determined on the basis of administrative

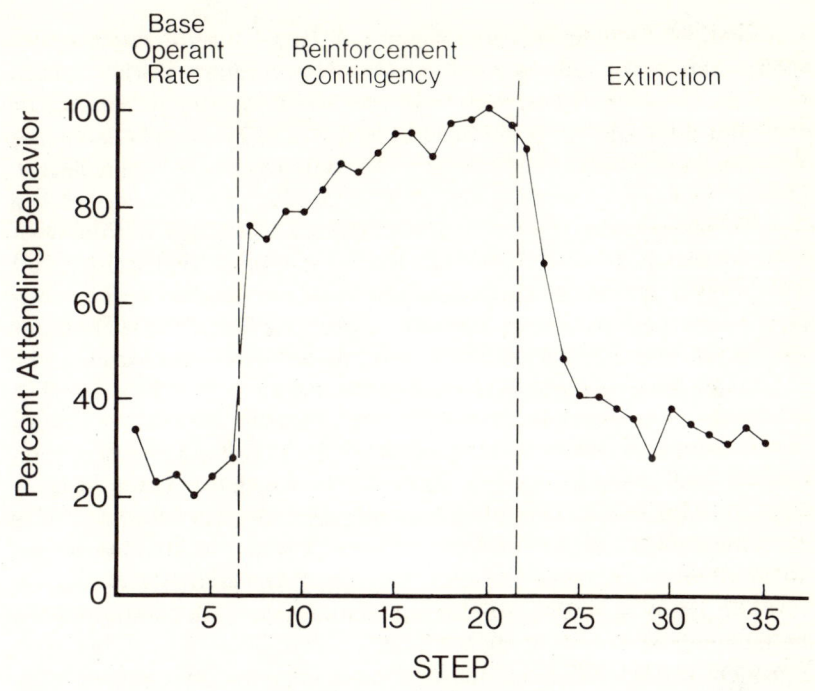

Figure 1. An ABA reversal design showing percentage of attending behavior during 10-minute observation sessions. (From Walker & Buckley, 1968; reprinted by permission.)

requirements or on the amount of time available for completing a study. However, from a research viewpoint, the termination of baseline and the beginning of treatment should be based on whether the level of behavior during baseline is *stable* or whether continuation of baseline is *not in the best interests* of the subject. The level of a behavior may be considered stable when it meets some criterion of regularity. A rule of thumb for determining stability is that the level of behavior for any one of the last five observation sessions must not exceed the average of those five observation sessions by more than 20%. For example, if the observations for the last 5 days were 10, 14, 8, 9, and 9, the average would be 10, and 20% of the average would be 2, so the range for stability would be 10 ± 2, or 8 to 12. One of the observations (14) exceeds this range so these data would be considered unstable; had the observation been 11 instead of 14, these observations would have met the stability criterion. If the baseline level of behavior is unstable, then the variations may obscure the effects of an independent variable. The consequence would be that one might incorrectly decide that the independent variable did not change the level of the dependent variable. The second decision rule for terminating baseline—when continuation of baseline is not in the subject's best interest—refers to situations where continued observation without intervention may be harmful to a child. Suppose, for example, that the three previous observation sessions of a child who bangs her head have shown 9, 26, and 37 head bangs per school day. These data do not meet the stability criterion, but, clearly, it would be harmful to allow the child to continue to bang her head so often. Consequently, the termination of baseline and the beginning of treatment would be wise. In a more general statement, this decision rule says that baseline may be terminated when the level of behavior is increasing if the purpose of the next phase is to decrease the behavior. Baseline may also be terminated when the level of the behavior is decreasing if the purpose of the next phase is to increase behavior.

In the first example of reversal designs there were three phases (ABA), but this is not the most common form of these designs. More frequently, applied behavior analysts go at least one step further and reintroduce the independent variable after the return-to-baseline phase. This yields the ABAB reversal design (see Figure 2). Knapczyk and Livingston (1974) alternated baseline and training phases in order to observe the effects of prompting an EMR junior high school girl to ask questions when she encountered trouble doing her reading assignments. Although the independent variable (directing the student to ask questions and providing immediate feedback whenever she did so) was applied only to one dependent measure (number of questions asked), Knapczyk and Livingston also observed the child's on-task behavior and reading performance accuracy. The lower two graphs indicate that prompting question asking also influenced these measures, and the upper graph indicates the direct effects of this treatment. The ABAB reversal design demonstrates a functional relationship even more clearly than the ABA design because the second introduction of the independent variable after the behavior has reversed to baseline levels replicates (repeats) the demonstration shown during its first introduction. Conceivably, in the ABA design some other uncontrolled variable may have occurred at the same time that the independent variable was introduced and this uncontrolled variable could have caused the change. In the ABAB reversal design, the reintroduction of the independent variable decreases the chances that this competing hypothesis can explain changes in the dependent variable. Another reason that the ABAB reversal design is widely used evolves from the first goal of applied behavior analysis and education, changing behavior. When the introduction of the independent variable causes a change in a behavior that needed changing, then it is beneficial to make this change. By reintroducing the independent variable, the behavior analyst not only replicates the change found between the first A and B phases, but the student is left in a better

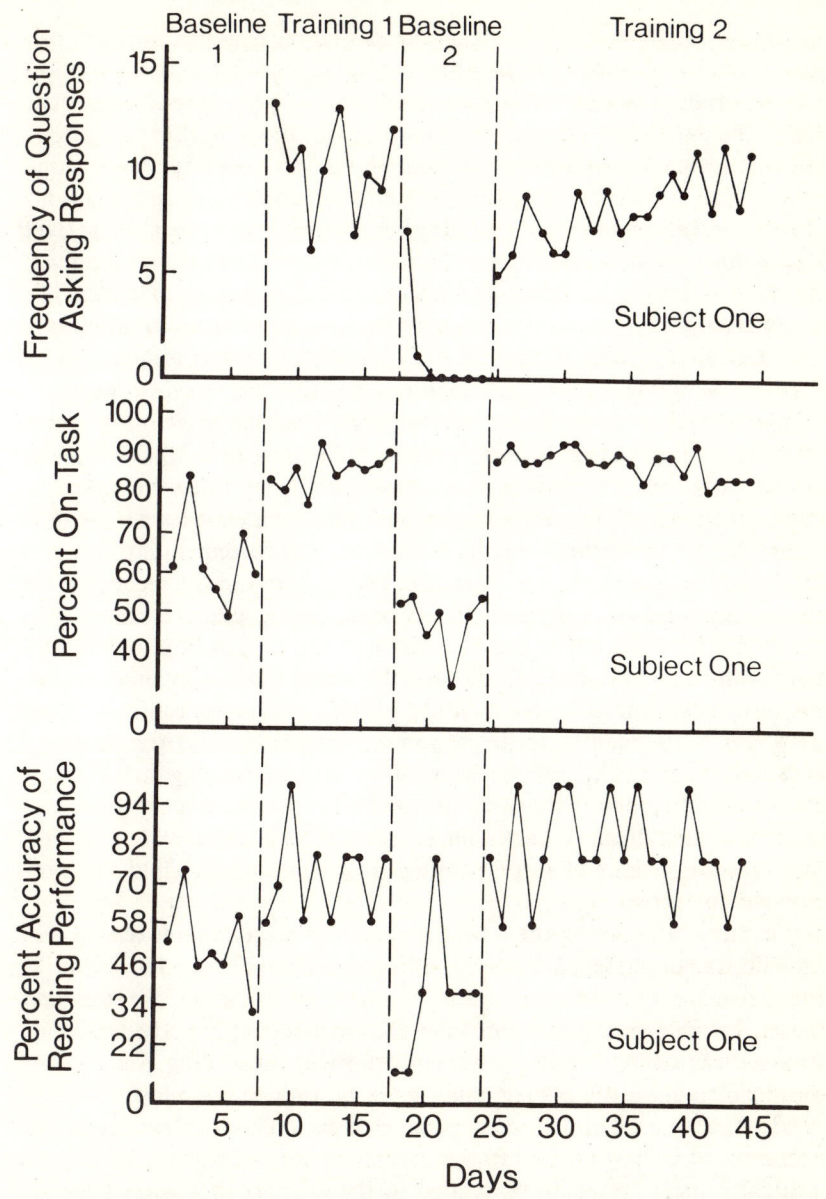

Figure 2. An ABAB reversal design showing frequency of question asking, percentage of time on task, and percentage of accurate responses to reading comprehension questions over 45 observations. (From Knapczyk & Livingston, 1974; reprinted by permission.)

position than the one in which he/she was found. Not reinstituting a successful and needed treatment leaves one in an ethically tenuous position.

There are several variations on the ABAB reversal design which primarily involve alterations in the first and third phases. The first variation is appropriate when the child does not know how to make the response that is the dependent variable. Usually this occurs in teaching situations where students are to learn to do something that they have never done before, such as write certain letters or numerals, add given number combinations, and answer particular kinds of questions. When the baseline level is zero, then a very short baseline period is appropriate. However, when the baseline level is not zero and when the objective is to teach students to do something more or less often or to do it in more or fewer situations than they already do it, then a short baseline is not appropriate.

The second variation is used either when the behavior is expected to reverse slowly or when there is little hope that the level of behavior achieved during the first treatment phase will reverse to the baseline level. In this variation, the programmer actually arranges a new treatment to change the B-phase level of behavior back to the baseline level. One procedure for accomplishing this is to schedule reinforcement so that it is contingent on the absence of the target behavior (when the second phase increased behavior). For example, Grimm, Bijou, and Parsons (1973) reported a procedure that taught a young handicapped boy to correctly match numbers and numerals. During the phase when individual teacher attention was withdrawn, the child's performance did not return to baseline levels. Subsequently, feedback and reinforcement for correct answers were also withdrawn, but the level of correct responding still did not reverse. Finally, incorrect responding was reinforced and the level of correct responding dropped back to near where it had been during baseline. At this point, Grimm et al. reinstituted treatment and the child again responded correctly.

A third variation on the ABAB reversal design maintains typical second and fourth phases, but alters the first and third phases. In this variation subsequent events are made noncontingent during the baseline phases. For example, if one were interested in assessing the effects of contingent and noncontingent token reinforcement on reading comprehension performance, the phases might be programmed as follows: During the first phase each child would be given a set number of tokens at the beginning of each day; during the second phase the number of tokens each child received would be related to the number of correct answers each child made to comprehension questions; during the third phase, at the beginning of each day, each student would be given the average number of tokens he/she earned during the last few days of phase two; during the fourth and last phase tokens would again be earned on the basis of number of correct comprehension answers. In the first and third phases, the tokens would not be contingent on correct answering, while during phases two and four, tokens would be contingent on correct responding.

In a fourth variation, multiple treatments are tried, each followed by a reversal to baseline conditions. For example, White, Nielsen, & Johnson (1972) studied three different timeout periods and a baseline period: baseline (A), a 1-minute isolation (B), a 15-minute isolation (C), and a 30-minute isolation (D). Since the sequential introduction of treatments is difficult to evaluate with single-subject designs because effects may be additive, White et al. had several children serve as subjects for several of the possible sequences of treatment. The treatment sequences were: ABACADA, ADACABA, and ACADABA.

The major advantage of the ABAB reversal design is that it can provide a strong demonstration of functional relationships. When the level of the dependent variable changes at the same time that the independent variable is introduced, withdrawn, and reintroduced, there can be little question that the reason it changed was the presence or absence of the independent variable. For education this is a great asset. Teachers can be certain that their teaching actions account for the changes in their students' behavior.

Among the disadvantages of the reversal design are that 1) the reversal may not be ethical, 2) the period required to reverse is one in which treatment is not available, 3) some behaviors do not reverse, 4) some behaviors do not stabilize, and 5) order effects confuse findings. The problem of *ethics* is summed up in this question: If baseline levels of the behavior were problematic, why return to baseline and, hence, raise the problem again? On the other hand, there may be cases in which the demonstration of a functional relationship is so important in terms of helping others that a reversal is necessary. The problem of *time* refers to the length of time required to obtain a reversal during which time the child receives no treatment. This problem of time is also an ethical one because it is concerned with withholding a presumably beneficial treatment. Fortunately, there are ways around these dilemmas that involve using one of the other designs discussed later in this chapter. The problem of *behaviors that do not reverse* refers to situations in which baseline levels of the dependent variable are not recovered. Differential reinforcement of other behaviors (DRO), as was used by Grimm et al. (1973), is an attempt to circumvent this problem. DRO is not always appropriate, however—as in the ethical dilemmas just described—and DRO is not always successful. The problem of *behaviors that do not stabilize* has been discussed. When baseline levels of the independent variable are judged unstable, the changes obtained during treatment must be greater than changes obtained when baseline levels are stable. The problem of *effects being obscured by order* refers to situations in which several treatments are introduced sequentially, as in the White et al. (1973) study. The problem is that one cannot be sure the effects of a later level of the independent variable would have been the same had it been introduced earlier. In this study, the effects of the 1-minute timeout were different when it was the first treatment than when it was the second or third treatment. When the 1-minute timeout came first, behavior was reduced by 61%; when it came after the 30-minute timeout phase, the 1-minute timeout actually *increased* behavior by 31%, when it followed both the 15-minute and 30-minute phases, the 1-minute timeout again *increased* behavior, this time by 67% in comparison to the preceding baseline. Obviously, the order in which levels of the independent variable are introduced in multi-treatment designs can have major effects on the dependent variable and may lead to inaccurate conclusions.

Multiple Baseline Design The multiple baseline design (Baer, Wolf, & Risley, 1968) provides a solution to many of the problems posed by the reversal design because the multiple baseline does not necessarily require a reversal. In a multiple baseline design at least two baselines are begun at the same time, the baselines are kept on different dependent variables (e.g., different behaviors of one individual, the same behavior of different individuals, or the same behavior of the same individual but in different settings), and the independent variable is introduced at different times for each baseline. In a sense, the multiple baseline can be thought of as separate AB designs with interventions that are staggered in time.

The multiple baseline design demonstrates functional relationships by showing that when the independent variable is introduced, the level of the dependent variable changes regardless of the behavior to which it is applied or when it is applied. When behavior changes at the first introduction of treatment, there is a suggestion of a functional relationship; but, the change may have been caused by other factors. When the change is replicated on the second dependent variable, however, the argument that change was caused by the independent variable is strengthened; and when the effect is observed again on a third dependent variable, one can be reasonably certain that a functional relationship has been identified. Borstein, Bellack, and Hersen (1977) assessed the effects of a social skills training package, including instructions, feedback, modeling, and rehearsal, on several behaviors of young children. Baseline data were collected on 1) the ratio of eye contact time to duration of conversation, 2) the loudness of speech, 3) the number of requests for an interaction partner to change an inappropriate behavior (e.g., ask another child who cut into line to take the appropriate place at the end of the line), and 4) an overall assertiveness rating. The social skills training package was then applied to each of the first three measures at different times: 1) to eye contact/ speech duration beginning with the fourth session, 2) to loudness of speech beginning with the seventh session, and 3) to number of requests beginning with the tenth session. As can be seen in Figure 3, each time the independent variable (the skills training package) was brought to bear on a new behavior, the level of the dependent variable changed. This is a powerful demonstration of the effectiveness of the treatment procedures. Figure 3 also shows how the level of the overall assertiveness rating changed; interestingly, the raters did not judge the subject's assertiveness to have changed until she began to make more requests for others to change their behaviors. (However, this does not necessarily indicate that the raters' judgments were dependent on changes in the child's requests; further analysis would have to be conducted in order to warrant this assertion.)

As was the case with reversal designs, multiple baseline designs require decisions on when to terminate baselines. In general, the same rules apply to the baseline of the first behavior as apply in the ABAB reversal design: Baseline may be terminated when stability has been achieved or when the level of the behavior is changing in a direction contrary to the subject's best interests. The rule for terminating baseline for the second, third, fourth, etc. behaviors is slightly different, however. Each of these behaviors may be terminated when the independent variable has produced a stable effect on the preceding behaviors. That is, after the intervention has shown a stable effect on the first behavior, the baseline for the second behavior may be ended and intervention begun on it; after intervention has shown a stable effect on the second behavior, the baseline period for the third behavior may be ended and intervention begun; this decision rule is applied for each behavior in sequence.

Deciding on the sequence for introducing intervention in the multiple baseline design is another problem that deserves discussion. Although there are no firm rules for setting up such sequences, there are logical and ethical considerations that provide some guidelines. For example, suppose that posturing (standing in a semi-contorted position), self-injury (biting wrists and head banging), and inappropriate noises (screaming, growling) are behaviors of a student that require change. DRO (differential reinforcement of other behavior, defined as providing reinforcement after a certain time interval has elapsed during which the behavior has not occurred) is a treatment procedure that has been successfully used with similar behaviors (e.g., see Repp & Deitz, 1974) and could be chosen as an intervention strategy in this case. Since self-injury is the behavior that probably presents the most immediate threat to the child, this is probably the wisest choice for the first behavior on which to intervene. Of the two

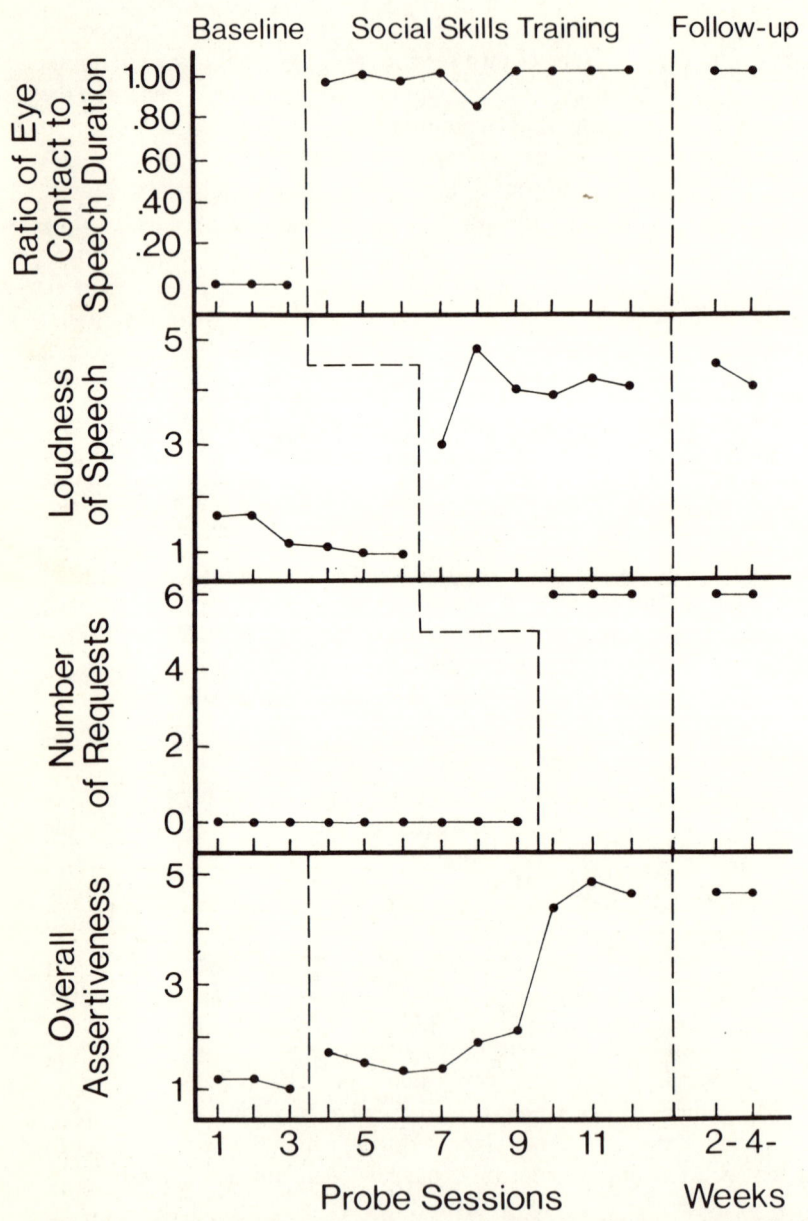

Figure 3. A multiple baseline across behaviors showing ratios of eye contact time, loudness of speech, numbers of requests, and overall assertiveness ratings observed during probe sessions. (From Borstein, Bellack, & Hersen, 1977; reprinted by permission.)

remaining behaviors, posturing and noises, noises may be seen as presenting the more immediate problem since the noises may disrupt other children and staff more than posturing. Ordering by priority the target behaviors on the basis of treatment needs is probably the most appropriate procedure for determining the sequence of interventions in multiple baseline designs.

Multiple baselines across behaviors of the same individual have been widely applied. For example, Barton, Guess, Garcia, and Baer (1970) evaluated the use of timeout in teaching eating skills. Stealing food from others, eating with fingers when utensils were more appropriate, inappropriate use of utensils, and "pigging" (eating spilled food) were successively treated. As the timeout contingency was introduced for each behavior, it continued to be in effect for each behavior to which it was previously applied. The results indicated that this subsequent event (timeout) rapidly reduced the level of each dependent variable when it was applied. In another multiple baseline program across the same individual's behaviors, Renne and Creer (1976) investigated the effects of a token reward system on three behaviors related to correct use of an apparatus for dispensing bronchodilator medication. The three behaviors—looking at the dial on the apparatus or eye fixation, correctly orienting the face and mouthpiece or facial posturing, and breathing deeply or diaphragmatic breathing—were successively treated. Figure 4 shows that the intervention had very clear effects on these behaviors.

In all of the above examples different behaviors of the same individual or individuals have been the dependent variables. In one variation of the multiple baseline design, however, the *same behavior* is the dependent variable, but the subjects are different. In a *multiple baseline across subjects,* as this variation is called, the logic and requirements remain pretty much the same. Figure 5 is an example of the multiple-baseline-across-subjects design. Frederiksen, Jenkins, Foy, & Eisler (1976) used this design to study the effects of role playing on social interactions. For Patient 1, all five target behaviors were treated: 1) percent of time looking at the person with whom the subject was talking, 2) number of irrelevant comments, 3) number of hostile comments, 4) number of inappropriate requests, and 5) number of appropriate requests. Then, after effects had been shown, the behaviors were then treated for Patient 2. The clear demonstration of the training procedures effects across patients brings to attention a special advantage of this design: multiple baselines across subjects demonstrate more general applicability of the treatment procedures without regard to individual subject differences.

In another variation of this design, the *multiple baseline across settings,* the same behavior of one subject is observed in different situations.

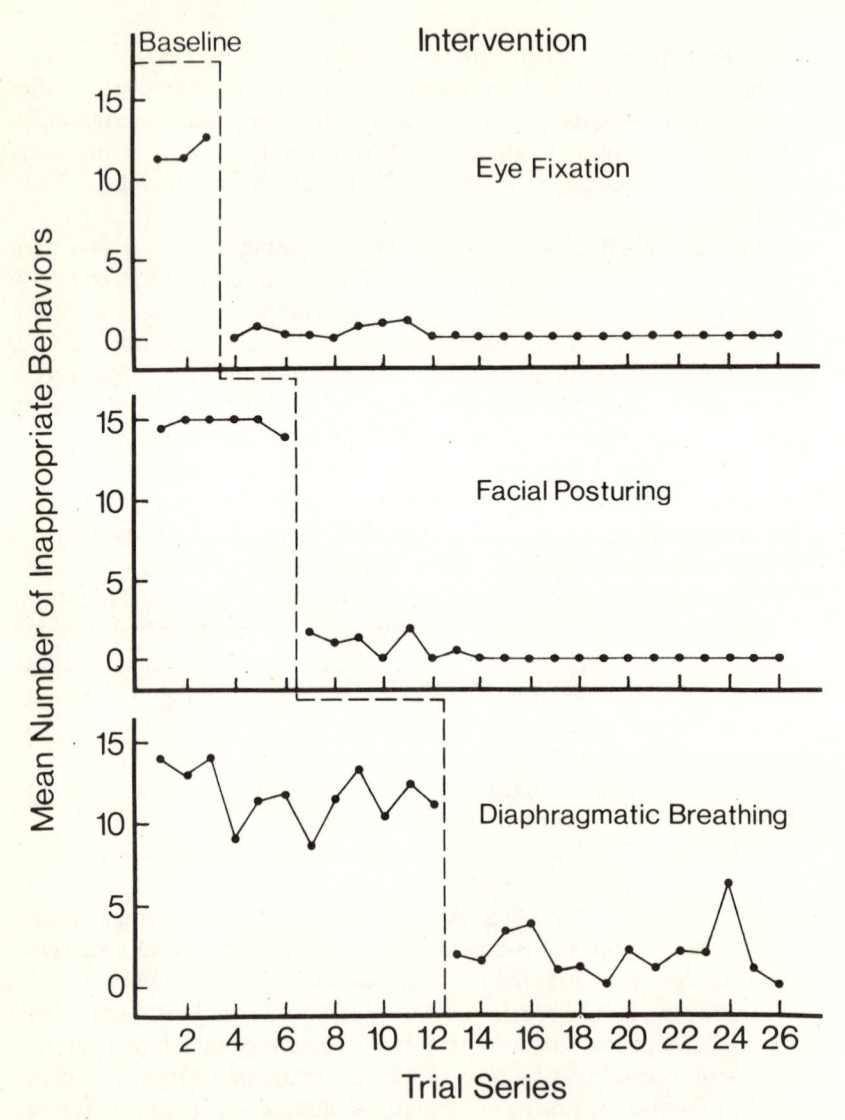

Figure 4. A multiple baseline design across behaviors showing mean numbers of inappropriate eye fixations, facial orientating, and diaphragmatic breathing during separate trials. (From Renne & Creer, 1976; reprinted by permission.)

Different settings, as used here, may refer to different rooms of the same building (e.g., kitchen, living room, den), different locations (e.g., classroom, playground, dayroom), or even to different people (e.g., teacher, aide, psychologist, parent) in the same place. Figure 6 is an example of

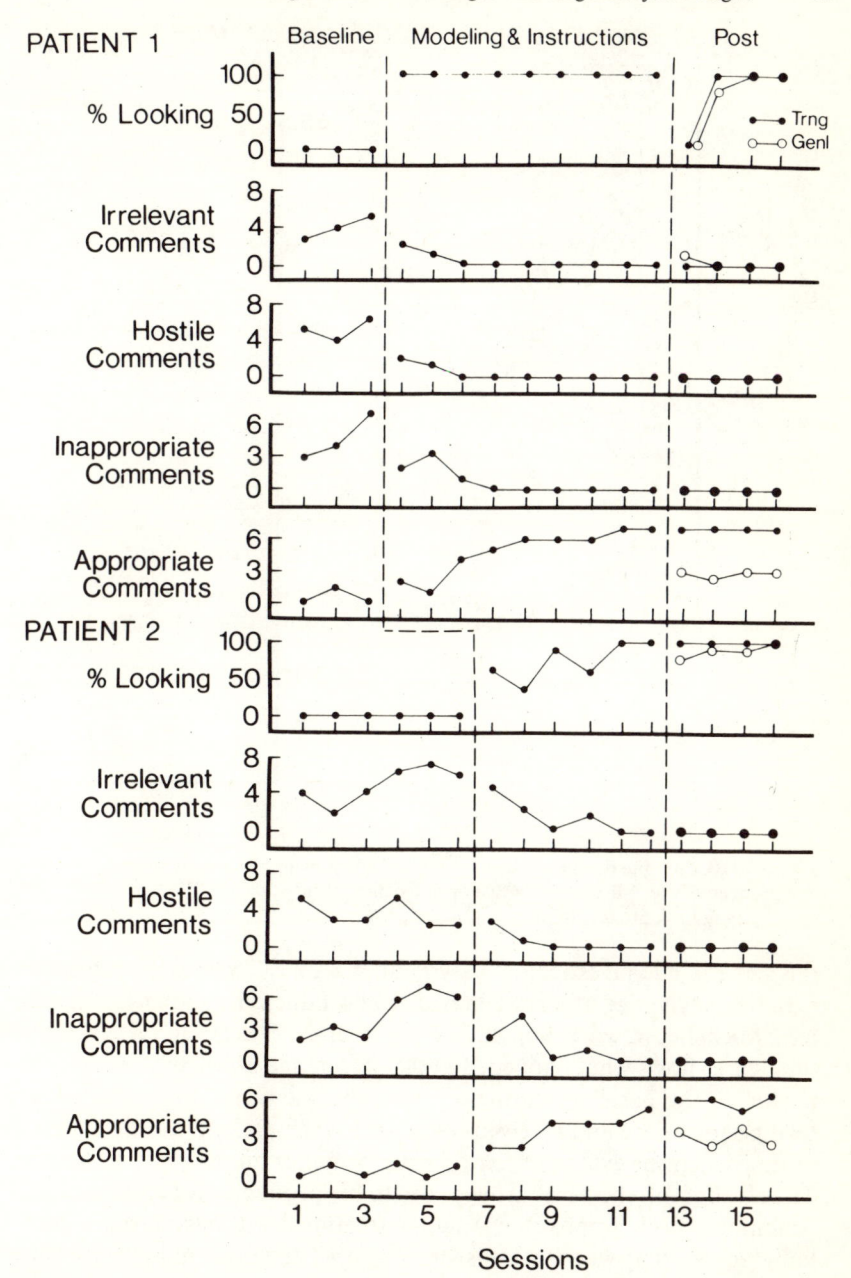

Figure 5. A multiple baseline design across subjects showing the behaviors of two children during 16 observations. (From Frederiksen, Jenkins, Foy, & Eisler, 1976; reprinted by permission.)

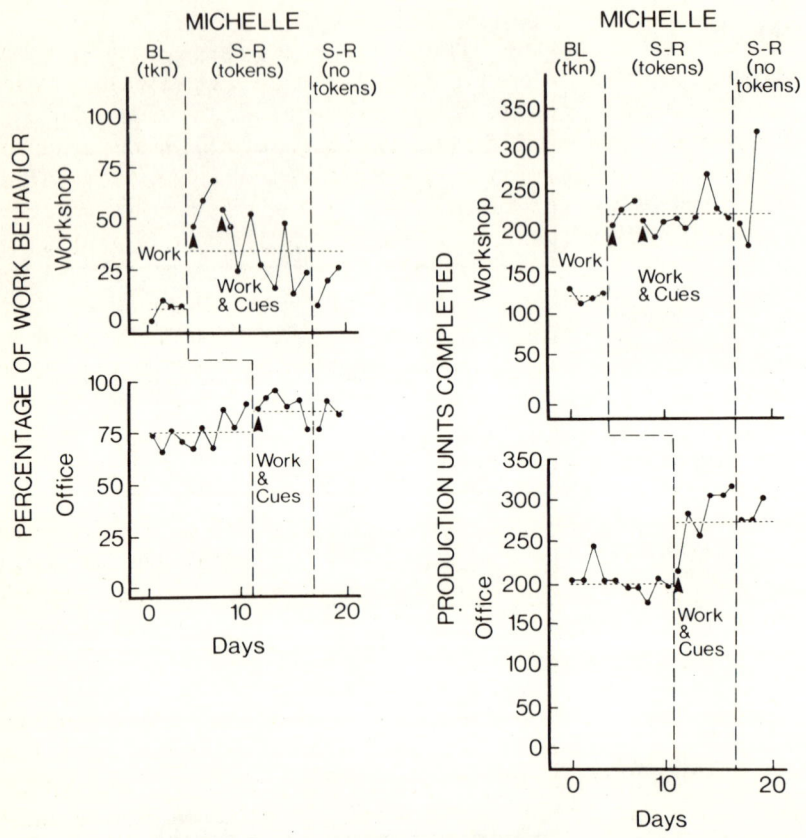

Figure 6. A multiple baseline design across settings showing percentage of work behavior and productivity for Michelle in workshop and office settings during 20 days of observation. (From Seymour & Stokes, 1976; reprinted by permission.)

this design. The investigators (Seymour & Stokes, 1976) were concerned with the percentage of work behavior and productivity shown by the subject, Michelle, in workshop and office settings. The graph on the left of the figure shows what happened to the percentage of Michelle's work behavior during baseline, during a period of time when she evaluated her own performance and received tokens for working, and during a period of time when she evaluated her own performance but received no tokens. The other graph shows what happened to her productivity across the same conditions. Both graphs show that the treatment was introduced sequentially across the two situations, making the design a multiple baseline across settings.

Some advantages of multiple baseline designs are: 1) the successive change in the level of behaviors only when the treatment is applied makes a strong case for functional relations between dependent and independent variables, 2) unlike the reversal design, a therapeutic change in behavior does not have to be reversed in order to demonstrate this relationship, and 3) the design provides an opportunity to study whether or not treatment effects generalized. For example, suppose that one chose to teach a student a system for attacking addition problems and wished to know whether the student would generalize using the system to problems on which training did not occur. The addition problems could be divided into three equally difficult groups and the child could be given 10 problems from each group each day. Hence, there would be baselines on problems in group 1, group 2, and group 3. Then, one could do the training on problems in group 1 and observe the effect of training; furthermore, if the child's performance on problems in groups 2 or 3 also changed, then the child may have generalized the use of the system. If the training did not transfer after it had been applied to only group 1 problems, then it could be applied to group 2 problems while group 3 problems were monitored for generalization. Similar applications of the multiple baseline design can reveal whether training in one setting transfers to the student's performance of the same behaviors in another setting. However, when the multiple baseline is used in this way, the argument for generalization is not ironclad because some competing hypothesis may explain the results; that is, another uncontrolled event may have interfered and caused the concurrent change in both baselines. This difficulty with using multiple baseline designs leads to another problem: when the design is used to demonstrate treatment effects rather than generalization, the behaviors observed must not be related. If the other behaviors change when treatment is introduced on the first behavior, then the design does not clearly identify a functional relationship. A further problem with the multiple baseline is that the length of the baseline periods for the second, third, or later behaviors may be countertherapeutic. When the delay that is necessary for later behaviors in the multiple baseline is not in the best interests of the student, then use of this design is inappropriate. Decisions on such matters can be made by ordering behaviors by priority or can be skirted by using another design.

Multi-Element Design In laboratory investigations of behavior, Ferster and Skinner (1957) used a multiple schedule design that has an applied behavior analysis analog: the multi-element design. Basically, the design uses several discrete stimuli, associates a different level of independent variable with each different stimulus, and assesses differences in the level of the dependent variable. Each of the stimuli acts as a sign announcing which level of the independent variable is currently in effect. In the multi-element design all conditions are present each day, as opposed to being alternately present or absent (as in the reversal design) or introduced in a staggered way (as in the multiple baseline). This does not mean that there cannot be a baseline condition; if there was one, however, it would be continued throughout the study.

Repp, Klett, Sosebee, & Speir (1975) investigated the effects of different variables in a token system. The dependent variable was the number of correct responses on a matching-to-sample task and there were four treatment conditions, each associated with a different color cue on the pages of the task. In the blue condition, tokens exchangeable for food were awarded for correct responses, while incorrect responses were ignored; in the red condition, exchangeable tokens were awarded for correct responses and deducted for incorrect responses; in the white condition, non-exchangeable tokens were awarded for correct responses and incorrect responses were ignored; in the green condition, no tokens were awarded or deducted. For each of the seven students, the sequence of conditions was varied daily. The results indicated that under the red condition, as compared to the blue condition, incorrect responding was reduced but correct responding was unchanged, suggesting that the effects of response cost procedures are specific to incorrect responding. Also, more responding occurred under the white condition than did under the green condition, suggesting that studies using baselines in which no tokens are awarded may overestimate the effectiveness of implementing token systems.

In another study using a multi-element design, Redd (1969) investigated the effects of adults reinforcing retarded children's behavior. Redd was interested in determining whether children learned to discriminate among people who dispensed reinforcement differently. In this case, the different stimulus conditions were different adults. In the first condition, the child was in a room with other children, but no adult was present. In the second condition, an adult who was in the room praised the target child and gave him candy when he played cooperatively with the other children. In the third condition, a different adult gave the target child noncontingent praise and treats. In the fourth condition, a third adult reinforced cooperative play for half the session and then gave noncontingent reinforcement during the second half of the session. (Conditions three and four are analogous to the careless reinforcement that most people practice.) The dependent variable was whether cooperative play occurred during the first 45 seconds after each different adult entered the room. When the adult who had dispensed contingent reinforcement in the second condition entered the room, the child played cooperatively with the other children. When the adult who had noncontingently reinforced the child throughout each session entered the room, the child did not engage in cooperative play. When the adult who had sometimes reinforced cooperative play entered the room, the child did not play cooperatively. However, after a while, if the child did not receive praise and candy from the third adult, he/she would begin to engage in cooperative play, as one might expect from the mixed contingent and noncontingent condition. This study shows very clearly that the way in which we reinforce children's behavior affects how they behave in our presence, even when the behaviors do not involve interactions with us.

Some advantages of the multi-element design are that: 1) a baseline condition is not necessary, although one can be used (as in the first condition of the Redd study or the green condition in the Repp et al. study), 2) all behaviors can be treated from the beginning of the study rather than having to wait for stable baselines, 3) levels of behavior do not have to be reversed, 4) several procedures can be compared simultaneously, and 5) component analysis of complex procedures can be conducted. Some disadvantages of this design are that: 1) having multiple conditions is not necessary when we are simply interested in assessing the effects of making an addition to a current program; 2) interrelationships among behaviors in each condition may obscure the contribution of any one condition, that is, when one is interested in determining which one of several procedures can be used to help children one needs to examine the contribution of that procedure alone, which may not be possible if other procedures are contributing to the effects; and 3) interrelationships among treatment conditions may cause multiple effects on the dependent variable.

Changing Criterion Design In the changing criterion design, 1) a baseline is established, 2) an independent variable is introduced, 3) a criterion for consequation is established (based on performance during the first few sessions of the intervention phase), and 4) the criterion is then systematically changed until a desired level of the dependent variable is reached. This design can be used to show that, as the consequation criterion changes, the level of the behavior changes. Hartmann and Hall (1976) characterized the changing criterion design in this way: "Each treatment phase is associated with a stepwise change in criterion rate for the target behavior. Thus, each phase provides a baseline for the following phase. When the rate of the target behavior changes with each stepwise change in the criterion, therapeutic change is replicated and experimental control is demonstrated" (p. 527).

Hartmann and Hall presented several examples of the changing criterion design, one of which was drawn from Hall and Fox (1977). In this study the dependent variable was the number of arithmetic problems completed correctly. After baseline, access to recess and playing basketball was made contingent on two correct answers. In each succeeding

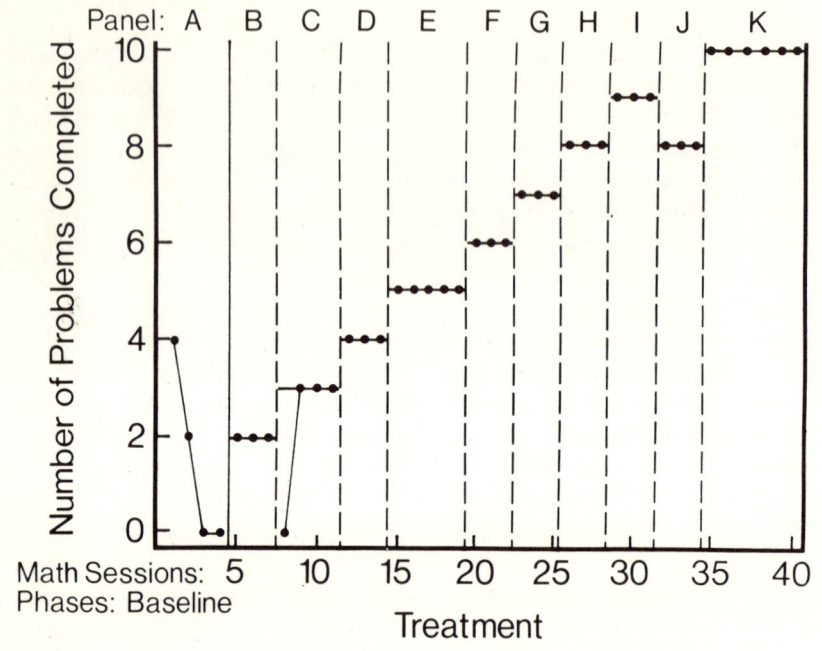

Figure 7. A changing criterion design showing the number of math problems solved correctly during 40 sessions. The criterion for each phase is shown by a solid horizontal line. (From Hartmann & Hall, 1976; reprinted by permission.)

phase, the criterion for earning recess and basketball was raised by one problem, until the ninth phase when it was lowered by one problem and the tenth phase when it was raised by two. As Figure 7 shows, whenever the criterion changed, the level of the dependent variable changed.

Figure 8 shows the results of a changing criterion design in which the experimenters (Deitz & Repp, 1973) changed the criterion for earning free time in order to reduce the frequency of students changing the topic of academic discussion. When free time was contingent on "topic switches" less than or equal to criterion, the level of "topic switches" decreased. In this example, a variation on the design is also illustrated: Deitz and Repp incorporated a reversal phase in which free time was no longer contingent on a criterion number of responses, thereby more clearly demonstrating the functional relationship.

As was the case in the reversal and multiple baseline designs, a decision on when to terminate baseline must be made. In the changing criterion design, this decision should be based on either stability or a countertherapeutic trend; however, this requirement is not as stringent as it is in

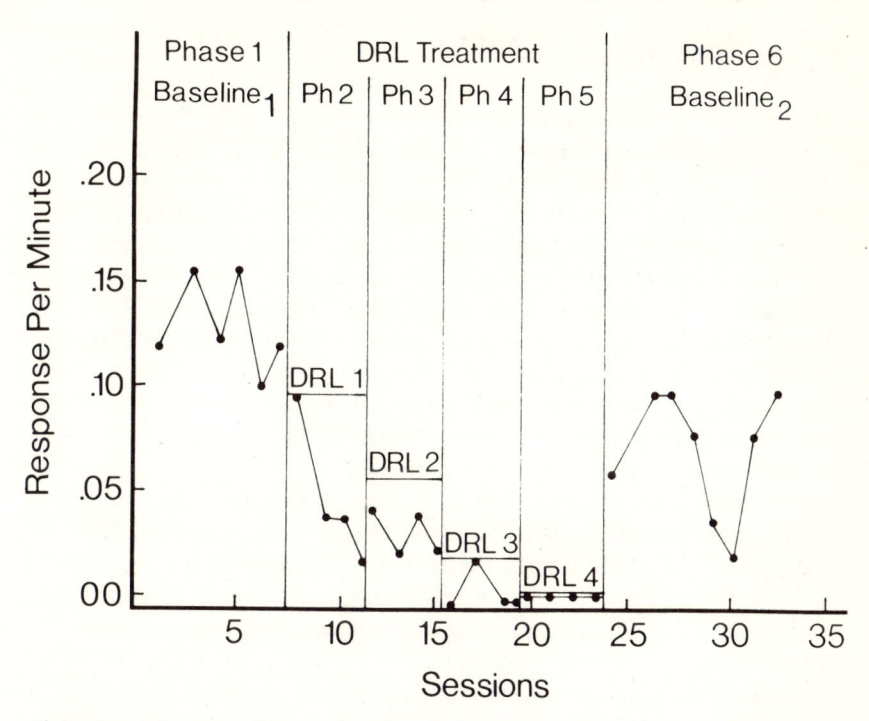

Figure 8. A changing criterion design showing the rate per minute of topic changes during 32 observations. (From Deitz & Repp, 1973; reprinted by permission.)

the other designs. A second decision that is necessary in the changing criterion design involves setting the criterion level. If the criterion is set at a level very much different from the current level of responding, the students' earning of reinforcement will be too infrequent to change behavior, and the procedure will not work. A simple way to determine the criterion is to calculate an average of responding for the last few days of baseline and use that as the first criterion. In this way the subjects will have a high probability of earning reinforcement. Later changes in criterion should be small enough that the students can be reasonably expected to achieve them, also.

Some of the advantages of the changing criterion design are that: 1) it does not require a reversal, 2) it requires only a short, or even no, baseline, and 3) it is very close to the desirable teaching technique of taking behaviors at their present level and gradually changing them to improved levels. The disadvantages of this design are that: 1) it does not allow procedure comparisons, 2) it does not allow component analyses, and 3) it can only reveal effects on single behaviors.

EVALUATING CHANGE

The designs discussed in this chapter allow applied behavior analysts to identify functional relationships. In general, the designs allow one to rule out competing explanations and to observe the effects of manipulations of the independent variable. Usually, the levels of the dependent measure are shown on a graph and are subjected only to interocular analysis. Statistical analyses are available and their application in applied behavior analysis has been widely debated (e.g., Baer, 1977a; Gentile, Roden, & Klein, 1972; Hartmann, 1974; Jones, Vaught, & Weinrott, 1977; Kazdin, 1976; Keselman & Leventhal, 1974; Kratochwill, Alden, Demuth, Dawson, Panicucci, Arntson, McMurray, Hempstead, & Leven, 1974; Michael, 1974a, 1974b; Thoresen & Elashoff, 1974). The main reasons that statistical analyses have been eschewed are that: 1) they usually require waiting until the entire study has been completed before judgment of effectiveness can be made, which is counter to behaviorist's desire to make more immediate data-based decisions; 2) large numbers of subjects are usually required in statistical analyses, but the interest of applied behavior analysts is on the behavior of individuals; 3) judgments of *statistical* significance focus on identifying small differences in the effects of treatments, although behavior analysts are not primarily interested in small differences; they are interested, instead, in identifying *large* differences of *educational* significance.

In place of statistical analyses, applied behavior analysts may perform arithmetical or visual analyses of data. Arithmetical analyses involve 1) comparing mean or median levels of the dependent variable for different phases (i.e., average of the baseline phase compared to average of the intervention phase), 2) comparing percent of change from phase to phase, 3) comparing ranges of the behavior for each phase, or 4) comparing slopes of adjoining phases. Although none of these procedures is complex, each one can provide a means for immediately examining the changes in behavior observed during changes in the independent variable.

Visual analysis of data is the most common method for evaluating the changes in behavior observed in applied behavior analysis studies. In general, behavior may 1) change in level when intervention is begun (i.e., get lower or higher), 2) stay at the same level, 3) change in slope (i.e., be going up or down), or 4) continue in the same direction. Figure 9 shows the various ways in which slope and level may combine and whether or not each combination reflects an increase (+), decrease (−), or uninterpretable change (?) in the level of the dependent variable, or whether it reflects maintenance of the level obtained during baseline.

In general, behavior can be said to have increased when the onset of intervention is accompanied by 1) an increase in the level of the behavior

Change in Slope from One Phase to the Next

	↗ (increase)	→ (same)	↘ (decrease)
↗ (increase)	+ A	+ B	? C
→ (same)	+ D	maintenance E	− F
↘ (decrease)	? G	− H	− I

Change in Level (mean, median, etc.) from One Phase to the Next

Figure 9. Possible combinations of level and slope changes from phase to phase and whether a given combination reflects an increase (+), decrease (−), or uninterpretable (?) change in behavior or reflects maintenance of the previous level of behavior.

and an increase in the slope, 2) an increase in the level of the behavior with no change in slope, or 3) no change in the level of behavior but an increase in the slope. In Figure 9 these outcomes are shown in cells A, B, and D, respectively. Behavior can be said to have decreased when the onset of intervention is accompanied by 1) a decrease in the level of the dependent variable and a decrease in the slope, 2) a decrease in the level of the dependent variable with an unchanged slope, or 3) no change in the level of behavior but a decrease in the slope. Cells F, H, and I show these outcomes. Behavior can be characterized as being maintained when both the level and slope remain unchanged, as represented in cell E. In some cases contradictory changes in level and slope make interpretation of results impossible. These cases are shown in cell C where an increased level of behavior is canceled by a decreased slope and in cell G where a decreased level of behavior is canceled by an increased slope.

CONCLUDING REMARKS

This chapter presents information on four designs (reversal, multiple baseline, changing criterion, and multi-element) commonly used in single-subject research, including some advantages and disadvantages of each of the designs. Because these designs are so commonly used in applied behavior analysis, they are often considered to be part of behavior treatment procedures. They should, however, not be so considered. They are, instead, research designs that are intended to answer research questions. In many cases, their use is antithetical to the ethical delivery of effective treatment. In these cases, those working with retarded persons should not confuse the purpose of treatment with the purpose of research.

REFERENCES

Baer, D. M. Perhaps it would be better not to know everything. *Journal of Applied Behavior Analysis,* 1977, *10,* 167-172.(a)

Baer, D. M. Reviewer's comment: Just because it's reliable doesn't mean that you can use it. *Journal of Applied Behavior Analysis,* 1977, *10,* 117-119.(b)

Baer, D. M., Wolf, M. M., & Risley, T. R. Some current dimensions of applied behavior analysis. *Journal of Applied Behavior Analysis,* 1968, *1,* 91-97.

Bailey, J. S. *A handbook of research methods in applied behavior analysis.* Tallahassee: Florida State University Press, 1978.

Barton, E. S., Guess, D., Garcia, E., & Baer, D. M. Improvement of retardates' mealtime behaviors by timeout procedures using multiple baseline techniques. *Journal of Applied Behavior Analysis,* 1970, *3,* 77-84.

Bliesmer, E. P., & Yarborough, B. H. A comparison of ten different beginning reading programs in first grade. *Phi Delta Kappan,* 1965, *56,* 500-504.

Borstein, M. R., Bellack, A. S., & Hersen, M. Social-skills training for unassertive children: A multiple-baseline analysis. *Journal of Applied Behavior Analysis,* 1977, *10,* 183-195.

Campbell, D. T., & Stanley, J. C. Experimental and quasi-experimental designs for research and teaching. In N. L. Gage (Ed.), *Handbook of research on teaching.* Chicago: Rand McNally, 1963.

Carnine, D. W. Phonics vs. look-say: Transfer to new words. *Reading Teacher,* 1977, *30,* 636-640.

Chall, J. *Learning to read: The great debate.* New York: McGraw-Hill, 1967.

Cossairt, A., Hall, R. V., & Hopkins, B. L. The effects of experimenter's instructions, feedback, and praise on teacher praise and student attending behavior. *Journal of Applied Behavior Analysis,* 1973, *6,* 89-100.

Dalton, A. J., Rubino, C. A., & Hislop, M. W. Some effects of token rewards on school achievement of children with Down's syndrome. *Journal of Applied Behavior Analysis,* 1973, *6,* 251-259.

Deitz, S. M., & Repp, A. C. Decreasing classroom misbehavior through the use of DRL schedules of reinforcement. *Journal of Applied Behavior Analysis,* 1973, *6,* 457-463.

Ferster, C. B., & Skinner, B. F. *Schedules of reinforcement.* New York: Appleton-Century-Crofts, 1957.

Frederiksen, L. W., Jenkins, J. O., Foy, D. W., & Eisler, R. M. Social-skills training to modify abusive verbal outbursts in adults. *Journal of Applied Behavior Analysis,* 1976, *9,* 117-125.

Garcia, E. E., & Trujillo, A. The effect of facial orientation during imitation maintenance. *Journal of Applied Behavior Analysis,* 1977, *10,* 95.

Gentile, J. R., Roden, A. H., & Klein, R. D. An analysis of variance model for intrasubject replication design. *Journal of Applied Behavior Analysis,* 1972, *5,* 193-198.

Gladstone, B. W., & Spencer, C. J. The effects of modeling on the contingent praise of mental retardation counselors. *Journal of Applied Behavior Analysis,* 1977, *10,* 75-84.

Grimm, J., Bijou, S. W., & Parsons, J. A. A problem-solving model for teaching remedial arithmetic to handicapped young children. *Journal of Abnormal Child Psychology,* 1973, *1,* 26-39.

Hall, R. V., & Fox, R. G. Changing criterion design: An alternative applied behavior analysis procedure. In B. C. Etzel, J. M. LeBlanc, & D. M. Baer (Eds.), *New developments in behavioral research: Theory, method, and application.* Hillsdale, N.J.: Lawrence Erlbaum Associates, 1977.

Hart, B. M., Reynolds, N. J., Baer, D. M., Brawley, E. R., & Harris, F. R. Effect of contingent and non-contingent social reinforcement on the cooperative play of a preschool child. *Journal of Applied Behavior Analysis,* 1968, *1,* 73-76.

Hartmann, D. P. Considerations in the choice of interobserver reliability estimates. *Journal of Applied Behavior Analysis,* 1977, *10,* 103-116.

Hartmann, D. P. Forcing square pegs into round holes: Some comments of "an analysis-of-variance model for intrasubject replication design." *Journal of Applied Behavior Analysis,* 1974, *7,* 635-638.

Hartmann, D. P., & Hall, R. V. The changing criterion design. *Journal of Applied Behavior Analysis,* 1976, *9,* 527-532.

Hersen, M., & Barlow, D. H. *Single case experimental designs: Strategies for studying behavior change.* New York: Pergamon, 1976.

Hopkins, B. L., & Hermann, J. A. Evaluating interobserver reliability of interval data. *Journal of Applied Behavior Analysis,* 1977, *10,* 121-126.

Jeffrey, W. E., & Samuels, S. J. Effect of method of reading training on initial learning and transfer. *Journal of Verbal Learning and Verbal Behavior,* 1967, *6,* 354-358.

Jones, R. R., Vaught, R. S., & Weinrott, M. Time series analysis in operant research. *Journal of Applied Behavior Analysis,* 1977, *10,* 151-166.

Kazdin, A. E. Methodological and assessment considerations in evaluating reinforcement programs in applied settings. *Journal of Applied Behavior Analysis,* 1973, *6,* 517-531.

Kazdin, A. E. Statistical analyses for single-case experimental designs. In M. Hersen & D. H. Barlow (Eds.), *Single case experimental designs: Strategies for studying behavior change.* New York: Pergamon, 1976.

Kazdin, A. E. Artifact, bias, and complexity of assessment: The ABCs of reliability. *Journal of Applied Behavior Analysis,* 1977, *10,* 141-150.(a)

Kazdin, A. E. The influence of behavior preceding a reinforced response on behavior in the classroom. *Journal of Applied Behavior Analysis,* 1977, *10,* 299-310.(b)

Kazdin, A. E., & Erickson, L. M. Developing responsiveness to instructions in severely and profoundly retarded residents. *Journal of Behavior Therapy and Experimental Psychiatry,* 1975, *6,* 17-21.

Keselman, H. J., & Leventhal, L. Concerning the statistical procedures enumerated by Gentile et al.: Another perspective. *Journal of Applied Behavior Analysis,* 1974, *7,* 643-645.

Knapczyk, D. R., & Livingston, G. The effects of prompting question asking upon on-task behavior and reading comprehension. *Journal of Applied Behavior Analysis,* 1974, *7,* 115–121.

Kratochwill, T., Alden, K., Demuth, D., Dawson, D., Panicucci, C., Arntson, P., McMurray, N., Hempstead, J., & Leven, J. A further consideration in the application of an analysis-of-variance model for the intrasubject replication design. *Journal of Applied Behavior Analysis,* 1974, *7,* 629–633.

Kratochwill, T. R., & Wetzel, R. J. Observer agreement, credibility, and judgement: Some considerations in presenting observer agreement data. *Journal of Applied Behavior Analysis,* 1977, *10,* 133–139.

Michael, J. Statistical inference for individual organism research: Some reactions to a suggestion by Gentile, Roden, and Klein. *Journal of Applied Behavior Analysis,* 1974, *7,* 627–628. (a)

Michael, J. Statistical inference for individual organism research: Mixed blessing or curse? *Journal of Applied Behavior Analysis,* 1974, *7,* 647–653.(b)

Neville, D., & Vandever, T. R. Decoding as a result of synthetic and analytic presentation for retarded children. *American Journal of Mental Deficiency,* 1973, *77,* 533–537.

Potts, M., & Savino, C. The relative achievement of first graders under three different reading programs. *The Journal of Educational Research,* 1968, *61,* 447–450.

Redd, W. H. Effects of mixed reinforcement contingencies on adults' control of children's behavior. *Journal of Applied Behavior Analysis,* 1969, *2,* 249–254.

Renne, C. M., & Creer, T. L. Training children with asthma to use inhalation therapy equipment. *Journal of Applied Behavior Analysis,* 1976, *9,* 1–11.

Repp, A. C., & Deitz, S. Reducing aggressive and self-injurious behaviors of retarded children through reinforcement of other behaviors. *Journal of Applied Behavior Analysis,* 1974, *7,* 313–325.

Repp, A. C., Klett, S. Z., Sosebee, L. H., & Speir, N. C. Differential effects of four token conditions on rate and choice of responding in a matching-to-sample task. *American Journal of Mental Deficiency,* 1975, *80,* 51–56.

Repp, A. C., Roberts, D. M., Slack, S. J., Repp, C. F., & Berkler, M. S. A comparison of frequency, interval, and time-sampling methods of data collection. *Journal of Applied Behavior Analysis,* 1976, *9,* 501–508.

Roos, P., & Oliver, M. Evaluation of operant conditioning with institutionalized retarded children. *American Journal of Mental Deficiency,* 1969, *74,* 325–330.

Seymour, F. W., & Stokes, T. F. Self recording in training girls to increase work and evoke staff praise in an institution for offenders. *Journal of Applied Behavior Analysis,* 1976, *9,* 41–54.

Sidman, M. *Tactics of scientific research.* New York: Basic Books, 1960.

Stimbert, V. E., Minor, J. W., & McCoy, J. F. Intensive feeding training with retarded children. *Behavior Modification,* 1977, *1,* 517–530.

Thoresen, C. E., & Elashoff, J. D. An analysis-of-variance model for intrasubject replication design: Some additional comments. *Journal of Applied Behavior Analysis,* 1974, *7,* 639–641.

Walker, H. M., & Buckley, N. K. The use of positive reinforcement in conditioning attending behavior. *Journal of Applied Behavior Analysis,* 1968, *1,* 245–250.

Webb, E. J., Campbell, D. T., Schwartz, R. D., & Sechrest, L. *Unobtrusive measures: Nonreactive research in the social sciences.* Chicago: Rand McNally, 1966.

White, G. D., Nielsen, G., & Johnson, S. M. Timeout duration and the suppression of deviant behavior in children. *Journal of Applied Behavior Analysis,* 1973, *5,* 111–120.

Yelton, A. E., Wildman, B. G., & Erickson, M. T. A probability-based formula for calculating interobserver agreement. *Journal of Applied Behavior Analysis,* 1977, *10,* 127–131.

III

Research on Mainstreaming

CHAPTER 5

Educational Provisions for Young Children with Down's Syndrome

John E. Rynders and J. Margaret Horrobin

One out of every six to seven hundred children born in the United States has Down's syndrome, a chromosomal anomaly that is generally associated with serious developmental impairment. Currently, as the most prevalent form of clinical mental retardation, it affects approximately one-quarter million families in the United States according to the Down's Syndrome Congress.

Down's syndrome children reared at home tend to do better developmentally than those reared in institutions (Centerwall & Centerwall, 1960; Stedman & Eichorn, 1964). This fact has increased parents' desire to raise their Down's syndrome infant at home and has helped to create a widespread movement to establish educational services that are centered in the child's local community. This movement has been accelerated by PL 94-142, Education for All Handicapped Children Act, which requires that a free public education, in the least restrictive environment possible, be offered to all handicapped children. No longer must new parents of Down's syndrome children think only in terms of institutional placement for their child; now parents can choose from an array of more normalized educational environments, including their own home and neighborhood school, should they elect to do so.

One result of this movement has been to place early education responsibility with the child's parents, a task that may overwhelm them with feelings of anxiety and uncertainty. Still, almost without exception, parents of Down's syndrome children harbor a hope for educational breakthroughs that will help their children develop more normally. And, relative to this hope, parents have been encouraged by evidence that early education programs can stimulate the development of Down's syndrome children in substantial ways.

EVOLUTION OF SOCIOEDUCATIONAL ATTITUDES

Historical Descriptions

Some historians trace the history of Down's syndrome back to 1866 when a physician, Langdon Down, described the condition in light of his interpretation of Darwin's thoughts on evolution. Down (1866) proposed that the syndrome represented a reversion to an earlier phylogenetic form of Oriental human (hence the term *Mongolism*). Although Down offered good clinical observations of the condition, the unwarranted racial overtones of his description of the syndrome have had unfortunate implications for socioeducational perceptions of this genetic disorder. The terms *mongol, mongoloid,* and *mongolism* have hung on tenaciously, although, at least in the contemporary professional literature, they have now largely been replaced by the term *Down's syndrome*.

Reports in the anthropological literature have also contributed to the misunderstanding of Down's syndrome. For example, the journal *Expedition* carried an article describing clay and stone artifacts (dolls, masks, statues) of the Olmec culture of Mexico and Central America (Milton & Gonzalo, 1974). Faces depicted in these artifacts, which are estimated to be around 3,000 years old, bear a striking resemblance to the facial features of present day Down's syndrome persons. Milton and Gonzalo speculate that Down's syndrome persons of that period were revered, perhaps idolized, because they were believed to be the offspring of a mating between a male jaguar and an Olmec woman. (Jaguars were worshiped by many ancient peoples because of their great strength and cunning. It is thought that the jaguar became a main totem in Olmec culture.)

With a history based in part on erroneous genetic theory and mysticism, it is small wonder that the condition has continued to carry with it a tradition of folklore and misunderstanding, which has often led to unfortunate perceptions, and in turn lowered expectations for Down's syndrome infants. For example, a mother of a Down's syndrome child recently related that, when her child was born in 1973, her husband, desperate for information, pulled the 1970 Encyclopaedia Britannica from their home library shelf and began to search it for information on the condition. Looking back on that incident now they can both laugh, though sardonically, about what he found: Down's syndrome was described under the heading "Monster." (Fortunately, the latest edition of the Encyclopaedia Britannica (1974) describes the condition under the heading "Down's syndrome.")

Recent Literature: Misinformation and Lowered Expectations

Misinformation lowers educational expectations about Down's syndrome children, and cannot help but reduce their educational opportunities. Unfortunately, misleading, if not inaccurate, statements continue to appear in the literature. In 1975, for example, in the widely read magazine *Psychology Today,* a prominent physician, Chief of the Reproductive Genetics Unit in an eastern university hospital, was quoted as saying, "You show me just one mongoloid that has an educable IQ...I've never seen even one in my experience with over 800 mongols" (Restak, 1975, p. 92).

A cursory look at the past 15 years of professional literature concerned with the educability of Down's syndrome children would suggest that the quoted statement of the Chief of the Reproductive Genetics Unit is accurate. However, a critical and intense look, one focusing on methodology, reveals some important problems that have contributed to a distorted view of educability.

Employing a computerized bibliographical search system, psychological, educational, and medical literature was searched systematically for studies on Down's syndrome persons that included data on intellectual and educational achievement. Studies dealing solely with medical aspects of Down's syndrome that included *no* measures of psychoeducational characteristics were excluded. In addition, this survey was limited to material published in the English language within the last 15 years. The initial search yielded over 650 references. Of these, 105 studies reported psychometric or other educational measures pertinent to the issue of the educability of Down's syndrome persons. From this body of studies the methodological problems were assessed. Details of our literature survey (Rynders, Spiker, & Horrobin, 1978) are not included here, but the major findings are highlighted.

Perhaps the overriding problem in studies of Down's syndrome persons is that the studies are conducted as if Down's syndrome persons are all very similar. This false assumption, which is likely to influence sampling procedures, has been reinforced by a number of persistent stereotypes. In support of this contention of overgeneralization is the finding that in the 105 studies that present data relevant to the issue of educability, information on a number of relevant or potentially relevant variables is not reported. These variables include:

1. Confirmation of diagnosis by chromosomal analysis (karyotype), including number of subjects with each specific form (i.e., trisomic, translocation, mosaic)
2. Sex of subjects
3. Residence—home or institution—and the period of time in each
4. Age at time of testing and the results presented for narrow age ranges
5. Basis for subject selection

The fact that these types of information generally are not reported in studies of Down's syndrome persons seems to indicate that many researchers think of Down's syndrome as being unitary and invariable, with little regard for the possibility of individual differences in traits and abilities.

Chromosomal Analysis Of the 105 studies in the literature that report psychometric or educational data, only 29 reported chromosome data on their subjects. (This is interesting since karyotyping has been available as a technique for nearly 20 years.) Of the 11,214 individuals included in these 105 studies, karyotyping was not reported for 9,292 or 82.9% of them. Nonkaryotyping is a problem because, without it, there is no way to rule out the possibility of a false-positive diagnosis. Furthermore, there is a controversy over whether intellectual abilities (and possibly other traits) differ among the three forms of Down's syndrome. In this regard, at least two studies indicate that persons with the mosaic form of Down's syndrome have higher IQ scores than those with the trisomic or the translocation form (Fishler, 1975; Rosecrans, 1968), but at least one other study did not find this to be the case (Kohn, Taysi, Atkins, & Mellman, 1970). Sometimes karyotyping is not feasible, or important, because of the nature of an experiment. Nonetheless, it is recommended that it be done far more routinely than it is done at present. (One should note that there are several unresolved problems related to the *procedure* of karyotyping mosaic individuals, e.g., number and specific types of body cells sampled, that further complicate the controversy.)

Sex of Subjects Regarding other information not reported or other research practices that reinforce the notion of little variability among Down's syndrome persons, in 63 of the 105 studies (60%), sex of the subjects is not reported. Few researchers in psychology studying the development and characteristics of normal children and adults would design a study or analyze data without taking the sex of the subject into account. Yet many researchers studying Down's syndrome persons, through their lack of attention to sex as a variable, seem again to be reinforcing implicitly the stereotype that all Down's syndrome persons are alike. Interestingly, at least two recent studies (Clements, Bates, & Hafer, 1976; LaVeck, personal communication) have found distinct sex differences in psychometrically assessed intelligence in Down's syndrome children.

Residency Concerning determination of residence of subjects, 25 of the studies do not report where the subjects reside, and these 25 studies represent the majority (78.6%) of the *subjects* for whom psychometric or educational data were available. Thus, drawing firm conclusions about educability expectations from the data reported in these studies is hazardous because they provide minimal data on the subjects' rearing histories.

Furthermore, where residence is reported (i.e., in 80 studies with 2,397 subjects), most of the studies (56%) deal with Down's syndrome persons in institutions, with another 14% reporting data on both home and institutionally reared persons. Stated differently, where residence is known, most of the data available are for individuals reared in institutions (i.e., 1,773 persons or 74% of these 2,397 subjects). In addition, little or no information is given concerning the quality of these institutions. For persons reared in poor institutions at least, there is now an enormous literature on the deleterious effects of institutionalization on development (cf. Blatt, 1973). Moreover, data from studies of Down's syndrome persons reared in institutions may tell little about developmental progress for individuals reared in, for example, more normalized environments.

Age Another problem concerning these studies is that many of them include data on Down's syndrome persons spanning quite large age ranges. That is, 46 studies (43.8%) report data for subjects from either infancy through age 18 or from infancy through late adulthood. In several of these studies, a large number of subjects have been rated or assessed on some ability or measure, and then a group mean is reported. Sometimes, of course, a group mean is the appropriate statistic to use. But here, again, there is often too little concern shown for individual variability or for the possibility of age as an important variable mediating differences between Down's syndrome persons. Likewise, subtle developmental differences correlated with age may be obscured by grouping data from very large age ranges.

Selection of Subjects The final variable mentioned concerns the selection of subjects for study. Often the research question dictates this selection. For example, a researcher may be interested in some characteristic of intervention for severely or profoundly retarded Down's syndrome persons. Similarly, a researcher may publish a report of case studies of Down's syndrome children with unusually high abilities. In both of these cases, subjects were *not* randomly selected. Due to this kind of selectivity, even a fairly exhaustive review of literature on Down's syndrome may not give an accurate picture of the true *incidence* of particular characteristics. In other words, there is no question that a selection bias can be appropriate for a particular experimental purpose, but unless the nature of the bias is explained carefully the professional literature becomes distorted.

Returning to the statement made by the prominent physician in the Reproductive Genetics Unit that in all his years he had not seen a Down's syndrome child with an educable IQ, the authors are tempted, based on results of the studies reviewed, particularly the preliminary results of several contemporary early education studies, to urge that physician to tell parents of newborn Down's syndrome children that their children's chances of having an IQ score in the educable range are 30%-55%. But, it is realized that probability statements based on incomplete descriptive and efficacy data are unwarranted. Nevertheless, based on the data we have presented, we would urge that physician *at least* to tell new parents of Down's syndrome children that 1) there is a definite possibility that their children will be educable on a psychometric basis, 2) there is a great deal of variability in Down's syndrome children's early developmental progress as well as in degrees and form of functioning and adjustment beyond early childhood, and 3) currently the limits of Down's syndrome children's educability are virtually unknown because past psychometric studies of educability have often been flawed, results from early education programs are just emerging, and traditional psychometric measures by themselves are too limiting. Such a portrayal is not only appropriately optimistic, it is also appropriately *fair*.

Recent Studies: Opening the Doors to Educational Opportunity

Several studies of early education for Down's syndrome children form the background for describing our work at the University of Minnesota.

Since 1971, Hayden and her associates at the University of Washington have been providing early education for home-reared infants and preschool-age Down's syndrome children, employing behavior modification techniques. The purpose of their program has been to maximize self-help, motor, social, verbal, and cognitive skills of the children and to give counseling and training to their parents. Specific objectives were developed for each child and criterion-referenced results showed that children mastered objectives with 85%-100% competency. Interestingly, children showed most progress in the areas of gross motor, social, and conceptual development, and least progress in language development. Along these lines, test-retest results for 17 children on the Denver Developmental Screening Test (Hayden & Dimitrias, 1975) reveal gains in the mean percentage of items passed in every area except language, where the mean percentage drops. This points up the difficulty of intervening effectively in the language area.

A study that has intervened quite effectively in the language area was conducted at Ohio State's Nisonger Center by MacDonald, Blott, Gordon, Spiegel, and Hartmann (1974). These investigators prepared parents of Down's syndrome children to be language trainers. Three children served as experimental subjects and three served as controls. The major objective was to increase utterance length and grammatical complexity in the children by preparing parents to foster their child's immediate generalization of language changes from imitation to parallel conversation through play activities, and by helping them to effect immediate transfer of training.

On the basis of experimental subjects' baseline performance on the Environmental Language Inventory (ELI), the "action + object" and "X + locative" rules were selected as the major classes for training. According to the authors, the "action + object" grammatical rule specifies that the experience of perceiving an action on a direct object is expressed in a child's language, generally with the action word preceding the object word, e.g., "throw ball." The "X + locative" grammatical rule indicates that when a child verbally expresses the location of a thing or an action (notated as X) the location word follows the word to be located, e.g., "ball there."

Results of the study indicated statistically significant increases in utterance length and grammatical complexity in imitation and conversation for all experimental subjects. An epilogue reports successful replication of the program with the original control subjects.

Matkin (1972), describing another language-focused early education program, reported that teaching, based on tasks of the Illinois Test of Psycholinguistic Abilities (ITPA), was helpful to Down's syndrome children. For example, in promoting auditory decoding ability, the teacher would say, "Tomorrow Mary is going shopping with her mother." Then the teacher would ask, "Who is going shopping, where is she going, and when is she going?" Results showed that children taught in this manner improved their performance levels on the ITPA and Peabody Picture Vocabulary Test.

A fourth study (Rhodes, Gooch, Siegelman, Behrns, & Metzger, 1969) was conducted with institutionalized children at Sonoma State Hospital. In this study, 10 institutionalized Down's syndrome children were compared with 10 home-reared Down's syndrome children, at chronological ages 2 and 5, on the Bayley Scales of Infant Development. Early Bayley outcomes uniformly favored the home-reared children. At 5 years of age, the institutionalized group began to receive a language enrichment program that was carried out in both the school and ward settings. When the institutionalized group receiving enriched instruction reached 8 years of age, there were no significant differences on the Bayley Scales between their performance and the performance of home-reared children. Differences favoring home-reared children remained on the Social Scale of the Bayley Scales throughout the entire project, however; overall, these findings are particularly encouraging because the population that "caught up" was an institutionalized one.

In summary, the studies reviewed in this section indicate that psychometrically-determined educability is not uncommon in Down's syndrome persons, and that a good deal can be done to stimulate their early development through education.

EXPECTATIONS OF EARLY EDUCATION PROGRAMS

Contemporary early education programs might be compared to the development of aircraft back in Charles Lindbergh's day. When airplanes of that era crossed the ocean successfully, no one involved in those early flights concluded that aircraft could not be improved. Similarly, while some early education programs have been reasonably successful in fostering positive educational development in Down's syndrome children, those involved in directing the programs would be very likely to acknowledge that early education programs can stand a great deal of improvement. Many have "flown by the seat of their pants" at times—as we have too—since the terrain of early education is not well charted. This is the state of the art-science called early education/special education. If we are honest, we will have to acknowledge that a great deal of research will be required to reveal programs that are successful, i.e., programs that will "fly" reliably and with beneficial effects on all "passengers."

PROJECT EDGE[1]

In 1968 the authors launched a longitudinal early education project for Down's syndrome infants, a family-centered project that began in the child's home with daily structured play sessions.[2] The idea was to promote

---

[1] Project EDGE (Expanding Developmental Growth through Education) is a longitudinal intervention study supported under Grant OEG-0-9-332189-4533-032 to the University of Minnesota Research, Development and Demonstration Center in Education of Handicapped Children, U.S. Office of Education, Bureau for Education of the Handicapped.

[2] The authors wish to thank parents in Project EDGE in Minnesota and Illinois who have given themselves so unselfishly to the cause of educational research for children with Down's syndrome.

the child's communication development through positive parent-child (usually mother-child) interaction, making features of the child's immediate environment, e.g., playthings, more engaging, more responsive to the child's activity, and generally more productive and pleasurable for mother and child to use together.

The goals of the EDGE Project were to:

1. Chart the development of individual Down's syndrome children and study their development in the context of their families' activities.
2. Evaluate the effects of a longitudinal, home-based, early education program, which emphasized the development of communication abilities through daily lessons involving structured play, and to conduct cross-sectional studies to verify principles that were incorporated in the home-based program.
3. Develop alternative ways of delivering early instruction to Down's syndrome infants.
4. Explore alternative ways of assessing development in Down's syndrome children.

Emphasis in this chapter is on the second goal.

Instructional Materials

Before the project began we asked ourselves, "How can enough play structure be provided so that a mother will feel confident that she knows what to do to stimulate her infant's development, without stifling her own unique maternal style?" An answer seemed to be to provide each parent with simple materials, each of which was accompanied by a lesson sheet containing printed descriptions of several short activities involving the materials, and a list of words, phrases, and sentences to be included in the activities. (Figure 1 provides a sample lesson for very young children, a Level I lesson.)

Lessons like those shown in Figure 1 provide enough structure to help mothers (and fathers) to be goal-directed but allow considerable freedom so that mothers can use the materials to suit their style preferences. Materials were chosen for their simplicity, play possibilities, and distinguishing characteristics, e.g., some make a sound, such as a tambourine and a set of animal sound boxes; some fit together in a sequence such as Kitten in a Keg; a doll, and a brush-comb-mirror set have social and self-care development value; and a bowl-boat-coin-sponge set illustrates that some objects float and some sink.

Conceptual Development

However, instructional materials were not the most important consideration in developing lessons; the *concepts* to be developed through the mate-

> **Expanding Developmental Growth Through Education (E.D.G.E.) Curriculum**
>
> 3.0–15.0 months
>
> Level I Lesson. Doll (#8)
>
> | **Activity** | **Vocabulary** (Minimum) |
> |---|---|
> | 1. To focus attention on the doll, play a game of peek-a-boo with the doll, hiding it behind the picture of the doll, behind mother's (M's) back, under child's (C's) leg, blanket, etc. | peek-a-boo
doll
where is the doll
here is the doll
behind, under, hiding |
> | 2. Point out the parts of the doll's body to C, comparing them to the corresponding parts of C's body. Help C to point to his body parts and to the doll's body parts. NOTE: As C "knows" the doll better, let doll "talk" to C. | face
hair
eyes, nose, mouth
arms, hands, fingers
legs, feet, toes |
> | 3. M makes the doll "dance" and then helps C "dance the doll." Show C that he can move his body parts as the doll does. NOTE: Chance for M to innovate a little! | dance
up, down
shake your arms (legs, hands)
wave
jump |
> | 4. Let C hold the doll as you show him the doll's bottle and how to hold it. Compare the doll's bottle to one of C's and let C drink from his as the doll does. | doll's bottle, (C's) bottle
big, little
hold
drink |
> | 5. To complete the activity, moving to a rocking chair, and holding C and the doll in your arms, rock them and sing to them. Then put the doll to bed, helping C cover the doll for "sleep." | doll's blanket, (C's) blanket
soft
rocking chair
goodnight (doll's name) |

Figure 1. EDGE lesson for children 3-to-15-months of age (revised).

rials were of central importance. But how were the concepts to be introduced to the very young Down's syndrome child? Sonquist and Kamii (1968) describe a framework designed to facilitate the transition from sensorimotor intelligence to conceptual intelligence, building a solid foundation for future development. They hypothesize that early educators need to work to effect this transition through two Piagetian dimensions: symbolization and the mastery of elementary types of relationships. The former helps a child to move from concrete sensorimotor intelligence to representational intelligence, and the latter enables the child to coordinate the relationships among things and events.

With respect to symbolization, in working with the doll in Figure 1, the lesson is begun by placing the doll on a color photograph of the doll and focusing the child's attention on both the doll and picture of the doll simultaneously, labeling them and pointing out their similarities. The mother also points to the word "doll" under the picture of the doll but draws no further attention to it. The photograph, having occupied perhaps 30 seconds of time, is put away because very young children are interested primarily in three-dimensional objects.

Mastery of elementary relationships, the second principle highlighted by Sonquist and Kamii, is facilitated by controlling vocabulary content in lesson activities. For example, again using the doll lesson as an example, earliest lessons give relatively greater emphasis to label and direct attribute vocabulary ("doll," "leg," "red"), progressing gradually to logicomathematical relationships, such as grouping and ordering relationships ("These are big," "These are the biggest"), and then to spatiotemporal relationships ("The doll is under the chair," "The doll is first").

THE SUCCESS OF PROJECT EDGE

Three types of evidence provide interrelated perspectives for judging program success:

1. Evidence that parent participants have been satisfied with the curriculum materials, feeling that their children respond well to them and that the materials are interesting and easy to use.
2. Evidence that the educational principles and practices which undergirded the program have merit.
3. Evidence that participating children have profited clearly and significantly from the early education efforts, particularly from the lessons.

Such perspectives, taken together, could be described as elements of a mixed strategy design (Wynne, Ulfelder, & Dakof, 1975), a design which calls for the use of multiple, intersecting, and overlapping indicators—indicators which are both formal and informal, and both process- and product-oriented.

In offering our findings, we have chosen to present data regarding parent satisfaction first, to give them some prominence, because data like these often receive short shrift in early education reports but merit much greater attention.

EVIDENCE OF SUCCESS BASED ON PARENT SATISFACTION

Parent satisfaction (a formative evaluation question) is equal in importance to posttreatment (summative) effects. Let us converge upon parent satisfaction from two approaches: 1) did parents think highly of the curriculum materials as they used them?; and 2) did parents observe that their children appeared interested in the activities, participating cooperatively in them when in use?

Formative Evaluation

Parent-participants completed curriculum evaluation sheets every day they used the lessons. At the top of the sheet, parents filled in the name of the lesson or lessons used on a given day, the amount of time spent on each, and the mood of their child entering the lesson, during the lesson, and after the lesson. In the body of the evaluation sheet, parents also noted their own reaction to the lesson.

The main purpose of collecting evaluations from the first group of nine parents enrolled in the project was to help us modify lessons, deleting the ones that created frequent problems. Some did. For example, we eliminated one lesson involving clay because several mothers observed that their children "ate" the clay, placing them and their children in a conflict situation (which could be avoided by introducing clay at a later time). We also substituted a four-piece puzzle and a number board (matching holes in discs to upright pegs) for a lesson involving a form board, attempting to increase the interest value of such tasks. Furthermore, a few new activities were developed to bring the total number of lessons in Level I up to 20.

Table 1 summarizes the reactions of mothers to the EDGE lessons. Only the ratings of the second group of nine mothers are presented since their evaluations were collected across the entire 30-month period. (The first group of nine mothers, after developing and piloting the original Level I lessons, were asked to focus their efforts on developing Level II and III lessons.)

Three aspects of Table 1 are noteworthy. First, parent ratings of the aggregated lessons tend, in general, to be quite good across the 30-month period. (One must acknowledge, however, that these parents' ratings are probably biased positively because they are in the experimental group.) Second, the ratings of child cooperation tend to be uniformly high across the 3-year period (in only two cases do they drop below the 70% level across the entire aggregated series). Third, there is a fair amount of variability, across mothers, in number of lessons given. We suggested, as a rule of thumb, that they present one lesson per day, but encouraged them to use child interest as their primary metric and to stay with a given lesson for several sessions if child interest was high.

In order to give a slightly different perspective on Level I lessons, the second group of parents was also asked to review the entire set of lessons, lesson-by-lesson, after they had completed the entire set, rating each one as "excellent," "acceptable," or "poor" (See Table 2). A second look at these earliest lessons seemed important since Down's syndrome children are a particularly "captive audience" at such an early age (3-15 months).

These first lessons received excellent to acceptable ratings most of the time, but there were some lessons which still needed considerable work. The refining process continued to the end of the project.

A final note on formative evaluation of lessons: high ratings of lesson quality or child interest should not be construed to mean that EDGE activities rated highly are the "best" in the universe. High ratings mean only that some materials fare better than others *within the set we chose*.

Instructional Management and Logistics

There was no cost to participants for any curriculum materials because EDGE was a federally funded project. Other parents could purchase all of the materials in Level I lessons (the first set of lessons) for around $40, and these materials would be the only materials they would need for Level II lessons. Hence, materials costs were modest. (Level II and III lessons will not be described because of space limitations.)

Time spent on EDGE lessons was limited to 1 hour each day, 6 days per week, and no lessons were given during normal public school holiday periods (except for summer vacation where we wanted to avoid a long interruption in the program). To ease possible scheduling problems, 1-hour lessons could be broken into segments as short as 10 minutes each, if parents chose to make them so, allowing lesson portions to be distributed more easily within the normal daily routine.

Another administrative procedure designed to minimize time and scheduling burdens was active encouragement on our part to turn one-half of the lesson sessions over to other members of the family, and to non-family persons after appropriate training under our direction. A further burden-lightening procedure was to help parents minimize the possibility of feelings of enmity developing between a nonhandicapped preschool sibling and the Down's syndrome child, enmity which could develop because of the special attention the Down's syndrome child received during lessons. How was this problem minimized? If the nonhandicapped child was very young, we advised the parent to work with both the Down's syndrome child and the nonhandicapped child at the same time, focusing structured play on the Down's syndrome child, but satisfying the nonhandicapped child's need for equitable attention. If, on the other hand, the nonhandicapped child was near school age, we advised the parent to let the nonhandicapped child become a "teacher's aide" so that the non-

Table 1. Summary of reactions to Levels I, II, and III Lessons by second group of mothers in EDGE Project

Mother	Child's reaction			Mother's reaction				Total number of lessons given[a]
	Cooperative	Changing	Uncooperative	Excellent	Good	Fair	Poor	
	\multicolumn{8}{c}{Level I Lessons (Approx. 3–15 mos.)}								
A	93%	0%	7%	9%	85%	6%	0%	697
B	88	10	2	27	64	8	1	592
C	75	15	10	0	21	66	13	709
D	87	12	1	83	10	7	0	387
E	92	4	4	21	67	12	0	543
F	82	14	4	24	45	24	7	360
G	84	10	6	39	50	7	4	135
H	62	22	16	42	41	15	2	687
I	94	4	2	11	87	2	0	369

			Level II Lessons (Approx. 15–21 mos.)					
A	78%	18%	4%	19%	62%	19%	0%	175
B	59	37	4	7	54	38	1	117
C	83	13	4	19	27	52	4	233
D	99	1	0	93	7	0	0	162
E	51	39	10	20	45	29	6	210
F	83	15	2	8	56	35	1	160
G	81	9	10	47	42	11	0	120
H	82	12	6	21	61	16	2	112
I	97	3	0	4	93	3	0	94

			Level III Lessons (Approx. 21–30 mos.)					
A	92%	7%	1%	17%	73%	10%	0%	378
B	88	15	0	20	60	20	0	391
C	85	10	0	39	48	13	0	88
D	99	1	0	85	14	1	0	299
E	88	11	1	26	58	15	1	329
F	87	12	1	30	49	21	0	166
G	79	7	14	32	49	19	0	82
H	91	8	1	34	58	6	2	89
I	100	0	0	1	95	4	0	76

[a]Number of lessons is not synonymous with number of daily *sessions* given.

Table 2. Reactions of second group of mothers regarding revised Level I Lessons, following approximately one year of use

Lesson number and name	Percent rated		
	Excellent	Acceptable	Poor
1. Blocks	78%	19%	3%
2. Gloves	71	29	0
3. Crayons/paper/finger paints[a]	53	24	23
4. Kitten in Keg	77	23	0
5. Paper, scissors, and paste	68	32	0
6. Mirror, brush, and comb set	77	23	0
7. Bowl, boat, sponge	54	39	7
8. Doll	76	24	0
9. Bubble soap and straw	68	23	9
10. Things that hold other things together (e.g., masking tape, a string, spring clothespin)[a]	54	37	9
11. Toy animals and sound boxes	83	16	2
12. Beads	77	18	5
13. Ball	81	17	2
14. Number learner[a] and four-piece puzzle	30 47	36 43	33 10
15. Jars and marshmallows	66	30	4
16. Tambourine and castinet	80	20	0
17. Toy tops	76	23	1
18. Stacking toy	91	9	0

[a]Divided into two sets of the same materials or revised extensively.

handicapped child would receive an equal share of the parent's attention. These simple management suggestions worked well according to the parents' reports.

EVIDENCE OF SUCCESS BASED ON VERIFICATION OF EDGE EDUCATIONAL PRINCIPLES

Educational principles of the EDGE Project, and attempts to verify them, are described in the two phases (in-home, preschool) of the EDGE program.

A Day in the EDGE Home Program: A Hypothetical Example Based on Fact

Philip and Rachel Smith's son, Jim, is a 1-year-old Down's syndrome child who has been in the study since he was 3 months of age. At home today he and his mother are scheduled to work with Level I Lesson #8 (the doll lesson shown in Figure 1). While Rachel selects the doll and other objects from her suitcase of materials and looks over today's lesson, an orientation to the principles incorporated in the lessons she uses is presented.

Principle 1: Each activity shall engage child and mother in affectionate, focused, and meaningful problem-solving oriented, sensorimotor, activity Rubbing, manipulating, and handling of objects and positioning of the child are important behaviors in each lesson. Piaget (1967) contends that early sensorimotor activity is a crucial foundation for later cognitive development; and Bricker and Bricker (1973) postulate that prelinguistic processes involved in sensorimotor interaction may constitute an essential basis for language development in the child as he/she matures.

Several researchers have found that physical handling accompanied by cooing and other forms of social attention by maternal individuals facilitates the general development, particularly of alertness, of institutionalized infants (Casler, 1965; White, Castle, & Held, 1964). Extending this point, Yarrow (1963) found a significant correlation between the developmental test scores of 6-month-old children living in foster homes and the ratings of the amount and appropriateness of maternal handling.

Mattick (1968) studied the effects of mother-child interaction on the exploratory behavior of Down's syndrome infants. In this experiment, groups of Down's syndrome and nonhandicapped children between 1-and-one-half and 3 years of age were presented with three prestructured opportunities to handle toy-like objects. In one condition a child was given objects to handle without the presence of the mother; in a second condition the mother was present with her child, but noninteractive (neutral); in the third condition the mother was present and interactive, i.e., she gently helped her child manipulate materials and talked with him/her about them in a pleasant conversational manner. The results demonstrated that both nonhandicapped and Down's syndrome children spent more time exploring objects visually and/or visually/tactually when the mother was interactive than when she was neutral. The least exploration of objects occurred when the mother was absent.

Obviously good communication stimulation, especially for an infant, must be regarded as more than just sensorimotor interaction accompanied by parent vocalizations. This view is probably self-evident, but an example may help give it emphasis: Rachel is carrying Jim around the room, showing him objects, altering his postural orientation, talking gently to him about what he is being shown, and rubbing his back gently. An observer who has a language orientation might view this event as a language stimulation; an observer who has a motor development orientation may say that changing the baby's position in space and rubbing his back are kinesthetic and tactile stimulation; another observer with a social learning bias might view this interaction as socialization. Those who view the child's development from a "whole child" perspective will say, "Rachel is stimulating motor, social, and language development simultaneously and interactively." This latter view is the most accurate one and the one we attempted to implement in the lessons themselves.

Principle 2: Related to Principle 1, each lesson shall engage mother and child in a manner that helps her to talk "educationally" with her child about the materials Several approaches to communication stimulation are possible. Hass and Hass (1972), in critiquing possible language stimulation approaches, caution educators to avoid a verbal bombardment or "language bath" approach where the quantity, not the quality, of what a mother says is most important. Also to be avoided is an approach that could be described as labeling only because labeling activity alone excludes natural and direct links to both richer and more mature language use.

The approach used in Project EDGE is probably best described as a structured communication approach in which semantic and syntactical features of language are modeled for the child in conjunction with an active and personal engagement of parent and child in enjoyable activities. The gist of the idea, as Bloom (1972) expresses it, is to help children learn notions of agent, action, and object as concepts because children interact in a world of actual objects, events, and event-object relations as they adapt to their environment. Schlesinger (1971) postulates that linguistic input to the child includes, in addition to linguistic data, its meaning through its association with specific situations. Thus, according to Schlesinger, the learning of language takes place through the child seeing people or objects acting on other people or objects and observing how the adult expresses these action-object/object-action relationships in speech.

Schlesinger's model suggests that the child has innate models of symbolic representation such as agent-action, possession, etc. However, the rules of these modes' rearrangement, expansion, or combination must be learned. Within this model the syntax provides the child with the linguistic-specific means of expressing the semantic relational concepts in a vast number of sentences. Syntax is learned by the child observing how the environmental utterances relate to given situations.

Carrying Schlesinger's ideas on language learning forward, in one of our studies (Buium, Rynders, & Turnure, 1974) we collected and analyzed weekly speech samples for 11 months from the language of three 4-year-old Down's syndrome children who were at the one-word utterance stage. The following experimental questions were posed: 1) Can the early utterances of Down's syndrome children be described by the same semantic relational concepts that were found to dominate nonhandicapped children's early utterances? In other words, does the Down's syndrome child represent experiences symbolically in any way that is different from the way nonhandicapped children do it? 2) Do the cognitive limitations of the Down's syndrome child appear to prevent him/her from attaining any of the semantic relational concepts used by nonhandicapped children?

Results showed that Down's syndrome children's utterances were accounted for by the semantic relational concepts that previously were found to appear in nonhandicapped children's early utterances; all the reported semantic relational concepts that were found to occur in normal children's language also were found in the language of the Down's syndrome child (Bowerman, 1973; Brown, 1973; Schlesinger, 1971). And, as had been predicted, semantic relational concepts followed a certain order in their appearance, perhaps an order related to cognitive demand (Bowerman, 1973) or related to an increased amount of specificity with which semantic functions are expressed (Miller & Yoder, 1973).

Generally our findings suggest that Down's syndrome children represent their experiences symbolically through the same modes of representation available for nonhandicapped children and that in contrast to the nonhandicapped child's language, there is a lag of about 2 years before these semantic relational concepts appear in the language of Down's syndrome children. The question of possible upper limits to the development of semantic relational concepts remains open because of the young age of the Down's syndrome children in the study.

The EDGE lessons were not a totally adequate representation of Schlesinger's model. In fact, we have some reservations about the age-match appropriateness of some of the objects employed, particularly some of the vocabulary words specified in several lessons. Rather than choosing vocabulary to parallel a well-established developmental sequence, such as Brown's (1973), we asked EDGE mothers to suggest words, phrases, and sentences that they felt were natural for them. A better strategy might be to aggregate words that mothers suggest for activities and then winnow that list by juxtaposing it against a well-known developmental sequence.

Principle 3: Parents should augment verbal instruction with other instructional techniques, as necessary, to elicit task solution, but in a hierarchical fashion so as to permit the child to exert his own problem-solving abilities to the maximum extent This principle responds to the question of how one links what the mother says and what she does so that the structured play activity is focused educationally, is socially acceptable to the child and parent and is free from verbal bombardment. In implementing Principle 3, directions at the beginning of the curriculum materials instructed parents to initiate an activity by first giving a child time to explore a material, then to verbally instruct him/her, then—if that did not produce the desired response—to continue verbal instruction while modeling the reponse, and then, if necessary, to gently guide the child physically through the response as the verbal directions are continued. While intended to help an enthusiastic mother or father meter the amount of intervention provided, this sequence also helps ensure that a proper response will be induced through augmentive techniques, if required, so that the child can be reinforced socially, for example, "There, Jim, you've put the beads together, good for you." Thus, the child receives consistent, positive reinforcement for "solving" a problem and, in turn, is set to do well on the next task, which in turn reinforces his parent, building a continuous series of positive feedback events (synchrony) between parent and child.

Two studies that we have conducted suggest that controlling the type and degree of instructional augmentation can be very helpful. Turnure and Rynders (1973) showed that instructional procedures such as modeling and manual guidance can be helpful in producing task solutions in institutionalized severely retarded persons who were unable to solve problems with verbal prompting (e.g., trial-and-error learning procedures), reporting that the procedures produce good retention and positive achievement striving behaviors. The task involved learning that a tool (simplified wooden rake) could be used to reach over an accordian gate to obtain a reward (small bag of M&M candies) beyond arm's reach. Children were assigned randomly on a stratified basis to one of three groups based on their performance in a discrimination learning pretask. One group received modeling without verbal instruction, another group received manual guidance without verbal instruction, and the third group received verbal prompting only. All three conditions were begun by allowing a child to solve the problem with a verbal prompt alone—a procedure which controlled for the possibility of a spontaneous solution. Results showed that subjects in both the modeling and manual guidance groups exhibited excellent task acquisition and retention, while those in the verbal-prompt-only group showed a high rate of task failure despite having four, 20-second trial blocks. At the close of the experiment, Turnure and Rynders placed the eight children who had not acquired task solution in the verbal prompt condition into the manual guidance condition, the condition which was slightly more efficient than modeling; all eight of these subjects attained solution in the first 20-second trial block. Turnure and Rynders caution that manual guidance should be used judiciously so as not to weaken the child's motivation to achieve, and is to be avoided altogether in instances where the child is repulsed by being touched.

Given the power of augmentative techniques, Rynders, Behlen, & Horrobin (1979) employed a hierarchy of augmentative techniques for typical preschool learning tasks. Verbal instruction was used as a constant instructional vehicle throughout a series of 16 tasks given to 3-year-old Down's syndrome children. An example of one task clarifies the hierarchical procedure: Teacher places a small, half-filled pitcher of juice and a plastic cup on a tray, sets it before the child, and says, "Go ahead" (verbal prompt). The teacher waits 15 seconds for an appropriate response (in this case, pouring any amount of juice into the cup) and if none is forthcoming says, "Listen carefully, and I will tell you what to do. Pour the juice into your cup" (verbal instruction). The teacher waits another 15 seconds and if the correct response does not occur, says, "Watch carefully and I will show you what to do. I am pouring the juice into your cup. Now you do it" (verbal instruction plus modeling). If this does not produce the correct response, the teacher then guides the child physically, saying, "I will help you. I am helping you pour the juice into your cup. Now you do it" (verbal instruction plus manual guidance). When task acquisition occurred at any point in the hierarchy, that particular task was terminated and a new one was begun until all 16 tasks were offered.

Results of the study (Rynders et al., 1979) showed that nonhandicapped children solved 80% of the problems with verbal prompting alone, while Down's syndrome children solved only 46% with verbal prompting alone. At the point of introducing verbal instruction to the two groups (for tasks not solved at the verbal prompt level), 72% solution was attained by the nonhandicapped group, while the Down's syndrome group attained 36% solution. Perhaps more important is the finding that nonhandicapped children left only 11% of the tasks unsolved after the three-part hierarchical instruction sequence, while Down's syndrome children left 36% unsolved. These differences on both task acquisition and task failure were significant statistically ($p < 0.05$). Thus, not only did Down's syndrome children have difficulty in acquiring solutions initially with verbal prompting and verbal instruction, but they also exhibited a relatively high nonacquisition rate even after a three-part verbally augmented hierarchical instruction sequence.

Looking at these findings we wondered if modeling and manual guidance might not have served as a distractor rather than a facilitator, considering the task failure rate of the Down's syndrome children. To investigate this possibility, a new Down's syndrome group was run with repeated verbal instruction alone, thus permitting us to contrast the influence of modeling and manual guidance. Interestingly, Down's syndrome children in this group had about the same rate of task failure as the augmented instruction group, with acquisition of 52% at the verbal prompt level, 46% at the point of first use of verbal instruction, and with a failure rate of 42% at the end of the entire repeated series. Differences between both of the Down's syndrome groups, compared with the nonhandicapped groups, favored the nonhandicapped group ($p<0.05$) on both higher frequency of acquisition and lower rate of nonsolution. However, differences between the two Down's syndrome groups were not significant on either acquisition or frequency of solution.

Results of the Rynders et al. study (1979) support our efforts to provide EDGE parents with an instructional scheme to help them to minimize the chances of verbal bombardment and non-focused verbalization, and to maximize task attention and acquisition.

Principle 4: Expose the child systematically to the fact that three-dimensional objects, photos of the objects, and the objects' labels have related meaning Bruner (1964) has pointed out the importance of helping a child move from a comprehension of objects, to pictures, and to printed words. Jim, at the age of 1 year, has little interest in photographs, except to mouth them, and no interest whatsoever in printed words. Therefore, Rachel merely places the real objects on their corresponding photographic representations, saying the words aloud, sounding them out phonetically, and using them in a simple sentence as she points to the objects in the photos. Then she sets the photos aside and begins to engage Jim with three-dimensional objects.

We have no "hard" data to support our use of this principle in EDGE lessons, but we have been encouraged by the interest EDGE children have in age-appropriate printed materials. Consistently, parents comment that their children develop a great interest in books. Perhaps systematic exposure of EDGE objects, paired with EDGE photos, has helped to foster that interest through photographic material. We are speculating on this, of course. Nevertheless, 1 year from now, Rachel may remark with a note of concern in her voice that Jim seems to be more interested in some of the photographs than in some of the three-dimensional objects that served as the subject matter for the photos. We will reassure her that this is what we had hoped would happen because it indicates progressive cognitive development. From that point on she will bind the photographs together and they will become Jim's first book.

Principle 5: Capitalize on the reinforcement value of relative novelty This principle focuses on the appropriate use of planned varitions in the lessons. Robinson and Robinson (1965), in discussing implications of Hebb's theory for education, note that this theory suggests that it is essential to control the degree of novelty for a child in order that the child's attention not be lost either through boredom (too little novelty) or through a surfeit of overwhelming new experiences (too much novelty). By combining the 20 Level I lessons in all possible pairs we obtained about 200 "new" Level II lessons, which are made up of the familiar objects of Level I lessons but can be used now in relatively novel ways. For example, the mirror, comb, brush lesson can be combined with the doll lesson so that the doll can be groomed by the child; the doll can wave so that the child sees it reflected in the mirror; the doll can be helped to wash the mirror and make it shine. None of these new and potentially interesting activities were available in the Level I lessons. Pairing of familiar objects is also useful because the child's attention can be focused on new ways in which two or more objects can be classified and related.

Parent reactions to Level II lessons were mixed (see Table 1). Hence, the pairing procedure used to capitalize on the reinforcement value of relative novelty was not very successful except in selected instances. We believe, nevertheless, that this is a powerful principle but that we did not implement it sufficiently.

A Day in the EDGE Preschool

At the age of 30 months, EDGE children's home instruction ended (except for daily, one-to-one, 30-minute reading sessions before bedtime). The preschool program, the second phase of the EDGE Project resembled any high quality regular preschool except that there was continued emphasis on concept utilization and communication stimulation throughout all of the activities. As can be seen in the outline of a typical daily program (Table 3) communication activities permeated all components of the EDGE preschool.

As each child approached 5 years of age, the age at which Minnesota law guaranteed public education for handicapped children (special education is now mandated at age 4 in Minnesota), the EDGE staff and the children's parents began to look at educational opportunities available in the parents' local school district with the hope of finding an excellent educational match between children's traits and the school's program. Frequently, EDGE staff members attended planning meetings with parents as they conferred with school officials about a child's placement options—a process which continues to this day.

Currently, all EDGE experimental children are in a public school program, most of them in classes for educable children, with a few in regular classes with resource teaching support, and a few in classes for trainable children.

EVIDENCE OF EXPERIMENTAL EFFECTS ON EDGE CHILDREN'S ABILITIES FOLLOWING 5 YEARS IN THE PROGRAM

An Experimental-Control (E-C) research design component was employed to enable us to compare the performance of children in the EDGE program (experimental group) with that of children not in the program

Table 3. Typical daily program in EDGE preschool

8:45–9:15	*Arrival:* Children arrive, remove wraps, and toilet themselves. (Most needed some help with toileting at the time of school entrance.)
9:15–9:45	*Circle Time:* Songs, stories, discussion of weather, "show and tell." Emphasis on concept utilization.
9:45–11:00	*Preacademic:* Arts and crafts and preacademic group activities. During this time, children are drawn out of the group, usually in pairs, to participate in Rebus (logographic) lessons (Clarke, Moores, & Woodcock, 1975), and other preacademic activities such as instruction using the Language Master.
11:00–11:30	*Adapted Physical Education:* Exercises, games, outdoor activities (if weather conditions permit). Emphasis on relating movement to verbal descriptors of the movement. Toileting.
11:30–1:30	*Activities of Daily Living including Lunch:* Materials used in the morning are put away; table set for lunch. Children help to clean up after lunch. Toileting; hygiene development (e.g., washing face, brushing teeth, removing clothing). Emphasis on task-related communication.
1:30–2:15	*Nap Time:* (or quiet rest time)
2:15–3:30	*Music and/or Creative Drama:* Finger plays, dress up time, phonograph records. Emphasis on verbal elaborations.

(control group). Because the structured play activities in the EDGE program had been designed so that they could be applied (with consideration for individual-child characteristics) to each Down's syndrome child in the experimental group, the hypothesis tested had to do with the impact of the EDGE lessons. It was hypothesized that there would be statistically significant differences in the communication (i.e., concept utilization and/or expressive language reflecting concept utilization) of experimental and control group children. In testing this hypothesis, fairly stringent conditions were set for the evidence since it would have to be powerful enough to justify asking future parents of Down's syndrome infants to provide several years of daily lesson periods. The following conditions were set to ensure appropriate testing of the hypothesis: 1) efficacy testing was to be conducted at each child's fifth birthday, 2) tests were to be administered to all project children who remained in the program through 5 years of age, and 3) testing was to be conducted by an experimentally blind examiner.

Selection of Control and Experimental Groups

For experimental-control comparison purposes, we chose to create a distal control group out of concern about the risk of treatment diffusion, i.e., where motivated C (control group) parents, in a common geographic area with E (experimental group) parents, could obtain curriculum materials, believing that an experimental educational program might be "the answer" to their child's problems.

We also chose to enroll E and C children consecutively without exception, providing they met screening criteria, because of the problems involved in assigning potential E subjects randomly to an E and no-treatment group but not being able to offer the experimental program (if efficacious) to waiting E children until they attained 5 years of age. Hence, we opened up enrollment in both Chicago and the Twin Cities during the same time periods, accepting all children on a consecutive basis who came to our attention during that period and met enrollment criteria.

At the time of EDGE Project entry, families in both the E (Twin Cities) and C (Chicago) groups were probably more interested in their child's development than would have been true of a totally randomly selected population of parents of Down's syndrome children. For example, nearly all of the parents in both groups belonged to an organization oriented toward handicapped citizens: In the Chicago area parents belonged to the Mongoloid Development Council (MDC) (now the National Association for Down's Syndrome). This association is committed to the furtherance of research and development activities for Down's syndrome children and their families and is action-oriented, having been involved in a number of experimental programs. Initial contact with 11 potential control group families was made for us by the director of the MDC, who went through the list of active parent members, identifying those having Down's syndrome infants between the ages of 3 and 9 months, and phoning or writing them to see whether they were interested in participating. If parents were interested, their names were given to our project's measurement coordinator who phoned each one to invite them to join, on a preliminary basis, for measurement-only purposes. All 11 families agreed. The reason they were invited on a preliminary basis was that additional screening criteria had to be met to ensure that families enrolled would not be unduly burdened with new obligations in cases where the family was stressed already, e.g., due to poverty. And, because these criteria were set up primarily to screen out E families who would be stressed by the addition of EDGE lesson responsibilities, it was obligatory for us to employ the same criteria to C families. These additional criteria, applied equally across the E and C groups, were:

1. Parents had decided to raise their Down's syndrome child at home for the first 5 years of life
2. Family not broken

3. Maternal IQ score 90 or greater
4. Parents' educational level at least 10th grade
5. Parents use English as a first language
6. Total family income at least $6,000 (unless one or both parents are students)
7. Family contains no more than three preschool-age children, including the Down's syndrome child

Child criteria that had to be met were:

1. Infant has Trisomy 21 (nondisjunction) form of Down's syndrome confirmed by karyotyping
2. Child must not be suffering from a serious health problem, such as a debilitating heart defect or major sensory problem

At the same time as potential C families were invited to participate, subject to passing screening criteria, enrollment for potential E families was begun. In the Twin Cities, most parents who came to our attention belonged to the local Association for Retarded Citizens (ARC). Most of these parents learned of the project through an advertisement placed in the local and state ARC newsletters or through phone calls from ARC officers. Sometimes they were contacted by a friend of a parent who belonged to an ARC group who referred the parent to us. During this initial enrollment we accepted (subject to screening considerations) the first nine families, consecutively, who came to our attention. All nine agreed to participate.

Approximately 1 year after the first enrollment period, a second enrollment period was established using the same conditions and the same criteria as before. And, 6 months after that, a third period (same conditions and criteria) occurred. Each time, nearly equal numbers of families were enrolled in both groups, and in no instances did any prescreened E or C family refuse to participate.

Across all of the enrollment periods, the application of the additional screening criteria to potential C families resulted in the exclusion (from the efficacy data, not from testing) of three children: one was excluded because the mother's IQ score was below 90; one was excluded because parents spoke English as a second language (we felt it would be difficult to monitor this child's language development); and one was excluded because the child had the mosaic form of Down's syndrome.

No potential E families were excluded on the basis of family variables or child variables, even though two children were enrolled who were below the age of 3 months at the time of entry, and also had very severe heart defects. Both of these children died in their first year of life. This illustrates how we attempted to minimize possibilities of experimenter bias favoring E children, in this case by enrolling all children between 1 month and 9 months of age who became known to us as potential E group members. If we had not enrolled every potential Down's syndrome child who came to our attention we might have introduced a selection bias since the second author was often the pediatrician who was the first point of referral in the Twin Cities area. Therefore, no potential E child was ever excluded for any child characteristics (although we would have excluded a child with nontrisomic Down's syndrome).

Characteristics of the Children and their Families

After the three enrollment periods, 23 E families and 20 C families had been enrolled. Of the 23 E children, two died in the first year of life and one died in the third year of life; two families withdrew during their first year when an early education program opened near their homes (both lived approximately 25 miles from the site of our soon-to-be-opened EDGE preschool), and one family, just 6 months before their child was due to graduate, withdrew their child in favor of another preschool program. Of the 20 C families, two sets of parents withdrew, saying that they did not wish to continue having their child tested. There were no deaths in the C group during the project.

At the end of the project there were 17 E and 18 C children. Of the 17 E children, 4 were female, 13 were male. In the group of 18 C children, 8 were female, 10 were male.

Characteristics of these 35 families and their Down's syndrome children at their first testing (12 months) are shown in Tables 4 and 5.

A comprehensive neurological assessment at 12 months of age revealed no significant differences (X^2) between E and C groups, nor between E and C males, or between E and C females. The variables assessed were 1) size, shape, and location of ears; 2) nose, mouth, and pharynx normalcy; 3) observed phonation; 4) reported phonation; 5) observed locomotion; 6) walking; 7) grasp; 8) sensation shown in extremities and trunk; 9) ability to follow light or object; 10) pupil reaction; 11) response to sound; 12) muscle tone of the right and left upper extremities; 13) right and left neck flexors; 14) right and left neck extensors; 15) muscle tone of right and left lower extremities; and 16) right and left muscle tone of the trunk. All children in both groups responded normally to sound and had normal pupil reactions. All E subjects followed a light or object visually, as did all but one C child (a follow-up shortly thereafter revealed normal visual tracking for this child).

Other variables measured at the time of the 12-month neurological assessment were head circumference, height, and weight. There were no

Table 4. Summary of descriptive statistics on experimental (E) and control (C)

Family characteristics		All Down's Syndrome subjects (Males and females combined)		Statistical significance[a]
		E N = 17	C N = 18	
Maternal age (years)	Mean SD Range	32.1 5.7 22–39	30.6 7.5 19–42	NSD[b]
Maternal IQ	Mean SD Range	114.0 10.5 93–133	112.0 8.6 92–128	NSD
Number of children	Mean SD Range	3.0 1.6 1–6	3.1 2.3 1–8	NSD
Mother education (months)	Mean SD Range	171.0 20.0 144–192	157.0 21.3 108–192	NSD
Father education (months)	Mean SD Range	190.6 29.7 144–240	170.7 20.0 144–216	<0.05
Total yearly family income (dollars)	Mean SD Range	12,441 4,703 6,000–22,000	13,892 4,957 6,300–28,500	NSD

[a]Difference between means tested for significance at 0.05 level using one-way ANOVA (University of Minnesota, SPSS—Statistical Package for the Social Sciences—1976)

significant differences in these dimensions between E and C groups, between E and C males, or between E and C females.

As Tables 4 and 5 reveal, aside from significant initial-group differences in fathers' education (E group versus C group) and differences in mothers' education (E males versus C males), families were quite similar on the variables measured. Regarding child variables, there were no significant differences in any of the psychometric characteristics in the two groups, either by group or by sex, at the 12-month assessment.

Measures were also taken of concept utilization performance when E and C subjects were 24 months of age. (Up to that age, attempts to solicit a sufficient number of reliable nonverbal responses met with little success.)

The concept utilization assessment instrument took the form of large pieces of illustration board on which photos of common household items (e.g., spoon, soap) were mounted. Questions probed the child's under-

Down's syndrome subjects when 12 months of age

	All Down's Syndrome subjects (Males and females separate)				
E Males	C Males	Statistical significance	E Females	C Females	Statistical significance
31.4	32.3		34.3	28.6	
5.6	7.8	NSD	6.6	7.2	NSD
22–38	19–42		25–39	20–39	
114.6	110.5		111.3	113.7	
8.6	10.3	NSD	16.7	6.3	NSD
97–128	92–128		93–133	108–128	
3.1	3.3		2.8	2.9	
1.6	2.4	NSD	1.7	2.5	NSD
1–6	1–7		1–5	1–8	
173.7	154.8		162.0	160.5	
19.8	23.6	<0.05	20.8	19.2	NSD
144–192	108–192		144–180	144–216	
186.5	169.2		204.0	172.5	
30.8	15.4	NSD	24.0	25.6	NSD
144–240	144–192		192–240	144–216	
11,884	13,855		14,250	13.938	
4,042	4,094	NSD	6,850	6,173	NSD
6,000–20,000	6,300–21,500		8,000–22,000	9,000–28,500	

[b]No significant difference

standing of labels for and attributes of objects and the relationships of objects one to another. There were no statistically significant differences between E and C groups, nor between E and C males, or E and C females at that 24-month point. Verbal output reflecting development of concept utilization (the gist of our expressive language concern) remained at a low level throughout the study.

A frequent criticism of early education studies has had to do with control group adequacy, especially where an E and C group are not drawn from a common subject pool. Of particular concern is the motivation factor. Prior to contact from us, C families had not only decided to raise their Down's syndrome child at home during his/her early years, but they also belonged to a group with a record of active involvement in various research and development projects. But, initial motivation is not the only issue; evidence of continuing motivation in control group families is of equal, perhaps greater, importance. To probe the factor of continuing

Table 5. Summary of psychological data on experimental (E) and control (C) ment)

		All subjects (male and female combined)		
Child characteristics		Experimental ($N=17$)	Control ($N=18$)	Statistical Significance[a]
Mental Development Index	Mean SD Range	732.8[b] 46.9 662–808	746.6 59.2 658–888	NSD[c]
Psychomotor Development Index	Mean SD Range	305.0[b] 38.7 242–375	289.0 37.2 217–358	NSD

[a]Differences between means tested for significance at 0.05 level using one-way ANOVA (University of Minnesota, SPSS—Statistical Package for Social Sciences—1976).

motivation, as well as other family variables, in the C group, a home interview schedule was administered when children were 3 to 4 years old. Pertinent to the issue of continuing motivation, one question asked: "Do you read to your child? If so, when did you begin and how often do you do it?"

Home interview findings revealed that 16 out of 18 C parents read to their children daily (one said that she did not read to her child at all, and one read to her child at least three times per week but not daily). Thirteen of the 16 who read to their child daily began to do so before their child was 2 years of age; the other three began reading to their child between their child's second and third year of life. One did not read to her child at all, and one did not begin reading to her child until the child was 3 years of age.

Also to be noted is the fact that C parents received no incentives from us, except a few inexpensive children's books at testing time (which they did not expect to receive), and a book *(The Family of Man)* at the end of the project as a final "Thank you." Taken together, these factors provide adequate evidence of good parent interest in C group children.

Comparisons Between E and C Groups at 60 Months of Age

As noted earlier, stringent standards were set for determining efficacy. Standards for determining efficacy required that statistically significant differences, favoring E children, would have to appear in concept utilization and/or expressive language outcomes reflecting concept utilization at

Down's syndrome subjects at 12 months of age (Bayley Scales of Infant Develop-

All subjects (males and females separate)					
E Male ($N=13$)	C Male ($N=10$)	Statistical Significance	E Female ($N=4$)	C Female ($N=8$)	Statistical Significance
730.2	753.9		741.5	737.5	
49.2	69.3	NSD	43.8	45.8	NSD
662–808	658–888		708–800	667–800	
306.6	278.7		299.8	301.9	
42.0	37.4	NSD	29.7	34.9	NSD
242–375	217–338		258–325	242–358	

[b]Scores are represented as the mathematical outcome of putting the total raw score of the test into ratio with child's exact age at date of test, and multiplying the result by 100.

[c]No significant difference.

60 months since the EDGE lessons were focused on these variables. To collect these data, an experimentally blind examiner administered the Boehm Test of Basic Concepts and an experimental language sampling instrument to both E and C children when they were 60 months of age.

The Boehm Test of Basic Concepts presented the child with a series of line drawings, one of which correctly depicted the concept of concern, e.g., "behind," "first." The Boehm test does not require a verbal response.

The language sample was solicited through a picture sequence format. Each series of pictures began with the examiner exposing a short series of conceptually related attractive pictures in a predetermined sequence with an invitation to the child to "Tell me a story about these pictures." If there was no response, the examiner said to the child, "I will tell you a story first. Now you tell me a story about these pictures." If there was still no response, the examiner asked the child to verbally label various objects as the examiner pointed to them. And, finally, if no response occurred, the examiner asked the child to repeat verbal models of object labels. Pretesting and, as necessary, pretraining, in tasks similar to those in the Boehm test and the language sample, assured us that all children understood task response requirements before formal testing began.

Table 6 summarizes the outcome of these two measures, as well as outcomes of the Stanford-Binet and Bruininks-Oseretsky tests. The Bruininks-Oseretsky, adapted for our use, sampled motor behaviors in domains such as dynamic balance, agility, and eye-hand coordination.

Table 6. Performance of experimental and control (E and C) Down's syndrome subjects on The Boehm Test of Basic Concepts, EDGE Language Sample, Stanford-Binet, and Bruininks-Oseretsky (adapted) measures at 60 months

		Measures		Statistical significance[a]
		E(N=17)	C(N=18)	
Boehm Test of Basic Concepts				
Decimal ratio scores[b]	Mean	198.5	151.1	
	SD	80.3	75.6	NSD[c]
	Range	0–379	33–379	
EDGE Language Sample				
Total words	Mean	31.7	33.7	
	SD	29.9	34.1	NSD
	Range	0–87	0–130	
Total elicited or spontaneous	Mean	27.2	29.8	
	SD	28.7	32.2	NSD
	Range	0–85	0–122	
Total imitated	Mean	4.5	4.0	
	SD	4.7	3.5	NSD
	Range	0–16	0–11	
Mean length of utterance	Mean	1.1	.89	
	SD	.5	.53	NSD
	Range	0–2.2	0–1.8	
Number of: One-word utterances	Mean	21.9	25.0	
	SD	20.7	25.8	NSD
	Range	0–77	0–101	
Two-word utterances	Mean	2.1	5.2	
	SD	2.2	10.7	
	Range	0–7	0–44	
Three-word utterances	Mean	1.2	.77	
	SD	2.3	1.8	NSD
	Range	0–7	0–7	
Greater than three-word utterances	Mean	.52	.06	
	SD	1.3	.24	NSD
	Range	0–5	0–1	
Stanford-Binet				
Decimal ratio score	Mean	167.5	133.2	
	SD	57.4	57.1	<0.05 (Program)
	Range	27–293	5–217	<0.05 (Sex)
Bruininks-Oseretsky				
Raw gross motor	Mean	58.9	43.1	
	SD	16.4	11.6	<0.05 (Program)
	Range	30–95	24–62	

Table 6 — *continued*

		Measures		Statistical significance[a]
		E(N=17)	C(N=18)	
Raw fine motor	Mean	13.8	12.3	
	SD	8.6	9.2	NSD
	Range	3–30	3–28	
Raw total	Mean	72.8	55.4	
	SD	18.4	17.5	<0.05 (Program)
	Range	44–117	27–84	

[a]Difference between means tested for significance at 0.05 level using two-way ANOVA (University of Montana, SPSS—Statistical Package for the Social Sciences—1976).

[b]Scores are represented as the mathematical outcome of putting the total raw score of the test in ratio with the child's exact age at date of test, and multiplying the result by 100.

[c]No significant difference.

As can be seen in Table 6, two-way ANOVAS (group × sex) revealed no significant group differences in our specified criterion variables (concept utilization and/or expressive language), measured through the Boehm and our experimental language test, although there were significant differences favoring the E group in IQ score and in motor ability as measured through the Stanford-Binet and Bruininks-Oseretsky tests.

With respect to sex differences, analyses showed significant sex differences only in the Stanford-Binet (see Table 6). These significant sex differences favored females over males in both groups on their decimal ratio IQ score (E males, mean 158.5, SD 59.0; E females, mean 196.5, SD 46.3; C males, mean 114.4, SD 59.5; C females, mean 156.8, SD 47.0). There were no significant differences in any of the interaction computations.

DISCUSSION AND A LOOK TO THE FUTURE

Implications of EDGE outcomes are not sufficiently clear at the time of this writing. On the one hand, it is clear that analyses conducted thus far do not support the dissemination of the experimental EDGE lessons. On the other hand, significant group differences in IQ score and motor performance, coupled with generally positive ratings of lessons by mothers, reports of good child cooperation during lessons, and verification through experimentation of most of the project's programming principles are interpreted as providing strong general support for our overall efforts as well as for the early education movement for young Down's syndrome children.

In the future, as done in the Nisonger Center study (MacDonald, et al., 1975), we plan to look at intra-individual differences in the E and C groups in order to understand them better. For example, inspection of the formative evaluation data shows clearly that some E parents report uniformly excellent cooperation in their children during EDGE lessons, while some do not. How do these data relate to child criterion outcomes? And, what more can we learn about this relationship by adding results from our home interview and other data?

Along these lines, we were curious about the possible impact of hearing impairments on IQ scores of our subjects. As has been noted earlier, 12-month descriptive neurological data revealed that all subjects responded normally to a simple screening test of hearing, but that is a far cry from the audiometric and functional hearing measures available later in the child's life. Hence, at the 60-month data point, having gathered extensive, longitudinal, audiometric, and functional hearing data, we asked an experienced speech and hearing specialist to examine each child's total hearing data record, responding to the question, "Would this child have been likely to have had difficulty hearing his/her parents speaking at a normal conversation level without hearing amplification during the first year of life?"

In making the decision, the specialist, experimentally blind to child group designation and to the hypotheses, and receiving individual packets of hearing data in a thoroughly mixed order, used a rating sheet, rating each child's hearing as "adequate," "questionable," or "inadequate." At the same time, she rated the confidence she felt in making the decision as "high," "medium," "low."[3]

After receiving the ratings, and following up on those whose hearing had been rated as questionable or inadequate and who received ratings of decision-making confidence below the high level, it was found that three children (1E, 2C) had hearing ratings below the adequate level and had IQ scores in the lower one-third of the total rank-ordered distribution of all subjects. (Obviously, this procedure is not valid as a bonafide efficacy measure because of its post-hoc nature and the arbitrariness in selecting the cut-off point in the distribution of IQ scores. Nevertheless, it augments data concerned with the thrust of the program and, thus, appeared useful to do.)

Running a two-way ANOVA (program × sex), with the three subjects removed (which by the way did not alter the 12-month pretest pattern, i.e., with these three subjects removed, there were no significant differences in child or family variables, except for father education level), revealed significant differences in IQ, and in gross motor and total motor

---

[3] Our thanks to Ms. Sue Marth and Professor Gerald Siegel, University of Minnesota, Department of Speech Science, Pathology and Audiology, for their help in the conceptualization of the post-hoc audiometric data summary.

scores favoring E children at 60 months just as was found in the analyses with all subjects included. And, interestingly, just as occurred at the 60-month analysis with all subjects included, there were no significant differences between groups in our target variables, i.e., concept utilization or expressive language. (There were no significant sex differences either.) Again, as with the main efficacy analysis, we believe that this outcome lends further general support for our overall program, as well as for the early education movement, but, again, does *not* support the dissemination of EDGE curriculum materials.

We will also continue to examine our data from a multiple analysis perspective, having noted considerable subject variability, from test to test, throughout the 5-year periodic testing sequence, which is not captured adequately in our final efficacy measurement alone.

But for now, let us ask the question, "Why didn't the EDGE lessons 'take' in terms of significant differences in concept utilization and expressive language outcomes?" There are a large number of possible explanations, of course. One could be that the linguistic aspects of the lessons were not developed or refined sufficiently, i.e., the match between a child's syntactic and semantic development and the lesson content for him/her was not adequate.

Then, related to the linguistic aspects of our work, there is the possibility that we should have given greater attention to children's expressive language, in general, attempting to solicit more of it and shape it toward a higher linguistic level.

Were we to repeat the project, more would be done to "fine tune" lesson content and give greater attention to expressive language. Relative to this point, Buium, Rynders, and Turnure (1974) have suggested the conceptualization for a program that consists primarily of pairing the systematic presentation of syntactical rules (that vary gradually in complexity) with situations designed to reflect the semantic-relational concepts available to the child at the time. As the child matures, opportunities are provided for the child to verbally manipulate staged situations—utterances pairs. We plan to experiment with this model in the future.

Viewing our outcomes from another perspective—that of design— we would employ more criterion-referenced measures to augment our norm-referenced measures if we were to begin the study today. Individual differences are just not captured sufficiently in the present design (although we thought they would be when we designed the program originally).

Finally, related to the design question, is the larger question of judging efficacy itself. We chose to take a conservative approach to judging efficacy, specifying that efficacy would be claimed only if statistically significant differences favoring E children occurred in targeted (criterion) outcomes, i.e., concept utilization or expressive language. There are some who might argue that we are being too conservative, that obtaining significant differences in nontargeted outcomes (e.g., IQ score) allows one to claim curricular efficacy. We would argue against such an interpretation for the following reasons:

1. Significant differences in nontargeted (precriterion) outcomes may signal the investigator that there was a general positive effect from the program, particularly if the formative data look supportive of the curriculum approach, but these general positive differences do *not* allow one to claim efficacy for curriculum materials that were designed to facilitate development in targeted areas; they produce significant differences only in the nontarget areas. Granted, there is some overlap between the IQ (nontarget) and concept utilization (target) measures we used, and, hence, their outcomes, but this overlap does not justify dissemination of curriculum materials which are "soft" in producing *clear, targeted* differences.
2. From a socioeducational standpoint, it would be inappropriate to publish a curriculum that has achieved only nontargeted significant differences when curriculum materials are now available which show more promise of producing significant differences in *both* targeted and nontargeted outcomes. At the beginning of this chapter, we compared the development of early aircraft to that of contemporary early education programs. Picking up on this analogy, parents of Down's syndrome infants don't need to "fly" our "single engine, propeller driven" curriculum when there are now a few "wide cabin jet" curricula available. To ask future parents to spend one hour each day on structured early education lessons should be done *only* when solid efficacy data reveal that such an investment is fully warranted. If one cannot be confident of a curriculum's efficacy, it should not be disseminated.

It is extremely exciting in these times to hear respected biomedical researchers say that the mechanism(s) which causes chromosomal nondisjunction will probably be identified (signaling the possibility of preventing the condition) in the next decade, given sufficient funding and orchestrated collaboration among researchers. Obviously, sufficient funding and orchestrated collaboration are not easy to obtain. Therefore, the Down's Syndrome Congress (a nationally recognized organization for parents and professionals) is working diligently for the establishment of a National Center on Down's syndrome. Such a Center would serve not only as an effective information agency but could also help to provide financial incentives and administrative impetus to study crucial biomedical, educational, and social problems.

Another exciting prospect is that of devising better (more creative, more predictive, more useful) ways of assessing the development of Down's syndrome individuals as they interact with their environment. Along these lines, Charlesworth and his associates at the University of Minnesota have taken an important ethological look at assessment. For example, Cicchetti and Charlesworth (1976) have videotapes of young Down's syndrome children using tools (e.g., a stick to pry a lid off a cocoa can) to reach a goal (candy). This ability is thought to relate to what the authors call "practical intelligence." Preliminary findings look very promising. In another recent study with Down's syndrome infants, Cicchetti and Sroufe (1976) showed how early affective (e.g., smiling behavior) and cognitive development are intricately linked.

Future studies like these, conducted with a creative developmental perspective and aimed at relating outcomes to everyday functional behavior, will supplement the information on the development of children with Down's syndrome gained from standardized tests and will also suggest ways to design more effective early education procedures for children with Down's syndrome and their families.

The years since 1866, when Langdon Down described the condition now known as Down's syndrome, have produced several exciting breakthroughs in biomedicine and education. Given sufficient planning and financial support, the research outlook for the remainder of this century holds the potential for more experimental breakthroughs than were produced in the entire past 100 years.

REFERENCES

Blatt, B. *Souls in extremis: An anthology on victims and victimizers.* Boston: Allyn & Bacon, 1973.

Bloom, L. Semantic features in language development. In R. Schiefelbusch (Ed.), *Language of the mentally retarded.* Baltimore: University Park Press, 1972.

Bowerman, M. *Early syntactic development.* Cambridge: Harvard University Press, 1973.

Bricker, W., & Bricker, D. Early language intervention. Paper presented at the National Institute of Child Health and Human Development Conference on Language Intervention with the Mentally Retarded, Wisconsin Dells, Wisconsin, June, 1973.

Brown, R. W. *A first language.* Cambridge: Harvard University Press, 1973.

Bruner, J. The course of cognitive growth. *American Psychologist,* 1964, *19,* 1-15.

Buium, N., Rynders, J., & Turnure, J. Early maternal linguistic environment of normal and non-normal language-learning children. *American Journal of Mental Deficiency,* 1974, *79,* 52-58.(a)

Buium, N., Rynders, J., & Turnure, J. *A semantic-relational-concepts based theory of language acquisition as applied to Down's syndrome children: Implication for a language enhancement program* (Research Report #62). Minneapolis: University of Minnesota Research, Development and Demonstration Center in Education of Handicapped Children, 1974.(b)

Casler, L. The effects of extra tactile stimulation on a group of institutionalized infants. *Genetic Psychology Monographs,* 1965, *71,* 135-175.

Centerwall, S., & Centerwall, W. A study of children with mongolism reared in the home compared to those reared away from the home. *Pediatrics,* 1960, *25,* 678-685.

Cicchetti, D., & Charlesworth, W. Unpublished manuscript, University of Minnesota, 1976.

Cicchetti, D., & Sroufe, L. A. The relationship between affective and cognitive development in Down's syndrome infants. *Child Development,* 1976, *47,* 920-929.

Clarke, C., Moores, D., & Woodcock, R. *Minnesota Early Language Development System (MELDS).* Minneapolis: University of Minnesota Research, Development and Demonstration Center in Education of Handicapped Children, 1975.

Clements, P. R., Bates, M. V., & Hafer, M. Variability within Down's syndrome infants. *Mental Retardation,* 1976, *14*(1), 30-31.

Down, J. L. Observations on an ethnic classification of idiots. *Clinical Lecture Reports London Hospital,* 1866, *3,* 259-262.

Encyclopaedia Britannica. Chicago: Encyclopaedia Britannica, Inc., Vol. 15, 1970, p. 763.

Encyclopaedia Britannica. Chicago: Encyclopaedia Britannica, Inc., Vol. 3., 1974, 648-649. (Micropaedia set.)

Fishler, K. Mental development in mosaic Down's syndrome as compared with trisomy 21. In R. Koch & F. F. DeLaCruz (Eds.), *Down's syndrome (Mongolism): Research, prevention, and management.* New York: Brunner/Mazel, 1975.

Hass, W., & Hass, S. Syntactic structure and language development in retardates. In R. Schiefelbusch (Ed.), *Language of the mentally retarded.* Baltimore: University Park Press, 1972.

Hayden, A. H., & Dimitrias, V. Infant preschool and primary programs for children with Down's syndrome. Paper presented at Children's Psychiatric Research Institute, Ontario, Canada, 1975.

Kohn, G., Taysi, K., Atkins, T. E., & Mellman, W. J. Mosaic mongolism. I. Clinical correlations. *Journal of Pediatrics,* 1970, *76,* 874-879.

MacDonald, J., Blott, J., Gordon, K., Spiegel, B., & Hartmann, M. An experimental parent-assisted treatment program for preschool language-delayed children. *Journal of Speech and Hearing Disorders,* 1974, *39,* 395-415.

Matkin, A. The development of psycholinguistic skills in a sample of children with Down's syndrome. Paper presented at national convention of Council for Exceptional Children, Washington, D.C., 1972.

Mattick, P. Effects of three instructional conditions upon the exploratory behavior of retarded and normal infants. Unpublished Ph.D. dissertation, University of Minnesota, 1968.

Miller, J. F., & Yoder, D. E. An ontogenetic language teaching strategy for retarded children. Paper presented at the National Institute of Child Health and Human Development Conference on Language Intervention with the Mentally Retarded, Wisconsin, Dells, Wisconsin, June, 1973.

Milton, G., & Gonzalo, R. Jaguar cult—Down's syndrome—were-jaguar. *Expedition,* 1974, *16*(4), 33-37.

Piaget, J. *Six psychological studies.* New York: Random House, 1967.

Restak, R. Genetic counseling for defective parents: The danger of knowing too much. *Psychology Today,* September, 1975, *9,* 21-23; 92-93.

Rhodes, L., Gooch, B., Siegelman, E., Behrns, C., & Metzger, R. A language stimulation and reading program for severely retarded mongoloid children. *California Mental Health Research Monograph No. 11.* State of California, Department of Mental Hygiene, Bureau of Research, 1969.

Robinson, H., & Robinson, N. *The mentally retarded child: A psychological approach.* New York: McGraw-Hill, 1965.

Rosecrans, C. J. The relationship of normal/21 trisomy mosaicism and intellectual development. *American Journal of Mental Deficiency,* 1968, *72,* 562-566.

Rynders, J., & Horrobin, J. Project EDGE: The University of Minnesota's communication stimulation program for Down's syndrome infants. In B. Friedlander, G. Sterritt, & G. Kirk (Eds.), *Exceptional infant* (Vol. 3). New York: Brunner/Mazel, 1975.

Rynders, J., Behlen, K., & Horrobin, J. Performance characteristics of preschool Down's syndrome children receiving augmented or repetitive verbal instruction. *American Journal of Mental Deficiency,* 1979, *84,* 67-73.

Rynders, J., Spiker, D., & Horrobin, J. Underestimating the educability of Down's syndrome children: Examination of methodological problems in recent literature. *American Journal of Mental Deficiency,* 1978, *82*(5), 440-448.

Schlesinger, I. M. Production of utterances and language acquisition. In C. A. Ferguson & D. L. Slobin (Eds.), *The ontogenesis of grammar: A theoretical symposium.* New York: Academic Press, 1971.

Sonquist, H., & Kamii, C. Applying some Piagetian concepts in the classroom for the disadvantaged. In J. Frost (Ed.), *Early childhood education rediscovered.* New York: Holt, 1968.

Stedman, D., & Eichorn, D. A comparison of the growth and development of institutionalized and home-reared mongoloids during infancy and early childhood. *American Journal of Mental Deficiency,* 1964, *69,* 391-401.

Turnure, J., & Rynders, J. Effectiveness of manual guidance, modeling, and trial and error learning procedures on the acquisition of new behaviors. *Merrill-Palmer Quarterly of Behavior and Development,* 1973, *19*(1), 49-65.

White, B., Castle, P., & Held, R. Observations on the development of visually directed reaching. *Child Development,* 1964, *35,* 349-365.

Wynne, S., Ulfelder, L. S., & Dakof, G. *Mainstreaming and early childhood education for handicapped children: Review and implications of research.* Washington, D.C.: Wynne Associates. (Report done for Division of Innovation and Development, Bureau of Education for the Handicapped, U.S. Office of Education, 1975.)

Yarrow, L. Research in dimensions of early maternal care. *Merrill-Palmer Quarterly of Behavior and Development,* 1963, *9,* 101-114.

CHAPTER 6

Research in Large-Scale Curriculum Development for Mildly Retarded Children

I. Leon Smith

CURRICULUM DEVELOPMENT VERSUS RESEARCH

Examination of the events affecting what goes on in classrooms for the mildly retarded over the past 50 years indicates that research and curriculum development have never been willing partners in the educational process. While many special educators and a few researchers have spoken about the progeny such a marriage should generate, few successful relationships have actually been consummated. In some cases, it has been argued that a trial separation is necessary with a reconciliation possible at a later, but typically unspecified, date. In other cases, divorce appears to be the only solution with both parties independently pursuing their own goals and objectives.

Differences in the historical development of educational research and curriculum projects probably account for the fact that these activities have not normally been found to operate together. In general, research has depended heavily on models borrowed from the physical sciences and

---

The research reported herein was supported by Contract #300-76-0050 from the U.S. Office of Education, Bureau for the Education of the Handicapped. However, the opinions expressed do not necessarily reflect the position or policy of the Office of Education, and no official endorsement should be inferred.

has not taken the reality of the classroom and the nature of day-to-day school experiences as important variables to study and monitor. Instead, research typically examines theoretically generated variables that can be manipulated and controlled in experimental settings. On the other hand, curriculum development efforts have traditionally been derived from practical, community- and school-based needs with little or no empirical underpinnings or support. Thus, the typical role of research has been to add to our fund of knowledge, while that of curriculum is to provide products and service.

Perhaps most important, the real differences in perspective can be summarized by the attitudinal polarities of those engaged in the two kinds of activities. Thus, the researcher argues that there is little scientific evidence to justify what goes on in schools, while the curriculum developer counters with the claim that most research has no application to the classroom setting. The consequences of these two positions probably explain why research and curriculum development have traditionally been separated in educational practice, with attendant reductions in the levels of accomplishment that could be achieved by their combination.

However, there is still room for optimism. The primary thesis of this chapter is that an effective merger of research and development is both possible and necessary, but on grounds other than what is commonly accepted as the usual approach to research activity. Much of what has passed for traditional research and development (frequently called R&D) in education can be characterized by big "R" and little "D." The major investment has been in the conduct of research with the acknowledgement that the results might ultimately lead to the development of products and materials. What typically happens, however, is that the research raises more questions than it answers, thereby requiring additional research to be conducted. Thus, the anticipated flow from research to development is diverted into more research. The cyclical nature of this process explains why many expected products never get developed. Another reason why accumulated scientific knowledge has not directly led to improvements in the quality of educational programs is that researchers are often unwilling or unable to apply what they have learned in order to achieve practical and useful goals and solutions. The big "R" little "D" strategy, then, tends to sharpen, rather than reduce, the problems inherent in translating the potential educational implications of research into the actual development of research-based products.

In contrast, the research approach that appears most relevant to the curriculum development enterprise is one characterized by big "D" and little "R." According to this view, the primary mission of the curriculum development project *is* curriculum development. However, the curriculum development project *does* have the added responsibility of dealing with the research questions that are encountered in and have an effect on the curriculum development cycle. At least theoretically, the complete cycle includes reference to the following major elements to be executed in a reasonably linear fashion: initial program development, dissemination of materials to selected sites, studies of implementation during product development, formative evaluation, revision, summative evaluation prior to publication, publication, marketing and dissemination, purchase, and postpublication studies of program effectiveness. At this writing, most curriculum development projects in special education are in a position to make only the most minimal response to researchable questions in these areas. The difficulty is partially due to the fact that the very presence of a research capability within the context of a curriculum development project is still regarded as unique, and to some extent, irrelevant to the primary mission. There is also some question as to who can and should ethically and financially assume responsibility for examining the questions that are raised at various points in the cycle. Will it be the developer, the publisher, the independent evaluator, or the consumer? Despite these overlapping responsibilities, however, there is no question that developers need to be in a better position to make data-based responses to questions in these areas than their current capabilities permit. (See Meyen and Altman, 1976, for a more complete discussion of these issues.)

TYPES OF RESEARCH ACTIVITIES

To summarize, then, our discussion points to the emergence of two qualitatively different types of research activity. One kind is referred to as *curriculum-directed* research because it examines questions that are generated by the curriculum development cycle. The second kind is called *curriculum-related research* because it seeks clarification of broad issues that extend considerably beyond what needs to be known in order to develop specific curricula. These distinctions do not mean that broad-based research designed to examine the cognitive, affective, and social behavior of mildly retarded students and their environments is irrelevant and unimportant. It is recognized that such research does, in fact, supply the general context and basis out of which most curriculum development projects in special education have emerged. It simply means that curriculum-related research cannot be used to resolve questions once curriculum purposes and priorities have been set.

There are several fundamental differences that serve to distinguish the two types of research that have been described. First, it can be stated that curriculum-directed research questions are likely to be raised by those working on curriculum projects, such as developers and media specialists. Traditional researchers who are less familiar with the curriculum development process are more likely to generate hypotheses that reside in the curriculum-related arena.

Second, the types of research can be distinguished on the basis of their use of existing psychological, sociological, and behavioral theories and related research findings. Curriculum-directed research generally examines theories and available research as a function of the question that may be unique for each program setting. On the other hand, curriculum-related research explores the question as a function of the theory that tends to be generalizable. In other words, the former type of work typically transcends a particular theory, while the latter is confined by a particular theory.

A third difference has to do with the importance of timing in the conduct of research. There should be a strong antedating quality associated with curriculum-directed research efforts. That is, curriculum-directed questions are raised prior to the need for the research answer so that solutions can be developed, tested, and made available as input to facilitate decision making. Curriculum-related questions, however, can be raised quite independent of specific curriculum development needs, and may be considered "timeless" in the sense that they are directed toward acquisition of knowledge that may have few immediate, socioeducational implications.

Finally, substantial differences exist in the way the results of the two types of research are applied and in the nature of the meaning associated with them. Curriculum-directed research is obviously intended to have an impact on decision making with respect to the achievement of program objectives. In order to ensure as much impact as possible, documents, reports, and communications must be prepared so that they can be understood clearly by members of the project staff who are not likely to be sophisticated in research methodology. On the other hand, the results of curriculum-related research are usually prepared for conspicuous consumption and with sufficient scientific rigor and style to guarantee publication in professional journals. In essence, then, the primary consumer of the former type of research is the curriculum developer and practitioner/consumer, and the researcher is the major audience for the latter type. Since the curriculum-directed studies are primarily useful within the curriculum development enterprise, the research efforts tend to be more unobtrusive and generally less well-known and acknowledged than traditional research activities.

For the sake of description and clarification, the two types of research are classified in highly idealized and non-overlapping terms. In actual practice, of course, real research tends to possess some qualities of both. However, since the concept of curriculum-directed research has received little attention, this chapter describes research that was initially designed to resolve issues that grew out of efforts to develop large-scale programs of instruction for mildly retarded children. Accordingly, no attempt is made to substantively review all large-scale curricula for the mildly retarded that have been supported by the Bureau of Education for the Handicapped over the past decade. The reader is referred to Soeffing (1975), Mayer (1975), Meyen and Horner (1976), Meyen and Altman (1976), and Goldstein (1975b) for descriptions and accounts of these programs. Specifically, two kinds of on-going curriculum-directed research are described along with implications regarding untapped areas of investigation that should be examined more completely in order to understand elements in the curriculum development cycle previously identified. The value of this type of activity is also discussed in relation to current practices in mainstreaming mildly retarded children. First, however, one needs to consider the curriculum development setting that supplied the basis for the research that is currently being conducted.

THE CURRICULUM SETTING

A curriculum is defined as an organized and structured set of learnings or knowledge that society judges to be relevant to the education of its children and youth. In this context, the curriculum guides for the mildly retarded that were developed a number of years ago can be considered as a very rudimentary attempt to provide more coherence and systematization to the educational process. The curriculum guide approach, however, did not go far enough. Teacher activities and actions were not specified with sufficient precision to ensure consistent use. This permitted wide variation in the implementation of the teacher guide and contributed to difficulties interpreting the results of studies concerning changes in pupil behavior. Comparisons between special class and regular class placement were also difficult because the differences in curriculum content and the degree of implementation were not examined and, therefore, their potential effects could not be estimated or controlled (Kaufman & Alberto, 1976).

While the need was not specifically directed toward the development of teacher-proof curricula, these experiences indicated that something more comprehensive was necessary. Accordingly, the curriculum guide approach was replaced by efforts to develop more complete curricula that included both highly structured knowledge that is important and a way or ways for the teacher to systematically transmit that knowledge to the mildly retarded learner. Ideally, then, the products of a curriculum development project should include the specification of both content *and* process.

At least one large-scale curriculum development project funded by the Bureau for the Education of the Handicapped has built-in systematic strategies that teachers utilize in order to deliver the content of instruction to pupils. This project is called the Social Learning Curriculum (Goldstein, 1974, 1975a). The program utilizes an inductive teaching methodology (ITM) and the term *curriculum* in this case includes the specification of both content knowledge and the process by which the teacher will transmit that knowledge. Operationally, the lessons are constructed and the activities are designed following inductive problem-solving principles. The intent here is not to produce a teacher-free curriculum in the sense that what the teacher does is completely determined; rather, the curriculum provides a systematic procedure for delivering instruction that can be modified and adapted to meet varying classroom conditions.

But what is induction, really? According to the classical definition, induction is the formation or production of a rule or principle based on repeated exposure to examples of that rule or principle. Each lesson is composed of a series of activities involving problem situations that the learner must confront. In assisting pupils through these problem situations, the teacher employs the ITM. The ITM is marked by a common organizing theme: the general movement of the learner through successive stages of awareness, beginning with the identification of a problem and concluding with the generation of principles for solving an entire class of related problems. The movement of the learner can be conceptualized as vertical, i.e., from a neutral point where a problem may not be recognized, to a mastery point where the problem is defined; hypotheses are considered and tested; and generalizations are derived and applied.

Specifically, the ITM consists of a highly structured five-step questioning sequence employed by the teacher to enhance the vertical progress of the student. These five steps are labeling, detailing, inferring, predicting-verifying, and generalizing. During the first two steps, instruction focuses on gathering and examining the relevant information concerning the problem situation. Labeling questions deal with the identification of the major aspects of the problem, while detailing questions encourage greater elaboration concerning the available information. The last three steps require the learner to deploy the established facts. Inference questions require the pupil to generate potential solutions to the problem. Prediction-verification questions encourage the production of probability statements or hypotheses regarding the adequacy of the solutions and the confirmation of the predictions through the use of reality-based procedures. Finally, generalizing questions require the students to produce a principle that is applicable to the solution of the specific problem, as well as to related types of problems.

The ITM is symbolically represented in Figure 1 as a sequence of wave-like clusters extending upward and outward toward a goal—the production of a generalization or principle, which is based on exposure to several related problem situations. The use of the wave analogy is intended to highlight both the individual buildup of each approach to the overall problem as well as the additive effect of the successive approaches to the problem. Each cluster of waves refers to teacher-pupil interaction and involves a single experience with an example of a specific problem area. Over the course of teacher-pupil interaction within each experience, the emphasis is seen to shift from the lowest inductive level, labeling, to the highest level, generalizing. The conclusions reached concerning each of the experiences are considered to be rules, or mini-generalizations, applicable only to that specific experience. Symbolically, the repetition of wave-like clusters represents the multiplicity of approaches to the development of an overall generalization related to the problem area under consideration.

The ITM is embedded within an instructional theory concerning the facilitation of general social competence and adaptation among retarded learners. According to the instructional theory, social competence is a function of two major elements, namely, critical thinking and independent action. Critical thinking involves the ability to utilize a store of social facts and concepts (content knowledge) within a systematic problem-solving framework that allows relevant associations to be made (process knowledge). Likewise, independent action is related to the ability of the individual to act upon the outcomes of critical thinking and to adjust behavior accordingly. The use of the ITM is designed to facilitate the acquisition of these two elements.

In relation to the goal of critical thinking, the ITM is the means by which content knowledge is delivered and through which a systematic problem-solving process is demonstrated. Concerning the goal of independent action, the active participation of the pupils required by the ITM provides the basis for utilizing both content and process knowledge in the classroom as well as practice for decision making in the real world. In summary, then, the ITM is specifically designed for use with retarded learners and consists of a more elaborate and structured account of what has been loosely referred to as inductive, discovery, and scientific methods of teaching.

I wish to apologize to the reader at this point for providing a very simple rendering of what is a complex process from the point of view of

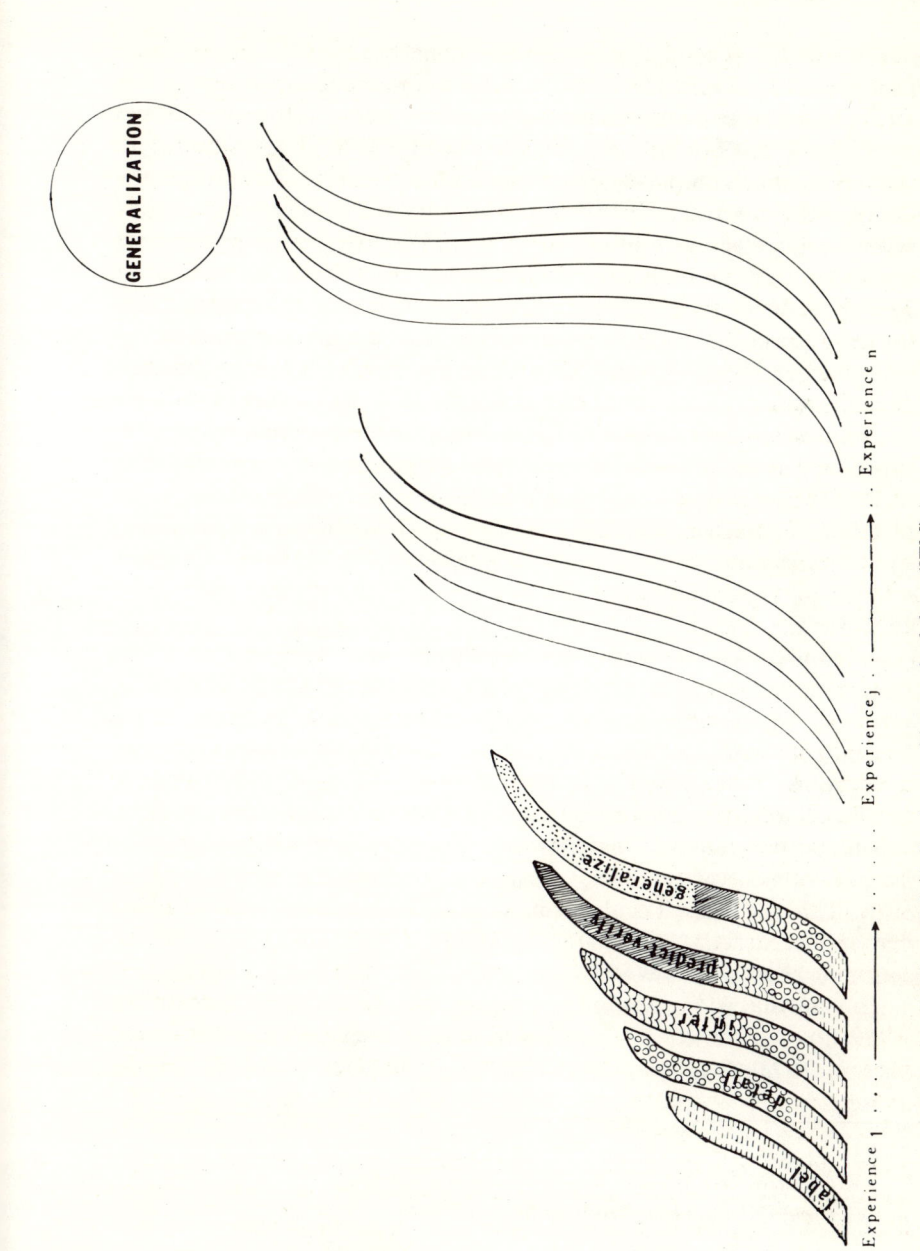

Figure 1. Symbolic visualization of the inductive teaching methodology (ITM).

curriculum theory and lesson development and structure. This is because I wish to address myself to a description and presentation of two on-going curriculum-directed research studies that grew out of efforts to develop curricula for EMR pupils based on the use of the ITM. Those who are interested in more completely exploring the historical development of the use of inductive teaching techniques with educable mentally retarded pupils are directed to the following sources. The first document of record is a dissertation by Goldstein (1957). While the ITM is not mentioned directly, many of the ideas that ultimately evolved into the methodology are either presented or can be inferred from various points in the dissertation. The development of the *Illinois Curriculum Guide for the Educable Mentally Handicapped* (Goldstein & Seigle, 1958) and its use in the well-known efficacy study of special class training on the development of mentally retarded children (Goldstein, Moss, & Jordan, 1965) provide initial evidence of a move toward greater specification of the methodology. The experimental teachers who used the *Illinois Guide* in the efficacy study were, in fact, trained in the application of inductive teaching techniques even though the concept of induction was not specifically discussed. Since the use of the teaching method appeared to be one of the factors contributing to the success of the special classes in the study, a research and demonstration project was then designed to systematically train teachers in what was, for the first time, referred to more formally as the inductive method and to examine its impact on pupil learning (Goldstein, Mischio, & Minskoff, 1969). The results of this study indicated that if inductive teaching is to have an effect, it should be systematically built into the instructional program and materials, thereby providing one rationale for the development of the Social Learning Curriculum referred to previously. This approach was also consistent with Minskoff's (1967) finding that simple teacher training in the inductive method outside the classroom does not seem to carry over to teacher behavior inside the classroom. A more complete description of the development, evolution, and use of the ITM with retarded learners along with instructional examples is found in Mischio (1973), Greenberg and Smith (1974), and Goldstein (1975c, 1976, in press).

CURRICULUM-DIRECTED RESEARCH STUDY I: ASSESSING INDUCTIVE PROBLEM SOLVING

Three assumptions appear to underlie the use of the ITM in the Social Learning Curriculum. The first assumption, concerning the relationships among the steps of the questioning sequence, is that there is an ordering between each of the steps such that the ability of individuals to respond at one step is prerequisite to the ability to respond at the next ordered step within the sequence. This type of ordering is a hierarchy because each succeeding step requires the abilities of the lower steps. Another way of saying this is that the lower order skills are gradually integrated to form higher order ones. The structure, management, and pacing of the teaching sequence are based on this general assumption. That is, when the teacher enters the questioning sequence at a given step, the transition to the next successive step is made only as it is evident that the class is capable of performing adequately at the preceding step.

The second assumption relates to the developmental nature of these critical thinking processes relative to the steps in the ITM. First, for each step or process there may be a threshold age below which performance is less than adequate. Second, for each step or process there may be an age where increments in performance become self-sustaining and the teacher no longer has to emphasize that step in the interaction. This assumption affects the emphasis placed on material presented to the students. Interactions among teachers and primary age students are directed more often than not to the first two steps in the problem-solving sequence (labeling and detailing), while interactions with intermediate age students are more frequently directed to the remaining steps in the problem-solving sequence (inferring, predicting-verifying, and generalizing) as guided by the familiarity of the students with the problem.

Although the assumptions concerning the ordering of steps and the developmental nature of the underlying processes may at first appear somewhat similar, a clear distinction is possible. The first assumption has to do with how pupil performance on the steps relates to each other without reference to other information about the learners. The second assumption concerns the relationship between performance on the steps and other types of "developmental" indices, such as chronological age and mental age. Both assumptions are inherent in the ideas regarding critical thinking that have been previously discussed. Empirical support for these assumptions would provide the teacher with an extremely powerful model for the purpose of planning specific kinds of instruction for specific pupils.

It is important to note that both assumptions are directly related to the process knowledge element in critical thinking and are only indirectly related to the social content knowledge element in critical thinking. However, both elements are, in fact, linked together. This is because the specific instructional material provides not only social facts but also the vehicle through which the process knowledge is transmitted. Problem solving is not taught in a vacuum; rather it is linked to content relevant to social adaptation, namely social adaptation concepts and facts that have both immediate and long-term value to the learner. Furthermore, this means that any assumptions concerning the underlying aspects of process knowledge should be valid when linked to *any* piece of social content and can be considered in this sense, to be "content-free."

Basic to the means used to foster the elements of critical thinking and independent action is a third essential assumption lying at the core of the inductive theory. The assumption is that the development of the prerequisite elements, namely *both* critical thinking and independent action, will affect the display of social competency in real-life situations. In other words, not only will there be a relationship between the vertical progress of students within the inductive sequence and their ability to think critically, but there will be an overriding relationship between these problem-solving processes and real outcome behavior. Due to the way in which independent action is defined, any assumption connected to it can only be considered in terms of outcome behavior. At the most concrete level, then, the last assumption suggests that basic knowledge elements of process and content can be provided and that with careful fostering these elements can lead to changes in real social behavior.

An assessment procedure called the *T*est of the *H*ierarchy of *IN*ductive *K*nowledge (THINK) was designed to permit the empirical examination of these assumptions and to provide a method for measuring the inductive problem-solving skills of EMR learners (Smith and Greenberg, in press, in preparation). The THINK is based on a translation of the ITM into a structure for a test instrument.

The measure consists of sets of 8½ × 11 inch, black and white line drawings. Each set consists of three cards depicting problem situations or experiences related to a specific social learning concept as symbolized in Figure 1. Each set also includes drawings that represent alternative resolutions to the three problem situations.

There are four separate sets of pictorial materials in the THINK, each relating to a different social learning concept or theme, namely, Sharing (theme 1), Object Substitution (theme 2), Dressing Appropriately (theme 3), and Responsibility (theme 4). The four themes are considered to represent universal social issues that primary and intermediate level EMR students would realistically encounter.

The administration of the THINK requires approximately 50 minutes per subject. Following a warm-up, which includes an explanation of the task, the subject is handed the first problem card from theme 1 and is told to hold it in an upright position on the desk. The accompanying resolution cards are placed face down to the subject's left. As the subject examines the card, the experimenter begins the interview sequence (see

Curriculum Research   159

Table 1. Overview of THINK interview procedure for each theme

Card shown	Questioning sequence
Problem card 1	Look carefully at this picture. Tell me everything you see in the picture. *Probe:* Tell me more. Tell me what you see happening in the picture. *Probe:* Can you tell me any more? How does he (she, they) feel right now? *Probe:* Why? What is his (her, their) problem? How can that problem be solved? *Probe:* Can they solve it another way? *Probe:* Any other way?
Resolution cards	What is the *very best* way of solving it? *Each resolution card is sequentially presented after asking:* How would it have worked if...*(description of the resolution)*? *Probe:* Were you correct?
Problem card 1	Now I want you to think very carefully. What did he (she, they) learn today about solving the problem of...*(statement of the problem)*?
Problem cards 2 and 3	Interview procedure is repeated as with problem card 1.
Problem cards 1, 2, and 3	*Pointing to each card as appropriate:* Now, I want you to think *very, very* hard. You told me the things that these people learned today. This person learned...*(appropriate learning statement)*, and this person learned...*(appropriate learning statement)*, and this person learned...*(appropriate learning statement)*. If you were telling other children how to solve these problems, could you tell me just one thing that would help them the most? Make it a good rule that would help them solve all these problems. Remember, I want *one* rule that would help other children solve all of these problems. *Probe:* Why is that important?

Table 1). When the administration of theme 1 is completed, all material is removed from view. The remaining themes are administered in a similar fashion. (See Greenberg (1977) for a complete discussion of these procedures.)

Table 2 contains the operational definitions of nine levels that served as the basis for scoring the THINK protocols and relates them to the five steps in the ITM. Elaboration and refinement in the number of scoreable levels were based on previous research (Greenberg & Smith, 1974).

Table 2. Operational definition of THINK levels and relationship to ITM sequence

ITM sequence	THINK level	Operational definition
Labeling	Label (L)	Name of object or individual
Detailing	Detail (D)	Descriptive qualities of objects or individuals
Inferring	Visual Inference (VI)	Statements involving relationships among people, expressed emotions, placement of action, and/or causal events leading to the problem
	Statement of Problem (SOP)	Inference concerning the nature of the unresolved conflict
	Solutions-Qualifications (SQ)	Statements regarding alternative hypotheses for the resolution of the unresolved conflict
	Best (B)	Solution judged to have the highest probability of solving the problem
Predicting-Verifying	Predictions-Verifications (PV)	Statements concerning the consequences of the alternatives
Generalizing	Learning Statement (LS)	Conclusion concerning the problem and its solution based on a single problem card and its associated resolution cards
	Generalization (G)	A principle concerning the resolution of the class of problems depicted in the theme

An investigation was then designed to empirically examine the three assumptions previously mentioned, namely, that the nine problem-solving processes are 1) cumulative and hierarchical, 2) developmental, i.e., age-dependent, and 3) related to ratings of social behavior.

Important additional issues that were examined involved the possible reduction in the actual number of problem-solving levels that would be needed in order to efficiently and adequately describe pupil performance as well as their relationship to measured intelligence. That is, could the levels be empirically combined to form fewer levels? Examination of these data were intended to make the process easier to conceptualize and to determine to what degree the THINK provides information that is different from traditional intelligence. This information was also designed to provide a clearer picture of the results that could serve as the basis for communication with curriculum developers and teachers using the Social Learning Curriculum.

In order to answer these questions, test data based on the THINK, the teacher rating scales of adaptive behavior, and the Wechsler Intelligence Scale for Children were collected from 120 EMR primary and intermediate level students. The sampling plan called for the selection of 20 pupils from each age level between 9 and 14, inclusive.

The hierarchical property associated with the nine levels of the THINK implies the existence of a simplex structure, an ordering of levels according to increasing complexity. Examination of the simplex structure indicated that a hierarchy among the first four levels is confirmed. A major break appears at the solutions-qualifications (SQ) and predictions-verifications (PV) levels suggesting that they may be empirically more complex and possibly non-unitary processes. The other violation appeared at the generalization (G) level where the inability to demonstrate the hierarchy may be due to the complexity of the process in relation to the age range of the sample. Very few pupils were able to perform at this level.

These results indicate that at least the initial steps in the inductive teaching methodology appear reasonable and suggest that teachers should emphasize mastery of the lower levels in the sequence before expecting adequate performance at the upper levels in the sequence. However, even though the knowledge that these specific inductive problem-solving levels are hierarchically acquired would imply and support a general instructional sequence, it does not directly specify how the behaviors should be taught. In other words, even though it is known that labeling behaviors should be acquired and probably emphasized first, does this mean that the teacher should focus exclusively on this level to the exclusion of the others? What are appropriate and reasonable distances between the levels at which students can perform and the levels at which the teacher is working? These questions suggest additional areas of research activity.

The second major question concerned the degree to which performance on the inductive levels follows a developmental or age-related pattern. Do older children tend to perform better on the levels than younger children? Is this true of all levels in the process? The answers to these questions would supply a base of information about building the ITM into the broad fabric of the Social Learning Curriculum, as well as some indication concerning the kinds of performance that might initially be expected from EMR pupils who are to receive instruction based on the methodology.

Examination of the results concerning the age-relatedness of the THINK supports a linear developmental pattern across all levels. From a more qualitative perspective, the verbal production of the sample in general appeared highly limited in light of the array of visual stimuli built into the test materials and the comprehensiveness of the interview format. The 9- to 10-year-old subjects often made responses related to the Label (L) and Detail (D) levels only. The 11- to 12-year-old subjects demonstrated a greater facility in producing responses that conceptually explained the context within which the problem occurred. However, their responses were less adequate at the higher inference levels. Although these subjects produced the greatest number of SQs, they did not always produce an adequate Best (B) from among the alternatives generated. The 13- to 14-year-old subjects appeared most capable of producing responses on all levels. However, even though the older subjects were most likely to respond adequately at the highest level, only 30% of the 14-year-old subjects produced appropriate G responses. Given the developmental nature of these processes, it is expected that an older EMR population would perform more adequately at that level.

Because younger, primary age EMR students can label and detail the elements of a problem, the teaching focus with such students appears to appropriately be on providing them with practice in distinguishing relevant and irrelevant details. Such practice is needed if the students are to begin to identify problems and make inferences about both their cause and resolutions. Middle, intermediate age EMR students can not only label and detail, but are capable of producing inferences related to problems as well. For these students, therefore, the teaching emphasis shifts to providing opportunities to increase the number of associations they form among problems. Thus, time is provided for students to personalize each problem and to compare it to previously experienced situations. So too, time is provided for comparisons among different problems so that additional information may be extracted from the related situations. Older, secondary level EMR students are capable of working through the processes in the inductive problem-solving sequence up to the generalization level. At that point, they need assistance in categorizing and comparing problem situations in order to produce abstractions.

An impression arising from an interpretation of the data concerns the ability of the sample to utilize directly presented information and/or feedback. Subjects could integrate novel material when it was provided under proper and structured conditions. Thus, it appears that it is pedagogically more sound to review in great detail rather than to briefly summarize for the students. In fact, the use of two modalities — visual and verbal — appears far more effective as a way of supplying information than the use of either modality alone. In fact, it is suggested that items such as reminder cards or summary sheets be employed as students are being encouraged to produce abstract generalizations. Care must be taken that the students do not use the visuals as literal guides. On the other hand, having enough information in view can free the student to leave the specifics in order to move to the general.

Does performance on the THINK actually relate to estimates of social competency? In order to answer this question, scores on the THINK levels were related to teacher judgments concerning the pupils' adaptability, social appropriateness of behavior, socialization skills, and ability to act reasonably. Other ratings related to academic competency and focused on attitudes toward school work, involvement in group activities, and willingness to persist in efforts to attain goals. Examination of these results indicate that performance on the THINK levels is significantly related to the teacher ratings. Specifically, the THINK levels explain approximately 20% of the variation on the teacher ratings, with the SQ and PV levels making the largest contribution.

These results suggest that the acquisition of the reasoning skills emphasized in the ITM should lead to the facilitation and enhancement of the social competency of retarded learners. Furthermore, instruction leading to the attainment of such skills appears to be a logical objective for children who seem to be able to acquire knowledge and have the potential to act on what they know, but seem to be unable to organize their thoughts and actions so that results are as good as they might be. Incorporating the ITM into the implementation of curricula appears to provide the teacher with a way for observing to what extent students require information as well as a procedure for determining how well pupils process information toward the generalized goal of social competency.

The last issue concerned the number of actual dimensions underlying the nine THINK levels as well as their relationship to that old standard, intelligence. This empirical strategy was employed in an attempt to make it easier to conceptualize the ITM from the point of view of curriculum development and instructional planning.

The data factor-analyzed in this fashion indicate that the nine THINK levels can indeed be reduced considerably without losing any important information concerning pupil performance (Smith & Greenberg, in press). In order to achieve a simpler view of problem solving based on the ITM, the nine original levels can be empirically combined to form three more basic factors or dimensions. One appears to be an information-storage and retrieval dimension, and the other two represent information-processing dimensions.

The information storage and retrieval factor is characterized most predominantly by the two lower levels of L and D and appears to refer specifically to behaviors associated with the overall process of initial data collection. This factor can be conceptualized as a "convergent" dimension in the sense that many different pieces of information are used or needed in order to achieve closure at this particular point in the process. The VI (visual inference), SOP (statement of problems), and SQ levels appear to define one information-processing factor suggesting that this dimension symbolizes behaviors associated with the overall process of initially exploring, mulling over, or ruminating upon the data. This factor is a "divergent" dimension because many different possibilities are being considered. A second information-processing factor is represented most clearly by the B (best), PV, and LS (learning statement) levels of the process indicating that the dimension involves decision-making behaviors associated with reaching a conclusion based on the data. Again, the notion of a convergent process is suggested here since the focus is on problem solution and rule-oriented behavior. From a very practical perspective, these three factors can be conceptualized as problem finding, problem exploring, and problem resolving.

How similar or different are the three factors underlying the THINK from a traditional test of intelligence? While the problem finding and problem resolving factors do tend to have slight to modest relationships with IQ, the data indicate that status on a standardized intelligence test is not a good indicator of the THINK processes associated with these two factors. With respect to problem exploration, intelligence test data tell virtually nothing about this THINK dimension. Thus, the THINK assessment appears to supply a picture of information processing that is not provided by or contained in our traditional measures of intellectual functioning.

In terms of the classroom, children may be more or less successful at the three different parts of the process. Some may be good problem finders, some may be good problem explorers, and some may be good problem resolvers. While the evidence suggests that good problem finders and problem resolvers do tend to have slightly higher IQs than poorer performers, the information also indicated that status on a standardized intelligence test is not a good indicator of pupil behaviors concerning problem exploration. The general implication of these findings is that the homogeneous IQ grouping of EMR pupils is likely to result in a very diverse group of learners in terms of reasoning abilities based on this problem-solving model. Unfortunately, the current version of the testing procedure described here is not in the shape where it can easily be administered and scored by practitioners. This is because it was initially developed and designed as a more research-oriented tool as is the case with most educational and psychological tests. One of the tasks for the future is to develop a more practically useful version that is less cumbersome but as functional.

However, this does not mean that work on the research version of the instrument is complete. Additional areas need to be examined in order to further refine, extend, and fully validate the THINK. For example, the findings concerning the hierarchical and developmental properties of the measure indicate that the inclusion of a broader age range of retarded students is needed to explore the limits of the assessment procedure and to develop a more comprehensive and representative picture of performance. The results also suggest that a reconceptualization of the SQ and PV scores is necessary. It would also be reasonable to design a format for mapping performance profiles on the hierarchy in order to permit comparisons both within and across individuals.

There appears to be no virtue and little benefit to be derived from such psychometric sophistication unless it can ultimately be shown to lead to some form of rational instructional intervention. In this case, the THINK assessment procedure dovetails with the objectives of the Social Learning Curriculum. Thus, the assessment of a hierarchy within which developmentally diverse pupils can be located will ultimately provide a very powerful mechanism for coordinating assessment and instruction.

In an effort to move the work in this direction, a modest series of investigations were designed initially to examine the relationship between pupil performance on the THINK and the behavior of teachers who are utilizing the ITM.

CURRICULUM-DIRECTED
RESEARCH STUDY II: CLASSROOM OBSERVATION

Contrary to many programs, an observational approach is uniquely justified in the case of the Social Learning Curriculum because it clearly specifies an implementation process and a particular teaching methodology that can be operationalized.

The Social Learning Curriculum Classroom Observation System (SLC-COS) was developed for this purpose. The SLC-COS allows for the systematic observation of the implementation of the Social Learning Curriculum. The SLC-COS consists of two instruments based on assumptions of the Social Learning Curriculum, namely, that teaching students to use an inductive problem-solving strategy within an enabling environment will facilitate critical thinking and independent action. The first scale, the Social Learning Environment Rating Scale (SLERS), is a 60-item instrument composed of teachers and student behaviors derived from the inductive problem-solving model of the Social Learning Curriculum (Warshow & Bepko, 1974). A second scale, the Social Learning Interaction System (SLIS) is a category system that uses a Flanders-type matrix (1970) to record teacher and pupil behaviors derived from the problem-solving model as well (Bepko & Warshow, 1974). It was expected that both the global classroom data collected with the SLERS and the more discrete data collected with the SLIS would represent a definition of the SLC implementation process in behavioral terms. Thus, the scales were designed to complement each other based on the kind of information they provide (see Table 3).

The primary purposes of developing the two observational scales for use with the Social Learning Curriculum are:

1. To monitor the inductive teaching delivery system that is built into the Social Learning Curriculum as specified by the developers.
2. To make explicit those aspects of the learning environment that are conducive to the use of ITM.
3. To provide feedback to the development staff for the purpose of revising curriculum materials and to provide a framework for teacher-supervisory interaction that would optimize the implementation of the Social Learning Curriculum (Bepko, Warshow, & Lehrer, 1975).
4. To investigate the interrelationships among Social Learning Curriculum variables, teacher implementation with regard to instructional strategies and learning environment, and student outcome measures.

The SLERS and SLIS were employed to collect observational data from 17 intermediate level EMR classrooms located in New York City. These 17 classes were observed once during the implementation of *each* of six lessons from a particular part of the Social Learning Curriculum. In addition, 4 or 5 pupils per class (total $N=77$) were randomly chosen and administered selected measures of problem-solving performance. The primary instrument employed here was the THINK.

Analyses of these data have been planned in three separate but related phases, only the first two of which have been completed (Smith,

Table 3. Overview of observation instruments

Instrument	Type	Source of information	Information areas
Social Learning Environment Rating Scale (SLERS)	Rating scale: Classroom observer, teacher, supervisor	Actual observations	1. Teacher behaviors that facilitate student critical thinking and independent action. 2. Teacher use and management of curriculum. 3. Student behaviors indicative of critical thinking and independent action.
Social Learning Interaction System (SLIS)	Verbal interaction scale: Coded-teacher-supervisor	Audio tapes	1. Percentage of teacher and student talk. 2. General measures of verbal interaction that facilitate or indicate student critical thinking and independent action.

1976; Schimoler & Warshow, 1978). The initial phase involved the SLERS and dealt with identifying and describing the primary qualities that define the instrument through the application of factor analytic procedures. In addition, an attempt was made to determine whether the underlying factors were uniformly present in all six lessons and whether they uniformly occurred in the 17 classes. The second phase concerned the relationships between the factor structure underlying the SLERS and the selected measures of learner characteristics. Phase III will involve the examination of the SLIS and its relationship to the two sets of data previously mentioned. Analyses of these data are currently being completed.

The factor analytic examination of the SLERS completed during Phase I generally supported the ITM underlying the Social Learning Curriculum.

A four-factor solution based on a principal components analysis with a varimax rotation was accepted as the optimal solution based on a relatively equal spread of the variation across the factors and their compatibility with the theoretical assumptions. These four factors were labeled problem emergence, problem resolution, application of learning, and social learning environment. The first three factors can be considered stages of the inductive problem-solving process, and the fourth may be interpreted as the classroom climate within which the problem-solving process unfolds. A more precise description of the four factors is provided below.

Factor 1: Problem Emergence

Problem emergence is characterized primarily by items that include labeling, detailing, and some of the inferring steps of the inductive strategy. The teacher, from an understanding of the objective of the lesson, structures activities so that the focus is on the emerging problem. The pupils identify (label and detail) elements in the learning situation that may be related to the emerging problem. Pupils are guided to infer the information that is relevant to the problem and to make associations between ideas. The teacher facilitates this step of the process by cuing so that pupils can connect previously obtained information in some meaningful way. After the problem, or content objective, is stated, pupils infer possible solutions to the problem.

Factor 2: Problem Resolution

Problem resolution is defined primarily by items relating to inference, prediction-verification, and generalization steps of the ITM. Pupils infer the possible consequences of acting on the solutions named in Factor 1. Based on this discussion, they predict the "best" possible solution. They verify this choice by trying out the solution. The pupils, working together as a group, abstract a rule or concept, which is then applied to a new problem situation.

In the stage of problem solving represented in Factors 1 and 2, the teacher is more actively involved in directing activities in which a generalization is formulated by pupils. Activities and questions provided by the teacher are responded to by the pupil and/or the class as a whole. In this way, pupils gain the experience preparatory to their functioning independently.

Factor 3: Application of Learning

Application of learning is characterized by items relating to the application of the problem-solving strategy without undue reliance on others. The teacher encourages student participation and independent use of the problem-solving strategy by providing additional relevant activities and materials, giving individuals the opportunity to demonstrate their new learning by solving a task-related problem, and allowing pupils free use of the resources and materials in the classroom. Students demonstrate the problem-solving strategy by working independently; by utilizing classroom resources, activity centers, and materials; and by applying the concepts and skills previously generalized to new problem situations. The full participation of pupils in the teaching-learning process is reflected in Factor 3. The pupils must apply a generalization understood from specific content within a lesson, demonstrate that they can use a problem-solving strategy on their own and employ the resources available to them.

In contrast to Factor 2, the pupils are now functioning primarily on their own with their peers while the teacher serves as a resource. Here the pupils are applying a problem-solving strategy with a greater degree of independence. This factor reflects a primary goal of the Social Learning Curriculum: the child must generalize social learning skills from the classroom to other situations outside of the classroom.

Factor 4: The Social Learning Environment

The social learning environment is represented by items having to do with the arrangement of the physical, social, and psychological aspects of the environment. There is freedom of movement within the classroom as pupils gather material and interact with each other. The psychological aspect of the environment is characterized by a respect for individual differences. Pupils are encouraged to trust their own experiences and feelings, to pursue their own interests and ideas, to make their own decisions wherever possible, and to be supportive of one another. This supportiveness sets the tone for constructive interaction. The social aspect of the environment stresses interaction with others. It is characterized by the belief that pupils can learn from each other (as well as from the teacher). For example, pupils are encouraged to interact to solve problems, or one student may be asked to respond to another within the questioning strategy.

The four factors, then, are consistent with the problem-solving model of the Social Learning Curriculum and are interpreted as a guide to the stages of the implementation process.

Additional analyses completed during Phase I suggested that these factors do not appear uniformly in the lessons nor were they uniformly implemented in the 17 classes observed. The six lessons appeared to differ the most on the extent to which Factor 3, problem resolution, is present with the factor being less prominent in early lessons and more prominent in later lessons. Since the lessons of the Social Learning Curriculum are, in fact, developmentally organized around the inductive problem-solving model, this finding did not seem unreasonable. Perhaps most important, the 17 classes were found to vary considerably on the social learning environment factor and to some degree, on the problem emergence, and application of learning factors. Overall factor comparisons indicated quite strongly that behaviors associated with Factor 1, problem emergence, occurred most frequently, while behaviors associated with Factor 4, application of learning, occurred least frequently.

In summary, then, the analyses completed during Phase I revealed considerable variation in the Social Learning Curriculum—variation that is understandably due to the developmental nature of the lessons and that is less understandably attributable to different implementation practices of teachers in classrooms. In terms of the latter, more formal attempts at facilitating the classroom implementation of the Social Learning Curriculum appear warranted. Toward this end, a modified version of the SLERS was developed for use by teachers and special education administrators involved in the field testing of the Social Learning Curriculum (Warshow, Smith, & Goldstein, 1976). The instrument, called the Social Learning Observation Record (SLOR), provides an organized, systematic method for observing Social Learning Curriculum classrooms. A specific feedback questionnaire was also constructed in order to provide curriculum writers with information from the SLERS that would assist in curriculum revision and development.

The four factors, problem emergence, problem resolution, application of learning, and the social learning environment, were then examined in relation to problem-solving performance on the THINK. Since the classroom was to be the primary unit for these analyses, preliminary checks were conducted to eliminate any factor and/or levels of pupil performance that did not demonstrate reliable between-class differences. Only three of the SLERS factors met this criterion, namely, problem emergence, application of learning, and the social learning environment. Concerning the measures of learner characteristics, only certain dimensions of THINK performance adequately differentiated the classes. The most recent analyses of these remaining variables speak to the highly specific nature of the relationship between classroom events and learner characteristics as opposed to more global effects—only particular factors appeared to be related to certain kinds of problem-solving performance. That is, classroom behaviors associated with problem emergence and the social learning environment were found to be significantly related to the aspects of problem solving that deal with identifying elements of a problem and making inferences about the problem.

SUMMARY AND DISCUSSION

Two on-going research studies have been described that were generated from the theoretical rationale underlying the Social Learning Curriculum. Based on the current state of knowledge concerning these data as well as the experiences encountered during the collection process, the following implications appear warranted.

First, while the assumptions underlying the Social Learning Curriculum seem to be justified, this does not mean that the program has been shown to achieve its primary objective, but only that these two individual tests of the organism have revealed that its heart is beating and is in the right place. This conservative interpretation is preferred because the data were collected under relational (correlational) rather than causative (experimental) conditions and based only on a small portion of the actual Social Learning Curriculum. Further statements must await revisions in the THINK and replication of the relationship between classroom implementation of the Social Learning Curriculum and student behaviors based on other parts of the program.

Second, the data indicate that each Social Learning Curriculum classroom is unique despite the fact that observations were conducted on the implementation of the same lessons. Since classrooms clearly differ, the implication here is that classrooms cannot and should not be aggregated in order to test for overall effectiveness of the Social Learning Curriculum or for that matter *any* program involving EMR pupils. (See Smith, 1974, for a more complete discussion of the effect of heterogeneity of special classrooms on the conduct of research.) The critical issue, then, is *not* really total program impact, but rather what actually happens when the portions of the program are utilized in various classrooms and what conditions actually facilitate optimal implementation in relation to learner behaviors. The expectation here is that teacher variables, i.e., experience, training, personality, and attitude, will be related to differential implementation and to program outcomes as well. Current work is moving in this direction.

Third, the results suggest that short-term studies of the implementation of specific Social Learning Curriculum lessons are more highly related to specific types of outcomes than to more global ones. This means that longitudinal studies need to be undertaken in order to examine the relationships between classroom implementation practices and more wide ranging outcomes for pupils who have gone through contiguous portions of the Social Learning Curriculum.

Fourth, a more definitive programmatic effort to facilitate the implementation of the Social Learning Curriculum in classrooms appears needed beyond the use of the SLOR. In order to provide for the continuous and developmental management of learning based on the Social Learning Curriculum, the endeavor must be integrated with and form the basis for teacher-supervisory-administrative relationships in the schools. Although such a strategy can certainly be evolved during the early stages of the development cycle, the critical need is to provide a basis for optimizing implementation and accountability once the curriculum has been published and adopted by practitioners.

While the value of product-process research has been recognized as an approach to evaluating educational programs (Soar, 1972; Stallings, 1974) and to studying teaching effectiveness (Gage, 1974), serious impediments to this type of research have been the lack of instructional strategies and student outcome measures related to specific curriculum content (Berliner, 1975; Joyce & Weil, 1972). The studies described illustrate that the Social Learning Curriculum provides a framework that maximizes the potentials of this type of research.

What implication does all of this have regarding current practices in mainstreaming mildly retarded children into regular classrooms? The kinds of curriculum-based questions raised in this chapter appear to be distinctly lacking in current concerns regarding mainstreaming. The primary reason for this lack of concern is that mainstreaming appears to have its source outside education proper; it is more an element in social change than a viable educational and curriculum-based practice. The real precipitating factor underlying the new surge of mainstreaming is legal and legislative; it is based on due process rights awarded parents and their right to challenge the decisions of the schools in every aspect of their child's experience, including placement. It is no coincidence that the stress on mainstreaming as a procedure burgeoned forth with the proliferation of parent-initiated court cases. It is no coincidence that some state legislatures mandated mainstreaming in one form or another shortly after it became clear that class action suits by parents were being successfully pursued. But where is the educational justification for the procedure? The current concept of mainstreaming appears to confound place or location where education is to be received with an actual educational program itself. We need to see placement issues and programming decisions as separate and distinct considerations. At the present time, the assumption appears to be that once mainstreaming has been accomplished, programming and curricular decisions are secondary, irrelevant, or unimportant. This author should like to argue that placement is more reasonably seen as a consequence of initially designating the total educational program in relation to unique learner needs. Placement, then, is an outcome of rational educational planning and goal setting; it is not the initial and primary educational issue. Accordingly, the selection of the program, the curriculum, and the methods of instruction should come under as much or more scrutiny than the placement decision itself. To put it another way, the pedagogic procedures that are designed to materialize educational and instructional objectives should meet the criteria for facilitation and only secondarily meet those criteria for logistical and managerial convenience. Thus, mainstreaming needs to be seen as one of a number of integrating alternatives and only as a means of accomplishing educationally important goals. The procedure has no intrinsic value and, therefore, no status as a procedure, except that in its implementation it contributes to meeting the curricular and instructionally based goals for those learners who are candidates for integration. Without this necessary connection to actual curriculum planning, mainstreaming is simply a procedure in search of substance.

ACKNOWLEDGMENTS

The author wishes to thank Herbert Goldstein, Sandra Greenberg, Gregory J. Schimoler, and Andrea Wilson for their suggestions, Sarah Oelberg for helping place the ITM in historical perspective, and Rochelle Mohr for her assistance in typing the manuscript.

REFERENCES

Bepko, R. A., & Warshow, J. P. The Social Learning Interaction System (SLIS). Unpublished monograph. New York: Yeshiva University, Curriculum Research and Development Center in Mental Retardation, 1974.

Bepko, R. A., Warshow, J. P., & Lehrer, B. Curriculum Research and Evaluation: Implications for Personnel Training. Paper presented at the annual meeting of the American Educational Research Association, Washington, D.C., 1975.

Berliner, D. C. Impediments to the study of teacher effectiveness. *Journal of Teacher Education, 27,* 1975.

Flanders, N. *Analyzing teaching behavior.* Reading, Mass.: Addison-Wesley, 1970.

Gage, N. L. Teaching as a human interaction, panel 2 report. In N. L. Gage (Ed.), *Conference on studies in teaching.* Washington, D.C.: National Institute of Education, 1974.

Goldstein, H. Social problems in mental retardation. Unpublished doctoral dissertation, University of Illinois, 1957.

Goldstein, H. *The Social Learning Curriculum: Phases 1-10.* Columbus, Oh.: Charles E. Merrill, 1974.

Goldstein, H. *The Social Learning Curriculum: Phases 11-16.* Columbus, Oh.: Charles E. Merrill, 1975.(a)

Goldstein, H. Many new curriculum programs for retarded children emerge. *The Centerline,* 1975, *1,* 10.(b)

Goldstein, H. Importance of social learning. In J. M. Kauffman & J. S. Payne (Eds.), *Mental retardation: Introduction and personal perspectives.* Columbus, Oh.: Charles E. Merrill, 1975.(c)

Goldstein, H. Curriculum design for handicapped students. *The High School Journal,* 1976, *59*(7), 290-301.

Goldstein, H. What research says to the teacher: Reasoning abilities of mildly retarded students. Reston, Va.: Council for Exceptional Children, in press.

Goldstein, H., Mischio, G., & Minskoff, E. Demonstration and research project in curriculum and methods (Final Report 32-42-1700-1700). Washington, D.C.: U.S. Office of Education, Department of Health, Education and Welfare, 1969.

Goldstein, H., Moss, J. W., & Jordan, L. The efficacy of special class training on the development of mentally retarded children (CRP No. 619). Washington, D.C.: U.S. Office of Education, Department of Health, Education and Welfare, 1965.

Goldstein, H., & Seigle, D. The Illinois plan for special education of exceptional children: A curriculum guide for teachers of the educable mentally handicapped (Curriculum Series B-3, No. 12). Springfield, Ill.: Office of the Superintendent of Public Instruction, 1958.

Greenberg, S. Assessment of inductive problem solving among EMR students. Unpublished doctoral dissertation. New York: Yeshiva University, 1977.

Greenberg, S., & Smith, I. L. Structural validation of a behavior hierarchy underlying an inductive teaching methodology (Research Report #3). New York: Yeshiva University, Curriculum Research and Development Center in Mental Retardation, 1974.

Joyce, B. R., & Weil, M. *Models of teaching.* Englewood Cliffs, N.J.: Prentice-Hall, 1972.

Kaufman, M. E., & Alberto, P. A. Research on efficacy of special education for the mentally retarded. In N. R. Ellis (Ed.), *International Review of Research in Mental Retardation,* 1976.

Mayer, W. V. (Ed.). *Planning curriculum development with examples from projects for the mentally retarded.* Boulder, Col.: Biological Science Curriculum Study, 1975.

Meyen, E. L., & Altman, R. Public school programming for the severely/profoundly handicapped: Some researchable problems. *Education and Training of the Mentally Retarded,* 1976, *11*(1), 40-45.

Meyen, E., & Horner, D. Curriculum development. In J. Wortis (Ed.), *Mental Retardation and Learning Disabilities (Vol. VIII).* New York: Bruner-Mazel, Inc., 1976.

Minskoff, E. H. Verbal interactions of teachers and mentally retarded pupils. Unpublished doctoral dissertation. New York: Yeshiva University, 1967.

Mischio, G. S. Inductive teaching techniques for the mentally retarded. *Focus on Exceptional Children,* 1973, *4*(8), 110.

Schimoler, G. J., & Warshow, J. P. Student-teacher dynamics of the Social Learning Curriculum classroom: The SLERS and student measures. Unpublished monograph. New York: New York University, Curriculum Research and Development Center in Mental Retardation, 1978.

Smith, I. L. Statistical realities of special class distributions. *American Journal of Mental Deficiency,* 1974, *78*(6), 740-747.

Smith, I. L. The factor structure and sources of variation underlying the Social Learning Environment Rating Scale: Monograph I. New York: Yeshiva University, Curriculum Research and Development Center in Mental Retardation, 1976.

Smith, I. L., & Greenberg, S. Hierarchical assessment of social competence. *American Journal of Mental Deficiency,* 1979, *83,* 551-555.

Smith, I. L., & Greenberg, S. Dimensions underlying a hierarchically-based assessment of social problem solving. *American Journal of Mental Deficiency,* in press.

Smith, I. L., & Greenberg, S. The *T*est of the *H*ierarchy of *IN*ductive *K*nowledge (THINK). New York: New York University, Curriculum Research and Development Center in Mental Retardation, in preparation.

Soar, R. S. An empirical analysis of selected follow through programs: An example of a process approach to evaluation. In I. J. Gordon (Ed.), *Early childhood education: The seventy-first yearbook of the National Society for the Study of Education.* Chicago: NSSE, 1972.

Soeffing, M. Where the action is: A look at four special education R&D Centers. *Exceptional Children,* 1975, *41*(6), 419-425.

Stallings, J. An implementation study of seven Follow Through models for evaluation. Paper presented at the 1974 annual meeting of the American Educational Research Association, Chicago, 1974.

Warshow, J. P., & Bepko, R. A. The Social Learning Environment Rating Scale (SLERS), Observational Manual: A Draft Version. New York: Yeshiva University, Curriculum Research and Development Center in Mental Retardation, 1974.

Warshow, J. P., Smith, I. L., & Goldstein, M. T. SLOR manual: A guide to using the Social Learning Observation Record. New York: Yeshiva University, Curriculum Research and Development Center in Mental Retardation, 1976.

CHAPTER 7

Regular Class Education of EMR Students, From Efficacy to Mainstreaming
A Review of Issues and Research

C. Edward Meyers, Donald L. MacMillan, and Roland K. Yoshida

This chapter reviews the education of educable mentally retarded (EMR) learners in regular class through various historical phases in which the basic question for research and practice consisted of an attempt to determine what was the best educational placement.

MAINSTREAMING AS NORMALIZATION

Mainstreaming is first seen as an educational application of the general principle of normalization, which refers to the ethic that all people are to be afforded the various rights and privileges that their condition does not specifically preclude. With respect to school placement of any exceptional learner including the EMR learner, the normalization principle is referred to as the least restrictive environment (LRE), meaning that the handicapped student's education is to be conducted with as much contact with nonhandicapped students as possible. The LRE may be perceived as a

---

This study was supported in part by the National Institute of Child Health and Human Development Research Grants No. HD-04612, HD-05540, HD-72847, and DHEW/CHD Grant No. 54-P-71117/9.

continuum from least to maximum contact. (For further elaboration see Chiba and Semmel, 1977.)

Mainstreaming, therefore, represents one form of LRE. No school whose enrollment included only handicapped students or any segregated self-contained special class on a campus with normal peers would be included in the LRE. However, the most common administrative arrangement for the conduct of the self-contained special class provides for some contact with the regular program pupils and activities. The typical EMR class for elementary level children is housed on the grounds of the regular elementary school; the EMR children are integrated for assembly, playground, physical education, and perhaps also for music and art. Even more integration occurs in the secondary school with its platooning of classes; the EMR students are integrated in such activities as art, music, physical education, and shop.

Mainstreaming *must* include the integration of handicapped learners with their nonhandicapped peers for instruction of basic academic subjects (e.g., reading, mathematics, English, language arts). Otherwise, the mere adherence to temporal integration, regardless of the curricular area, results in the handicapped child being integrated in nonacademics for half of the school day, which is precisely what went on prior to the litigation concerning retarded students. Thus, mainstreaming refers to the form of the LRE that has one of the following forms of regular class placement for special learners:

1. Regular class placement for about one-half of the average week. The special student is able to go to a special resource room or is helped individually by a tutor or aide.
2. Regular class placement most of the time. The degree and extent of special assistance are limited to occasional tutoring or counseling where most needed, or perhaps to periodic visits to a resource room.
3. Regular class placement with no provision of assistance directly to the special student. The teacher is assisted by a consultant with materials, instructional techniques, and/or guidance.
4. Unassisted regular class placement.

The unassisted student is included because the amount of mainstreaming assistance provided to students is sometimes so small that it may be meaningless, may be temporary or sporadic, and may exist only on paper.

HISTORICAL TRENDS
CULMINATING IN MAINSTREAMING *ZEITGEIST*

The groundwork for an adequate interpretation of issues and research currently being reported on mainstreaming requires some historical review of the education of the EMR learner. Before World War II, programs for EMR students were found in many places, primarily the larger cities, as a rule, on a legally permissive rather than mandatory basis. Although the depression of the 1930s tended to open the high school to vocational programs, making it more comprehensive in service, the trend toward high retention was thwarted by the employment opportunities for youth in the subsequent war period. Following World War II, largely because of parental lobbying and the endeavor to keep all youth in school, state after state expanded school districts and mandated some form of segregated education for those limited learners, now called EMR learners, who otherwise would have been early dropouts. (Programs for the trainable mentally retarded followed shortly.)

The segregated education movement found support in investigations of the status of psychometrically determined mildly mentally retarded students in regular classes (Johnson, 1950; Johnson & Kirk, 1950; Martin, 1953). These studies demonstrated the social isolation and the unhappiness of the retarded children in regular classes, leading to a claim that a better education would result if the students were placed in small, homogeneous groups with a specially trained teacher using appropriate materials and techniques. Such special classes became more available in most states. Almost as soon as they had become popularly established, the classes for the special education of the mildly retarded students came under empirical question. Johnson (1962) and then Dunn (1968) commented on the negative effects of such placements, although not acknowledging the adverse effects of the alternative—remaining in the regular class. Children with academic and social failure who score between 50 and 80 on an IQ test are children who have not experienced academically or socially successful histories in the public schools. Yet, when special classes cost much more money to operate because of the low pupil-teacher ratio, many teachers have felt it necessary to demonstrate their advantage.

The Efficacy Studies

Efforts to provide comparative evidence on the overall success of children in special classes as contrasted to similar children in regular grades are referred to as *efficacy studies*. These studies have been discussed, dissected, and dismissed in a series of lengthy reviews (see Cegelka & Tyler, 1970; Goldstein, 1967; Guskin & Spicker, 1968; Kirk, 1964; MacMillan, 1971; Quay, 1963). To summarize the compendium of results, these studies suggested that children profit in regular classes in terms of academic achievement, but that their social adjustment is poorer. However, these studies have been so thoroughly criticized on methodological grounds that one must be extremely cautious in drawing any conclusions from them.

The study of the efficacy of segregated classes for the education of the mildly handicapped was attended, as we know in retrospect, by a variety of problems that left critical questions unanswered. The *Zeitgeist* for the education of the mildly retarded, which first supported the establishment of such classes, switched to mainstreaming without adequate empirical information on comparative goodness of programs. Empirical ambiguity permitted other forces, both political and philosophical, to push the change, exemplified most famously in the enactment of PL 94-142, as well as in the *Larry P.* case, 343 F. Supp. 1306 (N.D. Cal., 1972).

The major criticism of these studies concerns inappropriate or biased sampling procedures, the particular instruments and procedures used to evaluate the outcomes of achievement and adjustment, and a lack of specificity concerning the "treatment" (regarding the teacher, the curriculum, and the special class). In considering these problems attention is focused on five studies: Blatt (1958), Cassidy and Stanton (1959), Thurstone (1959), Mullen and Itkin (1961), and Goldstein, Moss, and Jordan (1965).

Sampling Procedures With the exception of the Goldstein et al. study (1965), some form of matching of EMR students with regular class (RC) students was employed. Blatt (1958) matched, on the basis of CA, MA, and IQ, 75 EMR children in one school district that provided a program for EMR children with children in another district that had no EMR program. A similar procedure was used by Cassidy and Stanton (1959) in several school districts in Ohio. Some districts had EMR programs, which yielded the EMR sample, and RC samples were drawn from districts without such programs.

Several problems exist with such matching procedures. First, the Blatt (1958) and Cassidy and Stanton (1959) studies are to be faulted because the assignment to EMR programs within any school district is not random within an IQ range. In other words, there are selective factors that determine why one child with an IQ of 68 is placed in an EMR class and another is allowed to continue in a regular class. The results are that the two children matched on IQ are probably *unmatched* on virtually every other variable of importance (e.g., academic achievement, behavior, social adjustment) and that the variables on which the children are not matched are often more closely related to the outcomes that will be evaluated.

Mullen and Itkin (1961) matched 140 EMR and RC children (IQ range, 50 to 74) on the basis of age, IQ, sex, socioeconomic status, location of previous school attended, reading achievement, foreign language spoken in the home, presence of brain damage, and an adjustment rating. They still found that the procedure was biased in favor of the RC sample. All subjects were pretested, and gain scores in achievement and adjustment were compared after 1 year (140 pairs) and again after 2 years (64 pairs). Guskin and Spicker (1968) pointed out the problem of matching subjects on the basis of achievement or adjustment at the beginning of the study, rather than at the time of placement. They noted that if a child's rate of improvement in reading decreased after entering the special class (because of less emphasis and time alotted reading) then at the time of matching, the special class child would be matched with a RC child whose rate of improvement had been maintained over the duration. Hence, the matched pair would consist of an above average EMR student and an average RC student. While the reverse is also possible, the effects of the program would be washed out by the procedure used to achieve a match.

The final major problem with matching, as used in the efficacy studies, is the limiting effect it has on the generalizability of the findings. The five studies above employed IQ ranges from 50 to 80. Clearly, the vast majority of students found in RC populations were among the higher strata of this range, with very few cases in the 50s. Hence, few EMR children in the 50 to 65 IQ range could be used in the study for lack of RC matches. One cannot generalize findings from the matched groups to the original unmatched groups. The findings of most studies can be generalized only to children in the IQ range of 65 to 80 and little can be said about the efficacy of special classes for EMR children with IQs in the 50s or low 60s.

In order to avoid the problems of matching, Goldstein et al. (1965) went into 20 districts without special classes and tested 1,938 children entering first grade with a group test of intelligence. Children scoring 85 or below were then tested with the Stanford-Binet, and those scoring 85 or below on the Stanford-Binet were selected for the study. Fifty-seven children from the group were randomly assigned to four newly established special classes. Those who qualified psychometrically, but were not selected for special class placement, served as RC students. Thus, Goldstein et al. (1965), using this sampling procedure, were able to eliminate the selective bias inherent in matching, which afflicted other studies, by randomly assigning subjects from the population to either EMR or RC groups. At the same time, they controlled for differences in the preplacement experiences, such as degree of failure or ridicule the children might experience in the first few years of school. Nevertheless, the external validity of the study was threatened by the selection of the children prior to entry into first grade, before they had experienced difficulties in school. Typically, the child who has academic and behavior problems is referred by the teacher, evaluated, and placed (often having repeated a grade or so). Some of the children selected by Goldstein et al. (1965) might never have encountered school difficulty leading to EMR class placement.

To quote Guskin and Spicker (1968): "In dealing with primary special classes initiated for 6-year-olds, the Illinois study revealed little about the more common special class for children beyond the age of 8" (p. 239).

Sampling proved a difficult hurdle to overcome in the efficacy studies. The more naturalistic the selection of EMR class, the greater the threats to the internal validity of the study; the greater the control over independent variables achieved through random assignment and early placement, the greater the threat to the external validity. The one procedure that went unstudied would be to allow children to be referred naturalistically by teachers, to be evaluated and certified, and then to be assigned at random to EMR and RC groups. Any study employing only psychometric definitions of the EMR or the RC population does violence to the multidimensionality of EMR classes in the schools—classroom failure as well as low IQ.

Evaluation of Achievement and Adjustment An understanding of the findings of these studies requires some perspective regarding the differential emphasis in regular classes and special classes. In the regular class the emphasis continued to be placed on the mastery of traditional academic content areas (e.g., reading, arithmetic), whereas the special classes for EMR students tended to place less emphasis on the learning of academics *per se,* concentrating more heavily on the development of social and prevocational skills. As a result, it was virtually impossible to select a single dependent measure that was equally appropriate to both RC and EMR programs in terms of their differing goals. The problem is compounded in cases where there was a selective factor involved in sampling, where the very dependent measure used to evaluate the efficacy of placements (i.e., achievement) was the determinant that placed children of an IQ range in EMR classes and that would be retained in a regular class—a classical example of confounding of independent and dependent variables.

Findings regarding achievement are mixed, yet tend to favor RC samples. Blatt (1958) reported no reliable differences in achievement, but Cassidy and Stanton (1959) found RC children to score higher on measures of achievement. Both Thurstone (1959) and Mullen and Itkin (1961) analyzed gain scores in achievement. On initial measures, Thurstone reported that RC students were superior to EMR students on all measures of achievement except arithmetic computation. However, at the end of the second year there were no differences in gains for the two groups. When the achievement data on children of lower IQ (50–59) were analyzed separately, special class EMR students were found to have made significantly greater gains in achievement than their equal IQ counterparts in regular classes.

Mullen and Itkin (1961) found RC children to achieve significantly higher in arithmetic computation after 1 year; however, no other differences were significant. Note that this finding contradicts that of Thurstone (1959) where there was a failure to find a difference in arithmetic computation, while securing differences on all other achievement measures. Thus, the Thurstone (1959) and Mullen and Itkin (1961) findings are the mirror image of one another.

Goldstein et al. (1965) reported significant gains in IQ for both groups over the 4 years studied. The mean IQ went from 75 to 83 at the end of the study. Achievement differences between groups were not pronounced, although at the end of the first 2 years RC subjects were considerably higher in reading achievement. This advantage disappeared by the end of the study. Similarly, RC students were superior in arithmetic achievement at the end of the first year, but this difference also disappeared at the time of subsequent evaluations. Otherwise, no significant differences in academic achievement were found between the two groups.

Social adjustment was measured in a variety of ways. Blatt (1958) reported no differences in personality; however, Cassidy and Stanton (1959) did find differences favoring EMR students on some aspects of personality and social adjustment. Cassidy and Stanton used a teacher rating, as did Thurstone (1959), which is impossible to compare across settings because different frames of reference render comparisons meaningless. Thurstone also employed a sociometric device that demonstrated RC students to be more often isolated in the regular class. Again, across-setting comparisons on sociometric status defy interpretation.

Goldstein et al. (1965) examined the subjects' interactions in their neighborhood and reported that special class children were less inclined to interact with neighborhood peers. On a scale of self-derogation, EMR subjects were found to admit to more derogatory perceptions of themselves (Meyerowitz, 1962). (The interested reader might want to consult Guskin and Spicker (1968) for their analysis of the secondary analysis performed by Goldstein et al. on cases with IQs above and below 80 at the end of the first year. However, these findings are not considered here because it is a questionable practice to perform secondary analyses not provided for in the original sampling design.)

In addition to the question of matching dependent measures to the goals of the different programs, there are problems inherent in the measurement of achievement and adjustment with the children studied in the efficacy studies. How does one select the level of achievement tests to administer to children in EMR programs? Yoshida (1976) gives considerable attention to out-of-level testing of this sort. In the adjustment area, tests of personality typically entail vocabulary and concepts that are not possessed by many children in the EMR range at the ages studied. So the uncritical use of scales not standardized on handicapped populations renders the results questionable. Meyerowitz' (1962) Illinois Index of Self Derogation has unknown validity and reliability. Commonly, discussions of the efficacy studies have taken findings at face value regardless of the limitations in instrumentation.

Failure to Specify Treatments A major assumption must be made when using a between-groups design for comparing special class students to regular class students. One assumes that the between-groups variance is greater than the within-groups variance; or that special classes are sharing more in general than they overlap with what goes on in the regular class. However, Kirk (1964) and Goldstein et al. (1965) faulted all of the studies conducted before the Illinois study on the basis that they failed to spell out what constituted the "special class" in the efficacy studies. What was the special training of the teachers, what were the curricular emphases and instructional methods employed; in other words, other than an administrative arrangement, what was the definition of the special class? To correct this, the Illinois study (Goldstein et al., 1965) controlled what went on in the special class by using a specific curriculum guide taught by specially trained teachers.

Another problem with all of the studies reviewed herein is the unit of analysis, which was invariably the child. When the subjects in the study are nested in classrooms each taught by a different teacher there is a question of whether the appropriate unit of analysis is the child or the class. If the progress a child makes is primarily dependent upon the ability of the teacher rather than the administrative arrangement in which teaching takes place, then the more appropriate unit of analysis might be the class. If this option were used, then considerable degrees of freedom would be lost in any analyses and the probability of significant differences would be reduced.

Misapplication of Findings to Mainstreaming The uncritical interpretation of the efficacy studies has apparently led some to believe that EMR children can "do better" if they are placed in a regular classroom that has no special adaptations for them. It is reasoned that the RC children achieved higher scores in the efficacy studies when no special considerations were given them. The results regarding achievement in the studies reviewed here are not all that impressive with regard to achievement considering the mixed results, the questionable measures of achievement, the inappropriateness of a standardized achievement test to tap the major emphases in the special class, and the differences, although significant, were not very great.

Possibly more important is for the reader to look to the sampling bias in terms other than methodological oversights. We mean that the RC populations in the efficacy studies were in those classes for the very reason that they did not need special education—they were functioning, albeit at a marginal level, to the satisfaction of the teacher. These learners differ from the ones currently being considered for mainstreaming; the latter failed academically in the regular class and only then were they tested and found to score low on IQ tests. In a related sense, the IQ ranges in the efficacy studies also bear attention since the upper IQ children in these studies go well beyond the present upper cut-off for EMR students according to the recommendations of the American Association on Mental Deficiency (Grossman, 1973). The EMR students, as currently defined, are more like the lower level students reported by Thurstone (1959) and by Goldstein et al. (1965) in their secondary analyses. These lower level students clearly did benefit from special class placement.

Civil Rights Labeling Litigation and Constriction of the EMR Definition

Paralleling the progress of the efficacy studies was the growing concern over the effects of labeling a child as EMR on his/her academic achievement and social adjustment. It is an historic irony that the doubts about the wisdom of EMR placement began to arise when the special program achieved its heyday, in the so-called Kennedy era. In this era, there was increased consciousness of the special needs of mentally retarded citizens and a lusty expansion of services everywhere, abetted by federal subventions. The American Association on Mental Deficiency (AAMD) broadened its definition of mental retardation to include the so-called borderline group, thus enabling schools to place children with IQs up to 85 into special education classes (Heber, 1959) under the widely practiced principle that all who might need a special service should be so classified to be eligible to receive it.

The AAMD's definition (Heber, 1959) made another change causing the abandonment of the historic distinction between the mentally defective who as a rule tended to have palpable biomedical complications in addition to the markedly limited mentation and the "retarded" or "culturally familial" or "difficult to educate" persons with normal bodies. All were grouped under the term *mental retardation*. This misinterpretation might have tended to increase the pejoration of the label *mental retardation* toward the mildly handicapped because it could invoke imagery of dwarfed-bodied and back ward inmates, not mere slow learning normal children. School classes had often been labeled *special training classes*, but in the 1960s all school districts tended to accept the label *special classes* for the mentally retarded or mentally handicapped persons. It is not possible to judge how much this association under the one term contributed to the total pejoration, but it is of interest that Badt's study (1957) on the negative effects of segregated status came before the Heber (1959) announcement of change. It is possible that any labeling achieves stigma on its own.

Whatever the reason, history shows that the enrollments of EMR children climbed in the 1960s, and that this increase contained a severe overrepresentation of minority children. This situation led to some local litigation in which there was a charge of wrongful assignment and labeling, attributed to biased testing. These cases were locally handled, but the creation of the class action suit in federal court led to nationally publicized litigation and radical changes in the assignment of students to the EMR program (Meyers, Sundstrom, & Yoshida, 1974). Best known of the cases were *Diana,* No. C-70-RFP (RFP Dist. Ct. N.D. Cal., 1970) and *Larry P.,* 343 F. Suppl. 1306 (N.D. Cal., 1972).

This account of the history of change in California in what came to be called the EMR program was necessary because the student composition of such classes varied with swings of policy and priority. Illustrative is the clear difference between the characteristics of students in segregated self-contained EMR class at the time of this writing and students in such a class in the mid-1960s. Court-mandated changes in the assignment of EMR pupils had several effects. The enrollments in EMR classes in California were reduced to less than half of the existing level because the better learners were returned to regular classes, which resulted in a lower average quality of special class student. School districts became sensitive to the implications of litigation and tended to avoid any placement that might invite scrutiny or appeal. Hence, there was some nonplacement of students who experienced class failures that invited consideration of EMR assessment. Nonplacement was exacerbated by the *Diana* stipulation that ethnic group enrollments in EMR classes not be very disproportional to the group's total enrollment. No one to our knowledge has investigated the success of these marginal learners who remained in regular class. Presumably these students could be served by an expanded compensatory education program, or not labeled as EMR students in mainstreamed education, once PL 94-142 is more fully implemented.

Regardless of one's interpretation of history, the establishment of the least restrictive environment (LRE) principle was a culmination of powerful forces originating from divergent sources: professional, consumer, and legal. Likewise, the application of the LRE will remain a salient practice for a prolonged period of time. The principle of the LRE and its specific application, termed *mainstreaming* in this chapter, define the context in which school personnel must select an appropriate setting for delivering special education services to students. Thus, attention must be given to research on the divergent perspectives of mainstreaming and the effects of mainstreaming practice on student outcomes.

CURRENT LITERATURE ON MAINSTREAMING

The relatively new term *mainstreaming* is found in titles of the more recent investigations, especially those performed in anticipation of and following the passage of PL 94-142. Mainstreaming literature has tended to examine aspects of the integrated education of the EMR learner, much of it featuring academic success as well as self-concept and peer acceptance. Some of it explores teacher acceptance and attitudes, in their own right and as possibly affecting regular class peer attitudes. An excellent review of mainstreaming is provided by Corman and Gottlieb (1979).

Academic Success

Pre-, midway, and post achievement measures supplied data for Budoff and Gottlieb (1976) in a comparison of segregated and regular class EMR students, the latter receiving resource room help for academic subjects. Controlling for initial test scores, the investigators found no differences. The subjects, who were about 13 years old, were more mature than those in the typical planned study found in the literature, which tends to favor elementary ages. Walker (1974) tested children ages 9 to 11 in a similar comparison, finding superior gain scores for the mainstreamed group in reading but not arithmetic. This was an example of a study in which the treatment methods (i.e., the educational planning) were described for the resource room teachers. Similar gains in reading but not in other measured subjects were determined for 8-year-olds by Carroll (1967) in an older study of the late efficacy period.

Some studies that were different from the simple comparison of basic treatments (segregated versus regular class placement of EMR students) have been reported. For example, cross-age tutoring was employed together with some trappings of behavior modification with material rewards (Bradfield, Brown, Kaplan, Rickert, & Stannard, 1973). Sixth graders were tutors of nonEMR students and mainstreamed EMR students in lower grades. Subjects were few and results generally inconclusive, but the instructional ideas in the report are worth reading about. A different purpose was exemplified by Haring and Krug's (1975) pre-mainstreaming efforts, comparing randomly selected EMR subjects assigned either to an experimental or regular EMR group program. A variety of features in the experimental EMR program included intensive and highly motivating reading instruction with attention to specific consequences of the reading effort. The subjects in the experimental program gained far more than the control subjects. Furthermore, 13 of 24 experimental subjects but none of 24 control subjects were placed into regular classes. Of the 13, 10 were judged not to require special assistance.

Few of the reports of mainstreaming have carried information about the specific programmatic components—the real life test of a placement. We are aware that many school districts had made pre-mainstreaming efforts, but there is scant literature about their success.

Personal-Social Adjustment

Nonacademic variables were studied with the use of peer ratings, self-ratings, sociometric choices, teacher judgment, and sometimes by observation. A potential impasse in the contrast of data secured in peer adjustment inheres in the fact that the peers of integrated EMR students are "normal," while the peers of the segregated classes are EMR students. We delimit remarks here to studies that controlled this, using for example, schools in which both treatments were on the same grounds, permitting all students to be familiar with each other.

The general trend of these studies is signaled by Goodman, Gottlieb, and Harrison (1972) who found the segregated EMR students to be viewed more favorably by peers than the mainstreamed students. The result was found to be attributed to the lesser visibility or exposure of the segregated EMR students to regular class peers (Gottlieb & Budoff, 1973; Gottlieb, Cohen, & Goldstein, 1974; Gottlieb & Davis, 1973). These and other reports either fail to substantiate the anticipated superior acceptance of EMR students in mainstreamed placement or showed less favorable attitudes toward them.

These results cannot be attributed to just a matter of reacting to a label. Iano, Ayers, Heller, McGettigan, and Walker (1974) demonstrated the same degree of acceptance/nonacceptance of those labeled EMR and those not, provided that the nonlabeled received some special treatment. This result is consistent with one interpretation of the alleged effects of labeling indicated by MacMillan, Jones, and Aloia (1974), namely that regardless of the initial neutral quality of a group's designation, the group name acquires qualities attributable to the students in the group given the special treatments.

Most studies of the sort cited here have been performed in elementary school settings. Seriously in need of replication is the report by Sheare (1974) in the secondary school in which nonEMR peers exposed to EMR students in their classes demonstrated better attitudes toward EMR students than nonEMR students who had not been so exposed. This apparent variation is in need of replication, as are other reports in which sex, ethnicity, bussing, and architecture (e.g., open structure among other variables) have complicated the determination of social acceptance and attitude.

The self-concept of EMR students in segregated versus mainstreamed programs has been compared, most commonly by use of self-report and teacher ratings. The results are mixed. Some (Budoff & Gottlieb, 1976; Carroll, 1967) show a better self-regard among the mainstreamed, others such as Walker (1974) show little or no difference. Carroll's (1967) report indicated the segregated students to have more self-derogation on the Illinois Index. In any case, the self-regard types of reports show better status of integrated students in comparison with segregated students than the peer acceptance reports. Better self-regard and academic self-concept are related somewhat to receiving good supportive help (Budoff & Gottlieb, 1976). This finding is consistent with observed changes over time reported by Gottlieb, Gampel, & Budoff (1975) after integrated placement.

Teacher Attitudes Toward Mainstreaming

Some writers of reports on the self-concept and peer acceptance of mainstreamed EMR students by nonEMR peers have speculated that differences among the results of such studies could have been due in part to the teacher attitude toward accepting the special student. Variations in the preparation of teachers and in the number of special students a single teacher has to instruct are of course well known (e.g., Kaufman et al., 1978). Some direct investigations have been made of teacher attitude vis-à-vis instructing EMR or similar special students. Good reviews of the topic are provided by Gottlieb (1975) and Corman and Gottlieb (1979), so that only a couple highlights are mentioned here.

The general tendency of the regular class teacher is to be neutral or unfriendly about possibly receiving EMR learners (Gickling & Theobold, 1975; Shotel, Iano, & McGettigan, 1972), and for attitudes to decline with actual reception. Only one report (Guerin & Szatlocky, 1974) showed a majority of teachers to be favorable. Furthermore, most teachers tend to express anxiety with the anticipated problems, but report acceptance of a *fait accompli*. However, the teachers' vague fears before mainstreaming convert to negative attitudes formed by the behavior of the specific students they have. In short, both the teacher's attitudes toward the handicapped and the confirmation of those attitudes may affect the self-concept and peer acceptance of those students.

Compared with the majority of efficacy studies, these later explorations of mainstreaming show better design and a greater variety of dependent variables. Unfortunately most of them endured for only a year or so, without providing the information about what happened to pupils some years later, as did Goldstein, Moss, and Jordan (1965). Even the massive PRIME investigation, covered next, was of short duration.

THE TEXAS PRIME PROJECT

The most ambitious planned investigation of mainstreaming and its variables is known as the PRIME project, carried out in Texas as an intramural project of the Bureau of Education for the Handicapped (Kaufman, Agard, & Semmel, in press). The design of the study profited from imperfections in assumptions and procedure of the earlier efficacy studies. Particularly, PRIME followed the mandate of Kirk (1964) and others in describing within treatment variability as well as between treatment comparisons.

The study was possible because Texas had elected to step up its provision of special education by a considerable amount. The law provided that the districts choose either self-contained classes for EMR and other marginal learners, or to formulate mainstreaming plans, considerable freedom in the latter being permitted. Hence, the project could observe variation in practices.

Children in grades 3, 4, and 5 in elementary schools were selected with some intention to secure adequate numbers of the three principal ethnic groups, called Anglo, black, and Chicano. Compared were 356 mainstreamed EMR students, 356 normal contrast students (each selected by random process from the classroom of the mainstreamed student), and 273 nonmainstreamed EMR students. The EMR learners of both groups averaged about a year older than the normal students and males were more frequent than in the normal group. Other marginal learners were involved in the study but were not included in the present analyses.

Program Characteristics

Mainstreamed EMR students spent from 50%–100% of time in the regular program, depending on the district or school. Nonmainstreamed students were identified as EMR students if they received 50% or more of instruction from the special teacher, although there was some amount of academic instruction by a regular class teacher. Hence the study could not maintain in pure form the primary contrast indicated earlier as the essential basis for answering the simple question about mainstreamed versus segregated instruction for the academic subjects. Kaufman et al. (in press) also pointed to the relative newness of special education in so much of the territory covered, especially for mainstreaming, and of delays in implementing such services as resource teachers and resource rooms. Furthermore, the districts chosen for the study were among the earlier ones to request state assistance in setting up new programs, thus being districts with more progressive concern for the education of the handicapped. For these and other reasons this largest of studies could not supply unambiguous answers to many of the questions one can raise, but yielded much interesting information nevertheless.

Because of its extensiveness, the PRIME project showed the variability that the real world provides in the percent of total time a so-called self-contained class student spends in integrated conditions, in how variable is the time spent in the resource room by a mainstreamed student, and in how variable is the number of students mainstreamed to a given teacher. The number of students assigned to one regular class teacher varied from one to six or more, 19% in the "six or more" category. In spite of this the regular teachers revealed attitudes toward integration that were slightly superior to those of either teachers of self-contained classes or of resource teachers. They felt less well, however, than resource room or self-contained class teachers about adequacy of supportive services. They reported various problems in teaching the mainstreamed EMR students, principally the lack of time and appropriate materials, but also the uncooperative or the disruptive behavior of the EMR student. Twenty-nine percent (29%) of the regular class teachers reported that the presence of mainstreamed EMR students increased discipline problems in the class; smaller percents of the teachers reported lower class social cohesion and morale. Teachers' responses to the invitation to make suggestions were no surprise: smaller class size, teacher aide, more preparation time, and so on, including assistance in behavior management.

One-to-one instruction occurred in resource rooms and in the segregated classes, rarely in the regular class. In general the resource rooms had too many students for individualized assistance. Clearly, PRIME data revealed that more intensive instructional services were available to the handicapped learner in the self-contained classes or resource rooms than in the regular classes.

Classroom observation provided some contrasts in how the classroom time was spent. Nonmainstreamed students received the largest proportion of time (34%) in activities other than academic instruction, compared with 18% for normal and 25% for mainstreamed. It is expected in contrasts like these that the normal and the mainstreamed students should differ only a small amount since teachers are common for pairs. Instruction time in academic subjects was about the same across the three groups except for much less time devoted to science and social studies for the nonmainstreamed students.

Child Data: Achievement and Adjustment

Scores on standardized tests indicated the expected superiority of the normal subjects; the mainstreamed EMR students were slightly ahead of the nonmainstreamed students. However, the nonmainstreamed students made greater gains during the academic year between pretests and posttests. Teachers' marks (a comparison valid only for the mainstreamed versus normal students) confirmed the findings of the test scores.

Instrumentation was developed to secure self- and peer regard and other social and personality indicators. Attitudes toward reading and other subjects differed little between groups. Feelings about peers were obtained by the student's marking of smiling or frowning faces, which formed a 3-point Likert scale. Nonmainstreamed learners marked more smiles than the mainstreamed learners, and the mainstreamed more than normal learners. The mainstreamed learners were less well accepted by class peers than those in the segregated class but rejection was not universal and everybody had some friends. The general social-emotional picture of the mainstreamed learners was not so good as hoped, but better than some had feared.

Conclusion This largest of all planned studies of mainstreaming contains far more data than mentioned in this brief account. The investigators related various pupil, educational-environmental, and outcome variables to each other in an attempt to explain variances in the data. Nevertheless, it would be difficult to conclude from PRIME that the mainstreaming treatment was superior to the segregated treatment except on philosophical grounds, given a commitment to as much normalization as conditions permit. At the cost of apparently a weaker self-concept, the mainstreamed students were holding their own on other variables in contrast with the segregated. If one assesses PRIME as a normalization experience, one notes that the "normal" students were subaverage on the average in both IQ and family socioeconomic status and hence not ideal role models. It is, of course, a common finding to locate the majority of EMR students in such below average school neighborhoods. Another note that the PRIME authors make pertaining to the export of the results is the high proportion of Spanish-surnamed students in Texas.

THE CALIFORNIA DECERTIFICATION STUDIES

Two studies have been conducted that took advantage of the "natural experiment" that resulted from the court-mandated reassessment of all California EMR students (*Diana* v. *School Board of Education,* No. C-70-RFP (RFP Dist. Ct. N.D. Cal., 1970).

The court mandates and agreements between litigants and the defendent school authorities (local and state) led to a succession of legislative enactments. In addition to providing for the reassessment and the use of "nonbiased" instrumentation, the state also changed guidelines for cutoff IQ for admission, from the previous maximum of 75 (plus or minus a standard error of measurement, thus up to and including 79) to two standard deviations below the mean. This normally means a maximum IQ of 68 on the Binet and 70 on the Wechsler scales, again with allowance of some error of measurement. The effect was to reduce EMR student registration in California by somewhere between 11,000 and 14,000 cases within the period 1969 to 1972, the uncertainty being due to no one's knowing: 1) how many reassigned students were cases of pending placement but not placed in view of new guidelines, 2) how many students were removed without formal decertification, and 3) how large was the usual proportion of students leaving school by dropout or graduation.

Why the Decertification

Diana v. *State Board of Education* case was a class-action suit claiming Mexican-American students had been wrongfully assigned to EMR classes by an inappropriate measure, the standardized individual intelligence test. Early in 1970 the court provided in stipulations with the defendant school district and the State Board of Education for certain relief as requested, one being mandatory reassessment of all California EMR class enrollees by the use of testing procedures in the child's home language or by performance testing, and so on.

The court, cognizant of the well-known ethnic overrepresentation in EMR classes, placed a burden on the schools to correct it. A period of rapid decertification occurred from 1969 through 1972, some thereafter, cutting total EMR class enrollment from over 55,000 to 35,000 by 1973. The carefully defined and gathered data secured in the 12 districts of the investigation indicated that 45% of the then current 1969–1972 EMR students had been decertified. This reduction was due mainly to a lowering of the qualifying IQ by the State Board. However, mandated change in testing and admission criteria had not effected much change in ethnic representation. Table 1 presents the percentage of Anglo, black, and Spanish-surname students enrolled in all California school programs and in EMR classes during 1969, the initial year of decertification, and 1973, the academic year in which all reassessments and reassignments of students were completed. The absolute frequency of EMR students declined from 55,519 to 35,110. The change in the proportion of minority students was relatively small; the decrease was from 55.3% to 48.0% for both black and Spanish-surname groups. This result seems disappointing in

Table 1. Statewide EMR enrollment, October, 1969 and June, 1973

		Percent Anglo	Percent black	Percent Spanish surname	Total
1.	Total California public school pupils (1969)	72.4	8.9	15.2	
2.	Percent of ethnic group which was in total EMR (1969)	43.1	27.1	28.2	55,519
3.	Percent of ethnic group which was in total EMR (1973)	50.0	25.0	23.0	35,110

Source: Allan Simmons and Leslie Brinegar. *Ethnic survey of EMR classes, 1973.* Sacramento: California State Department of Education, 1973.

terms of "equal" representation. Nevertheless, one cannot overlook the significant decline in EMR class enrollments that affected all ethnic groups as well as the very high percentage of minority students in some districts who were in fact decertified as a result of the new state guidelines.

This brief history is provided to show the setting of the decertification study and the powerful influence of such litigation in promoting the mainstreaming aspects of PL 94-142, as well as the clauses for "protections in evaluation procedures" in the rules and regulations. The decertified students certainly were educationally failing students in regular class. They had been considered, in the then prevailing rules and practices, to be better served in special EMR class, but now were returned to the regular program. Their level of success was grist for the research mill. One motivation for performing the studies was to determine the relative efficacy of various means of providing transition assistance to the students upon their return, as also mandated in the *Diana* stipulations. However, this help was so hastily improvised and of such irregular delivery as not to provide for the answering of questions. Nevertheless, a variety of other questions could be addressed.

The Meyers et al. Study

The Meyers et al. (1975) study sampled 12 districts chosen to represent urban and suburban areas, northern and southern California, large and small districts and to show either a variety in predominant ethnic membership or an ethnic balance in a district. Two "districts" were actually two of the administrative areas of the huge Los Angeles district which enrolls nearly one-fifth of all California public school students. Inter-ethnic comparisons were possible for some variables because all three primary ethnic groups were represented in two of our sampled large districts. The study did not enter the two districts involved in the two major litigations, *Diana* and *Larry P.* A complete description of the sampling has been provided in Meyers et al. (1975).

In the first phase of the study, the complete psychological and cumulative record files were examined to produce the actual EMR registrations for the period in question, thus providing the sampling bases for the study of educational progress later of both the decertified (D) and nondecertified (EMR) groups. The second phase was the study of the then current success of the sampled students. Stratified random sampling within ethnic and sex groups was made to secure D subjects. Any student was excluded whose return to the regular program was due to influences other than the mandated reassessment. All D students were matched in their own school districts with a nondecertified EMR student of the same sex, ethnicity, and either grade level or program level. This was to control for differences that might have been due to those factors. The D students were also matched as above with a regular class peer (RC) who had never been in special class. This matching with the RC peers was performed at the time of the study (Meyers et al., 1975) from 2 to 6 years after the D student had reentered the regular program. The RC student was selected to be in the lower half of the class in which the D student was enrolled, based on a criterion group test performance as the Iowa Test of Basic Skills or current academic marks.

Current status data were secured for all three groups of students, D, EMR, and RC, as follows: standardized reading and mathematics on the Metropolitan Achievement Tests (MAT), teacher marks in academic subjects and citizenship, and current adjustment and attendance status. Cumulative records and psychologists' files permitted a comparison of D and EMR students in regular classes before EMR placement, during that placement, and at reassessment time. Finally, teachers were surveyed concerning their perceptions of: a student's current level of achievement and adjustment, the general level of the class in which a D or EMR student was enrolled, and a general evaluation of the transition program.

The D and EMR groups were also compared in another respect. When the EMR student's matching cases were drawn and were found not to be enrolled at the time that the current study was to be made, they were replaced by the new "draws," but the unenrolled EMR student's registration was sought to determine whether or not he was attending school.

Before discussing the current status of the D and EMR groups, it is important to address issues regarding the circumstances that led to their placement into special education. The *Diana* and the *Larry P.* cases charged that children were tested with biased instruments and by examiners who could not make due allowance for cultural differences, resulting in a stigmatizing identification as mentally retarded and placement in the EMR program, itself a deprival of the right to an appropriate education for a nonretarded person. As in much similar litigation, the defendant school districts and the State Board of Education did not choose to make a serious defense against the allegations.

Regardless of the reasons for failure to defend themselves against the charges, the defendants, by accepting the charges, appeared to prefer a court mandate to effect an improvement in the alternatives that the school could provide for children with learning disabilities. However, failure to present an adequate defense permitted the schools to be painted in an unfavorable light. It was not brought out that psychological assessment is generally conducted after the child has been brought to the attention of the school as being a school failure in achievement or adjustment. The intelligence test serves only to confirm the child's eligibility for the EMR program as required by law. Given the focus on the IQ, an attempt was made to determine whether, in hindsight, there were differences in characteristics of the D and EMR students that could have prevented possible misclassification.

An examination of the psychologists' files at initial EMR student placement revealed some small and statistically significant IQ differences at initial EMR student placement (Meyers, MacMillan, & Yoshida, 1978). However, the significance was due primarily to the large numbers of cases, so that the group differences accounted for very little of the total variances, as measured by omega squares. Also, an examination of the cumulative records revealed no systematic difference between D and EMR groups in teachers' marks for academic subjects or citizenship, years in the regular program before EMR group placement, and age at EMR placement. The data show that children were given a good try in the regular class before being placed in the EMR class, that IQs differed only a little between those who were later to be decertified and those not, that cases for referral did not systematically differ to indicate that the "higher grade" EMR students were placed because of deportment difficulties and that teachers' marks before EMR placement did not differ.

The IQ difference at reassessment was of course greater because IQ was the criterion to distinguish the groups. Furthermore, the decertification decisions appeared to have been based almost exclusively on IQ.

The grade equivalents for various reading and math subtests and total scores on the MAT were selected as the achievement measure. The MAT scores were subjected to analyses of variance and covariance using the program level (e.g., elementary, junior high, senior high) as a covariate. In analyzing the data we were interested in testing whether the D, EMR, and RC groups differed from one another.

For all school districts in which it was possible to do the testing, the results revealed a monotonous regularity. The means of the RC groups were highest, the D next, and the EMR groups lowest for both reading and mathematics. The results, treated as direct comparisons of groups with and without statistical corrections for program level, indicated a tested superiority of the D group over the EMR groups, a kind of validation of their return to the regular program. Yet the fact that they tested below the RC groups' matches indicates that they were not strong students. The mean achievement level of the D students was approximately 4 years below their grade placement. Their placement, considered age-grade wise, was nearly 2 years below that expected on an annual promotion basis. The age-grade placement of the RC subjects was a little over one-half a year more favorable. The RC group did not provide a very severe comparison for the D group, as the typical D student was placed into the least advanced English or reading and mathematics class, if in secondary school, and the RC student match was selected from the lower half of that class. That is to say, while the D group had lost two years in placement the RC group had lost about a year and a third. In spite of the fact that the RC group was not a severe criterion for the success of the D group, the RC group was probably the consequence of the relatively low status of the class group as a whole. On a question about the proportion of the class reading at or above grade level, 58% of the teachers responded "very few."

Questions about the help the transition program provided tended to be answered with responses that if it existed, they or the student benefited little or not at all; some were surprised to learn there had been one. If they had opinions about the variety of help given, they most often mentioned paraprofessional aides, followed by a resource teacher.

As a study of the effects of mainstreaming, the Meyers et al. study leaves much to be desired. No random assignment of EMR students to regular class was made, thus introducing the interpretive problems that had been encountered with the efficacy studies. Furthermore, there was little knowledge to be gained about the effectiveness of so-called transition assistance (with varieties like those listed in the mainstreaming literature). However, there was unquestioned external validity in the investigation. The study sampled hundreds of decertified students to determine their success in comparison with matched regular class peers, and also compared them with nondecertified EMR students. The investigation secured current status of the students at a point about 2 to 6 years after the reassignment to regular class. Hence the enduring results of the decertification were determined. Unlike the short-lived planned experiment with high internal but questionable ecological validity, this study did have the latter in abundance.

The Keogh et al. Study

The second study of the California decertification program is reported by Keogh and Levitt (1976) and Keogh, Levitt, Robson, and Chan (1974). It was limited to the junior high grades (7, 8, and 9) in the schools of the third largest metropolitan area of California, in an area of the state not entered by the Meyers et al. investigation. Search of the EMR students' files for 1970-1972 identified 153 students enrolled in such grades, this being 57% of the 267 who were known to have been reassigned to regular programs and were now in the junior highs. No comparison with nondecertified students was attempted. Rather, each reassigned student was compared with four regular class students drawn from the required English class, these being matched for sex and ethnicity, otherwise randomly drawn from the class.

The results were generally considered discouraging. Seventeen percent (17%) of the D students had been returned to some special program; others were lost in one way or another, or were in custody or suspended status, leaving 78% of the initial study group. The teachers rated the former EMR students as poor in academic subjects and as having social adjustment difficulties—all data of course in comparison with the class as a whole. The measured achievement in reading and arithmetic was consistently and significantly poorer than that of the match cases or of the other comparison sample. This was true even for the students who had been placed in rather low achieving classes.

The low teacher regard was obtained in the knowledge that over 95% of the teachers did not know that the reassigned student had once been in special class, but their judgments of academic attainment were consistent with empirical test results. In terms of grade placement of their test score, the results of the Keogh studies tended to confirm the results secured by Meyers et al. In general, there was no profound difference in the determinations of Keogh and associates from our more comprehensive study; the former used a stricter comparison with regular class, drawing randomly from the entire class rather than from the lower half, as had been done by Meyers et al. As a consequence, the "success" was seen to be at a relatively lower level. Neither study could be concluded to say that the "mainstreaming" had been successful in academic terms for very many, unless success would be defined as barely getting along.

Interpretation of the Decertification Studies

The authors developed this section with knowledge of a series of unpublished investigations or observations made in California when decertification with transition assistance was at its peak. These studies were as a rule district-sponsored, some with ESEA Title VIB funding. Most had to do not with the politics nor the statistics of reassignment but rather with how the decertified students fared with respect to the transition help provided. Inasmuch as many districts provided no help whatsoever and others were known to have provided help on as minimal a basis as funds permitted, the reports one heard about were surely the product of more progressive districts.

None of such information which in the writer's awareness produced conclusions much different from that secured through the two studies reported above, except for some successful local instances of the employment of resource teachers or teacher aides. Such reports were about "how well" the assistance worked out, but typically there was no comparison group of unassisted decertified EMR students to provide a basis of comparison.

If the transition period experience is to be considered an experience for what works in mainstreaming, the California effort was disappointing. The programs were admittedly hastily generated, and morale for their support was sabotaged in the knowledge that support would be time-limited. This sabotage was exacerbated by an unanticipated interruption of funding through a legal fluke. Most districts which for 2 years had tried to operate a program threw up their hands at the time of this interruption. Altogether, the mainstreaming literature gained little or nothing from these studies on service delivery issues except how not to provide special help.

On the positive side, both of the major reports determined that a majority of the students returned to the regular program tended to cope at least to the degree that they remained in school well into the secondary years. If one takes pessimism from the fact that some minority had to return to EMR class or to other special placement, optimism can result from the "success" of the majority. That success as we saw was earned without much benefit of special assistance.

How well should mainstreamed students do? If the relative success of the decertified students is to be taken as a promise, certain considerations are involved. The decertified EMR students tended to perform better than nondecertified EMR students. If one mainstreamed those EMR students who had been left in special class, the success level would have been diminished. As of this writing, the severe reduction in EMR placements has made the contemporary EMR class seem to be a sure loser in mainstreaming. Thus one can predict more surely if one knows which of the broad spectrum of competence and general adjustment within the broad definition of EMR is subject to the mainstreaming effort. If one selects those EMR students of the higher level including the so-called borderline, then the evidence from the California studies indicates that a solid majority will succeed at least to the extent of staying with the regular class, surviving it, so to speak. As we have seen, they did so with little or no transition (read mainstreaming) assistance.

DISCUSSION

The chapter began with the statement that the fundamental research question the public and most of the school people ask is whether the student who has a mental limitation is better educated in a segregated, self-contained class or in some mainstreamed integration program with the regular class and its students. This was the issue when it appeared from the early studies that demonstrated the unhappiness of marginal learners in the regular program. It was the issue during the period of the efficacy studies. Those studies were inconclusive, partly because most were of inadequate methodology and partly because the determination of the better placement depended on the outcome variables most favored by the interpreter of the empirical results.

The single greatest need pointed out by the efficacy studies was to examine what goes on *within* the programs being compared. The simple mainstreamed versus nonmainstreamed question cannot by itself lead to useful conclusions without specification of the assumptions of each program, the curriculum and methods, the time allocations, and other factors within each program, not to mention teacher skill, attitudes of teacher and administrator, and other variables. In fact, the empiricism has been so confused that decisions have had to be based in large part on the political and philosophical persuasions of the decision makers.

The current era of research in mainstreaming followed the efficacy studies. It has been conducted under new conditions required by litigation. One change was a refinement of who was to be identified as EMR. Another was to observe the principle of least restriction, hence mandated integration of handicapped students. Two varieties of studies ensued, one the controlled, experimental contrast of mainstreamed with nonmainstreamed students. The other was the "natural experiment," the study of learners placed into mainstream in contrast with those not so placed. Running across these two designs were further investigations of teacher acceptance and attitude, measurements of self-regard and social acceptance as well as of academic progress in different placements, and to a lesser degree, comparisons within each treatment. Precious little of the latter, however, was placed under study except in the PRIME investigation.

Given all this investigation and debate, what may now be concluded regarding the simple question, is mainstreaming better than segregation on any but a philosophical basis? What can be concluded about the auxiliary issues, such as the comparative good of the placements, given different educational priorities? What are optimal time allocations to individualized educational treatment in regular class and resource room? These and many other questions are asked. We answer some and list the still doubtful ones.

CONCLUSIONS

It appears to be true at the present time that almost any form of treatment of the identified marginal learner in which some academic instruction is provided by the regular teacher in the regular program may be called mainstreaming. This was true, as shown in the Texas PRIME study, that mainstreaming must involve considerable instruction of academic subjects by the regular teacher and with mixed handicapped and nonhandicapped pupils. To segregate the EMR or other handicapped groups for separate academic instruction fails to comply with the principle of least restriction. The regular teacher merely becomes an EMR teacher in that case; so does the resource teacher if that teacher likewise has only the EMR students. Thus, it appears that a lot of so-called mainstreaming, including some unknown proportion of that in PRIME is merely the "temporal" integration for nonacademic instruction.

Within mainstreaming are many variations, ranging from no special assistance at all on a continuous or a transition basis up to the spending of 50% of the time out of the regular classroom. Similarly, segregated self-contained classes continue to vary from complete segregation up through mixing the EMR students with nonEMR students in the less academic subjects of instruction.

Fundamental decisions to provide mainstreaming appear to come more as a response to the current *Zeitgeist* of least restrictive alternative and as a response to mandated caution in identification and placement than to empirical information for decision making. Both of the largest of all studies, the California decertification study and the Texas PRIME project, showed hurried placement without adequate preparation or factual support.

Some empirical points can be made and can serve for guidance in the future, whatever the *Zeitgeist* may become. It appears impossible to avoid labeling when identifying for special need. Labels may vary in their inherent pejoration, but the report of Iano et al. (1974) and the indications from other studies are that children will react to the characteristics of any subgroup singled out for special services whether a traditional handicap name is employed or not. Thus to render individualized instructional service in mainstreaming cannot avoid some effects of labeling.

Teachers react with neutrality or negativism at the prospect of having handicapped learners in their classrooms. After having had them, however, they become accepting, and their attitudes are determined by the presence or absence of special assistance tailored to individual cases and to behavior problems in mainstreamed individuals. Teachers generally take a less than enthusiastic view of inservice preparation, although according to PRIME, it was the most common form of help afforded the teachers. The regular class teachers who have had former EMR pupils for a year or more tend to perceive them as just very slow learners with some tendency to have behavior problems. Nearly three-fourths of the teachers in the California study reported no particular or outstanding difficulty with the decertified, but as a whole, did not regard them as competent students, even as seen against the usually low class norm. The 29% who said extraordinary help had to be provided mentioned both academic and deportment difficulties.

If asked what kind of help they would like for educating a mainstreamed EMR child, teachers tend to specify smaller class size, ways of coping with extreme academic failure, and ways of taming the misbehavior of the EMR student.

It continues to be true that interpretation of the value of one placement versus another depends in part on the dependent variables one emphasizes. However, it has been demonstrated that EMR students in regular programs receive lower peer acceptance than segregated EMR students from nonhandicapped peers. The belief that nonhandicapped students' contact with, or exposure to, handicapped learners will promote more positive attitudes is not supported by the evidence. The insightful studies of Gottlieb and associates suggest that it is the actual academic ineptitude and misbehavior of mainstreamed (or nonmainstreamed) EMR students, as perceived by nonEMR peers, which are apparently causative of low social regard and not handicapped status *per se*. It remains unclear whether unconscious teacher dislike or suspicion can influence peer regard negatively. This finding remains an uncertainty at the secondary level.

Unanswered Questions

There appears to be no unambiguous answer to the primitive question of whether segregated or integrated placement is superior. Answers depend in part, as we have insisted, upon one's philosophy. If the principle of least restriction is paramount, which is presently true and is expressed in laws, then the answer appears to be a commitment to mainstreaming under all but difficult conditions.

This conclusion is tempered with some other considerations. Take first the extreme depopulation for the EMR classes in California. The remaining EMR students were *not* decertified when there was much political and other pressure to send all possible EMR students back to regular programs. They obviously were the ones most in need of special help and would have been the least likely to be successful in regular class competition. For example, it has been shown in the decertification study, that their response to being given the standardized achievement test administered to their grade placement level is one of despair. If mainstreaming is philosophically or politically contemplated for these students, "the remainder EMR students," it will face extraordinary difficulty. The majority of the decertified students were "successfully" returned to regular programs in California in spite of inept or absent transition programs. However, this definition of success was one of survival; the academic D students' gap generally remained 3 or more years behind placement, and placement was nearly 2 years below age expectancy. Given an acceptance of the survival definition of successful decertification, then the return was not a bad decision.

A few definitive problems may be listed that require further investigation as to their impact on success of integrative placements. One is that relatively little is known about the secondary education scene with respect to many of the investigated issues. The California decertification study had largely secondary level subjects, but was by its nature not a review of mainstreaming parameters in their own right. Another problem to follow is the intriguing dynamics brought out by Gottlieb and Iano and their associates about such factors as: the nature of exposure to nonEMR students of EMR students, the EMR students' visibility in receiving special services with or without labels, the teachers' attitudes related to the acceptance of the handicapped as well as service delivery issues and architectural arrangements, team teaching, and multigraded models of instruction.

Final Analysis

Three statements may be made regarding the availability of special education services. The first is that decisions will rest not so much with conclusions reached from empirical investigation as from the swing of current priorities. Right now the *Zeitgeist* is and has been at peak for least restriction and individualized programming, but this situation may be dampened by future political, economic, and other imperatives. The waxing and waning of priorities and pressures will cause changes in the extent that special help is traded off against both prohibitive costs and the need to avoid labeling or designating some people *special.*

Second, no one is able to predict whether the current taxpayer revolt as evidenced by the passage of Proposition 13 in California will stifle the progress in the delivery of special educational services. The brave plans of PL 94-142 call for considerable local involvement and both indirect and direct costs, apart from funding by the states and from the federal level. It is probable that implementation of the more costly provisions of PL 94-142 will be slowed. With respect to marginal learners, budget tightening is expected to result in unassisted or minimally assisted mainstreaming of marginal pupils to the maximum extent of teacher tolerance. This negative note is a realistic one as we read the tenor of the time of this writing.

Finally, in spite of efforts to avoid labeling or making any special designations of people to receive special services, to provide services itself designates the receivers as "special" with consequent effects on acceptance by the public or the student body at large. Negative effects can never be entirely avoided, and "hard to teach children" will not cease to be a special concern.

REFERENCES

Badt, M. I. Attitudes of university students toward exceptional children and special education. *Exceptional Children,* 1957, *23,* 286-290.

Blatt, B. The physical, personality, and academic status of children who are mentally retarded attending special classes as compared with children who are mentally retarded attending regular classes. *American Journal of Mental Deficiency,* 1958, *62,* 810-818.

Bradfield, H. R., Brown, J., Kaplan, P., Rickert, E., & Stannard, R. The special child in the regular classroom. *Exceptional Children,* 1973, *39,* 384-390.

Budoff, M., & Gottlieb, J. Special class students mainstreamed: A study of an aptitude (learning potential) X treatment interaction. *American Journal of Mental Deficiency,* 1976, *81,* 1-11.

Carroll, A. The effects of segregated and partially integrated school programs on self concept and academic achievement of educable mental retardates. *Exceptional Children,* 1967, *34,* 93-99.

Cassidy, V. M., & Stanton, V. E. *An investigation of factors involved in the educational placement of mentally retarded children: A study of differences between children in special and regular classes in Ohio.* (U.S. Office of Education Cooperative Research Program, Project No. 043.) Columbus: Ohio State University, 1959.

Cegelka, W. J., & Tyler, J. L. The efficacy of special class placement for the mentally retarded improper perspective. *Training School Bulletin,* 1970, *65,* 33-65.

Chiba, C., & Semmel, M. I. Due process and least restrictive alternative: New emphasis on parental participation. *Viewpoints. Bulletin of the University of Indiana,* 1977, *53*(2), 17-29.

Corman, L., & Gottlieb, J. Mainstreaming mentally retarded children: A review of research. In N. R. Ellis (Ed.), *International review of research in mental retardation,* Vol. 9. New York: Academic Press, 1979.

Dunn, L. M. Special education for the mildly retarded: Is much of it justified? *Exceptional Children,* 1968, *35,* 5-22.

Gickling, E. E., & Theobald, J. T. Mainstreaming: Affect or effect. *Journal of Special Education,* 1975, *9,* 317-328.

Goldstein, H. The efficacy of special classes and regular classes in the education of educable mentally retarded children. In J. Zubin & G. A. Jervis (Eds.), *Psychopathology of mental development.* New York: Grune and Stratton, 1967.

Goldstein, H., Moss, J. W., & Jordan, L. J. The efficacy of special class training on the development of mentally retarded children. (U.S. Office of Education Cooperative Research Program, Project No. 619.) Washington, D.C., 1965.

Goodman, H., Gottlieb, J., & Harrison, R. H. Social acceptance of EMRs integrated into a nongraded elementary school. *American Journal of Mental Deficiency,* 1972, *76,* 412-417.

Gottlieb, J. Public, peer, and professional attitudes toward mentally retarded persons. In M. J. Begab & S. A. Richardson (Eds.), *The mentally retarded and society: A social science perspective.* Baltimore: University Park Press, 1975.

Gottlieb, J., & Budoff, M. Social acceptability of retarded children in non-graded schools differing in architecture. *American Journal of Mental Deficiency,* 1973, *78,* 15-19.

Gottlieb, J., Cohen, L., & Goldstein, L. Social contact and personal adjustment as variables relating to attitudes toward EMR children. *Training School Bulletin,* 1974, *71,* 9-16.

Gottlieb, J., & Davis, J. E. Social acceptance of EMRs during overt behavioral interaction. *American Journal of Mental Deficiency,* 1973, *78,* 141-143.

Gottlieb, J., Gampel, D. H., & Budoff, M. Classroom behavior of retarded children before and after reintegration into regular classes. *Journal of Special Education,* 1975, *9,* 307-315.

Grossman, H. J. (Ed.). *Manual on terminology and classification in mental retardation.* Washington, D.C.: American Association on Mental Deficiency, 1973.

Guerin, G. R., & Szatlocky, K. Integration programs for the mildly retarded. *Exceptional Children,* 1974, *41,* 173-177.

Guskin, S. L., & Spicker, H. H. Educational research in mental retardation. In N. R. Ellis (Ed.), *International review of research in mental retardation* (Vol. 3). New York: Academic Press, 1968.

Haring, N. G., & Krug, D. A. Placement in regular programs: Procedures and results. *Exceptional Children,* 1975, *41,* 413-417.

Heber, R. F. A manual on terminology and classification in mental retardation. *American Journal of Mental Deficiency Monograph,* 1959 (Suppl. 64).

Iano, R. P., Ayers, D., Heller, H. B., McGettigan, J. F., & Walker, V. S. Sociometric status of retarded children in an integrative program. *Exceptional Children,* 1974, *40,* 267-271.

Johnson, G. O. A study of the social position of mentally handicapped children in the regular grades. *American Journal of Mental Deficiency,* 1950, *55,* 60-89.

Johnson, G. O. Special education for the mentally handicapped—a paradox. *Exceptional Children,* 1962, *19,* 62-69.

Johnson, G. O., & Kirk, S. A. Are mentally handicapped children segregated in the regular grades? *Journal of Exceptional Children,* 1950, *17,* 65-68, 87-88.

Kaufman, M. J., Agard, J. A., & Semmel, M. I. *Mainstreaming: Learners and their environments.* Baltimore: University Park Press, in press.

Kaufman, M. J., Gottlieb, J., Agard, J. A., & Kukic, M. B. Mainstreaming: Toward an explication of the construct. In E. L. Meyen, G. A. Vergason, and R. J. Whelan (Eds.), *Alternatives for teaching exceptional children.* Denver: Love Publishing, 1975.

Keogh, B. K., & Levitt, M. L. Special education in the mainstream: A confrontation of limitations? *Focus on Exceptional Children,* 1976, *8*(1), 1-11.

Keogh, B. K., Levitt, M. L., Robson, G., & Chan, K. S. *A review of transition programs in California public schools.* Unpublished Technical Report SERP 1974-AZ. No. 3586. Sacramento: California State Department of Education and UCLA, November, 1974.

Kirk, S. A. Research in education. In H. A. Stevens, & R. Heber (Eds.), *Mental retardation: A review of research.* Chicago: University of Chicago Press, 1964.

MacMillan, D. L. Special education for the mildly handicapped—Servant or savant? *Focus on Exceptional Children,* 1971, *2,* 1-11.

MacMillan, D. L., Jones, R. L., & Aloia, G. F. The "mentally retarded" label: A theoretical analysis and review of research. *American Journal of Mental Deficiency,* 1974, *79,* 241-261.

MacMillan, D. L., Meyers, C. E., & Yoshida, R. K. Regular class teachers' perception of transition programs for EMR students and their impact on the students. *Psychology in the Schools,* 1978, *15,* 99-103.

Martin, Sr., M. A. Social acceptance and attitudes toward school of mentally retarded pupils in regular classes. Unpublished doctoral dissertation, University of Southern California, 1953.

Meyerowitz, J. H. Self derogations in young retardates and special class placement. *Child Development,* 1962, *33,* 443-451.

Meyers, C. E., MacMillan, D. L., & Yoshida, R. K. Validity of psychologists' identification of EMR students in the perspective of the California decertification experience. *Journal of School Psychology,* 1978, *16*(1), 3-15.

Meyers, C. E., MacMillan, D. L., & Yoshida, R. K. *Correlates of success in transition of MR to regular class.* Volume I and II (Appendix). Final Report. Pomona, CA.: California University, Los Angeles, Neuropsychiatric Institute; Pacific State Hospital 1975. (ERIC Document Reproduction Service Nos. EC 081 038 and EC 081 039.)

Meyers, C. E., Sundstrom, P. E., & Yoshida, R. K. The school psychologist and assessment in special education. A report of an Ad Hoc Committee of Div. 16. *School Psychology Monographs,* 1974, *2*(1), 3-57.

Mullen, F. A., & Itkin, W. Achievement and adjustment of educable mentally handicapped children. (U.S. Office of Education Cooperative Research Program, Project SAE 6529.) Chicago: Chicago Board of Education, 1961.

Quay, L. C. Academic skills. In N. R. Ellis (Ed.), *Handbook of Mental Deficiency.* New York: McGraw-Hill, 1963.

Sheare, J. B. Social acceptance of EMR adolescents in integrated programs. *American Journal of Mental Deficiency,* 1974, *78,* 678-682.

Shotel, J. R., Iano, R. P., & McGettigan, J. F. Teacher attitudes associated with the integration of handicapped children. *Exceptional Children,* 1972, *38,* 677-683.

Thurstone, T. G. An evaluation of educating mentally handicapped children in special classes and in regular grades. (U.S. Office of Education Cooperative Research Program, Project No. O.E. SAE 6452.) Chapel Hill: University of North Carolina, 1959.

Walker, V. S. The efficacy of the resource room for educating retarded children. *Exceptional Children,* 1974, *40,* 288–289.

Yoshida, R. K. Out-of-level testing of special education students with a standardized achievement battery. *Journal of Educational Measurement,* 1976, *13,* 215–221.

CHAPTER 8

Students' and Teachers' Perceptions of the Mentally Retarded Child

Gary N. Siperstein and John J. Bak

> Mentally retarded people are not able to comprehend what life really is. They are unable to function as normal people because of brain disease or damage. I know this from viewing them doing their menial tasks and from books I have read. They got that way because of a lack of air during birth, thus their brain damage, or because of freak mutations like too many chromosomes—just one extra will do it. They are outwardly obvious, that is, they have cloudy haircuts, outdated clothes and cheap eyeglasses. They feel nothing. They haven't the capabilities to understand what they are.
>
> —an 11th grade boy

Misinformation about mentally retarded persons abounds. In virtually all segments of our society, there exist ill-defined notions of what mental retardation is, how it is caused, and how mentally retarded persons look,

---

© *1978 Gary N. Siperstein and John J. Bak*
This research was supported in part by Grant No. OEG-0-078-02-92 from the United States Office of Education, Bureau of Education for the Handicapped and Grant No. HD 08439-01 from the National Institute of Child Health and Human Development. Points of view or opinions stated do not necessarily represent official Office of Education, BEH, or NICHD policy. The authors wish to thank the principals and teachers of the Newton, Melrose, and Lowell, Massachusetts school systems and the teachers enrolled at Lesley College and Boston State College for their assistance and cooperation. The authors also extend special thanks to Marilyn Fichman for her assistance in data analysis.

act, and feel. This misunderstanding is alarming when we consider the fact that handicapped persons are becoming increasingly well integrated into our communities. Every day there are more opportunities for people's misconceptions to spawn harmful feelings and behaviors—serious threats to successful integration.

Recent federal legislation (Education for All Handicapped Children Act, PL 94-142) has mandated that handicapped children be educated in environments that are least restrictive to their development. In order to maximize the benefit of these environments, teachers and administrators must effectively plan for the social as well as the instructional integration of handicapped children. As educators design programs aimed at facilitating the social integration of handicapped individuals, including those who are mentally retarded, they must consider the nature and extent of the public's misinformation about such individuals. Currently, however, our knowledge of people's misconceptions is incomplete. Gottwald (1970) conducted an extensive survey of adults' knowledge of mental retardation and found several widespread misconceptions. These mistaken notions are similar to those documented over 50 years ago by the National Committee for Mental Hygiene, Inc., and then again over 30 years later by Winthrop and Taylor (1957) and Polonsky (1961). In their 1926 publication entitled *About Feeblemindedness,* the National Committee set forth the following ideas under the heading "What Some People Still Believe":

1. That feeblemindedness is a mental disease.
2. That feeblemindedness can be cured like many mental diseases.
3. That feeblemindedness is always inherited.
4. That sterilization of the feebleminded is the best solution of the problem.
5. That the feebleminded are a menace and should all be kept in institutions.
6. That the feebleminded are unteachable and a total loss to society.
7. That the feebleminded are all equally defective.
8. That the feebleminded are readily recognized as such.
9. That the feebleminded have no "feelings" and do not realize their condition.

Although it is difficult to assess changes in the prevalence of these misconceptions over a period spanning five decades, we can say that the public's knowledge of mental retardation, as represented in these past reports, is still incomplete and inaccurate. Most people still do not know what mental retardation is. A commonly accepted definition was prepared by Heber (1961) for the American Association on Mental Deficiency. This definition, broadly based in order to accommodate the diversity among retarded persons, describes mental retardation as referring to "1) subaverage general intellectual functioning, which 2) originates during the developmental period, and 3) is associated with impairments in adaptive behavior." We do not mean to suggest that everyone should know this clinical definition. Even psychologists disagree over what the exact definition should be. We mention it here because we plan to see how well people's information about retardation aligns with this definition. The alignment ought to be close among those persons who must frequently interact with mentally retarded persons.

The reports mentioned above have not surveyed populations which are, or which will soon be, in contact with mentally retarded persons. Our study was conducted in Massachusetts, where a state law, similar to the federal PL 94-142, establishing the right of handicapped persons to a public school education, had been in effect for several years. We chose to question children, special education teachers, regular education teachers, and prospective teachers because they are the people who have the most contact with newly integrated retarded children. One of the goals of our survey was to determine the state of people's knowledge about mental retardation in a location where people are increasingly in contact with retarded persons.

The integration of mentally retarded children into regular classrooms by no means ensures their social acceptability in their new environment. In fact, these children face far more severe social challenges in normal environments than they ever did in segregated ones. Regular class teachers' and children have predominantly negative attitudes toward retarded children (Baldwin, 1958; Copeland & Weissbrod, 1976; Dentler & Mackler, 1962; Johnson, 1950; Johnson & Kirk, 1951; Lapp, 1957; Marge, 1966; Rucker, Howe, & Snider, 1969; Warren, Turner, & Brody, 1964), which reflect similar attitudes in the community at large (Efron & Efron, 1967; English & Palla, 1971; Gottlieb, 1974). Teachers, children, and other members of the community also place impairment of intellectual functioning at the bottom of hierarchies composed of different disability groups such as the physically handicapped, the blind, and the deaf (Appell, Williams, & Fishell, 1963; Kleck, Richardson, & Ronald, 1974; Kvaraceus, 1956; Strong, 1931; Whiteman & Lukoff, 1964).

It is not surprising to find that teachers and other community members share negative attitudes toward the integration of mentally retarded children into the schools. While both groups have been found receptive to community integration, they have been shown not to favor it in the classroom (Siperstein & Gottlieb, 1978). The impact of these negative attitudes, especially those of the teacher, can be quite harmful to mentally retarded children.

Teachers bring to the classroom specific attitudes concerning students differing along racial, economic, or handicapping dimensions (Brophy & Evertson, 1976). Different expectations arise for individual students in line with teachers' attitudes. These expectations then lead teachers to treat students differentially in ways that help bring about the outcome they expect, the self-fulfilling prophecy (Brophy & Good, 1974; Rosenthal & Jacobson, 1968).

Since teachers' attitudes toward mentally retarded persons are generally negative, their expectancies for retarded children are usually poor. Consequently, the performance of retarded children is poorer than it has to be, their self-concepts suffer, and teacher-student relationships are not enjoyable. Negative attitudes can also have an adverse affect on student-student relationships.

If a teacher consistently exhibits unfavorable attitudes toward a mentally retarded child, it can safely be assumed that many nonretarded students in the class will eventually develop similar attitudes and behave correspondingly. Investigations have revealed that children model teachers' behavior and values that are incidental to the curriculum objectives (Bandura & Walters, 1963; Feshbach, 1967; Rosenblith, 1959, 1961; Ross, 1966). Gallagher (1967) has shown that when teachers' attitudes toward handicapped children are more favorable, their students are more accepting of handicapped peers. This is especially true of children at the elementary grade level, where much of the integration of the retarded is occurring.

An often heard hope of many educators is that teachers' negative attitudes and behaviors will disappear after they have had experience with mentally retarded children. Research findings do not support this expectation conclusively. Some studies indicate that increases in teachers' knowledge of and exposure to retarded children lead to more favorable attitudes (Condell & Tonn, 1965; Efron & Efron, 1967; Skrtic, Sigler, & Lazar, 1975); others give no such indication (Monroe & Howe, 1971; Panda & Bartel, 1972; Semmel, 1959).

There does not seem to be a direct cause and effect relationship between teachers' knowledge of mental retardation through experience and positive attitudes toward mentally retarded persons. However, in the studies mentioned above, those teachers who did have positive attitudes also did have substantial information about mental retardation. This strongly suggests that *knowledge of mental retardation is necessary* for teachers to have a positive attitude toward retarded children, *but it is not sufficient* to ensure that their attitude will be positive. Other factors, such as the amount, nature, and perceived voluntariness of the contact, will finally determine the favorableness of an attitude (Jordan, 1968). Accurate

Table 1. Frequency of males and females at each grade level

Grade level	Male	Female	Total
4–6	150	165	315
7–9	240	240	480
10–12	120	120	240
			Total = 1040

information only sets a stage for the development of a positive attitude, but it is important that this stage be set, and set properly.

School systems nationwide are either starting or expanding inservice training programs for teachers who need to improve their skills in dealing with handicapped children in general and mentally retarded children in particular. Established programs for training new teachers are initiating new courses that prepare student teachers to work with children with special needs. In order for classroom integration to have the best chance of working, teachers must have proper knowledge of mental retardation. Training programs will be most effective when they address the specific misconceptions that both teachers and children have about mental retardation.

The results of our survey document the accurate impressions, as well as the misconceptions, that children, special education teachers, regular education teachers, and prospective teachers have about mentally retarded children. This information should be of particular use to these groups of people and to others who are concerned about the welfare of retarded children in our communities.

RESULTS OF THE CHILDREN'S SURVEY

We distributed our questionnaire on mental retardation to 1,040 students in grades 4 through 12 in three elementary, two intermediate, and two secondary schools. Younger students were not surveyed because they did not have the writing skills needed to adequately answer the questions. Among those participating, there was equal representation of boys and girls (See Table 1).

Students received the questionnaires in study halls and in regular subject classes. They were told that it was a survey, not a test, and that there were no right or wrong answers, which was to discourage the copying of others' answers. After completing the questionnaires, students returned them and were then debriefed about the survey and mental retardation.

The questionnaire consisted of eight items; six were open-ended and two required a yes/no response:

1. If a boy or girl is called mentally retarded, what does that mean to you?
2. How did you find out about mentally retarded people?
3. What do you think are the most common causes of mental retardation?
4. As far as you know, can anything be done at this time to prevent mental retardation?   YES   NO
5. If you answered "yes," what can be done to prevent mental retardation?
6. Do mentally retarded boys and girls look different from other boys and girls?   YES   NO
7. If you answered "yes," describe in your own words how a mentally retarded boy or girl looks.
8. How do you think mentally retarded boys and girls feel?

The wording of the questions was slightly modified for students of different ages to ensure the appropriateness of the questionnaire in the elementary, middle, and secondary grades.

The questions were the result of extensive pilot testing. In our initial surveys, we found that many students were reticent to describe a mentally retarded person when only asked the broadly phrased question, "What does it mean to call a boy or girl mentally retarded?" Some students described the appearance, feelings, and behavior of mentally retarded children, while others described only the behavior. Therefore, we decided to use both the broader question and the more specific questions concerning physical appearance and feelings in order to make certain that a complete representation of students' stereotypes was received.

For the purposes of analysis, the children's answers were placed into categories that were developed for each question. These categories were broad enough to include all the different traits and terms used by students in answering each question. Interrater reliability for the categorization schema was established and the children's answers were summarized in frequency distributions. This procedure allowed us to see how often children in each grade gave one particular type of answer. Tests of statistical significance were not especially useful in analyzing the data because the large number of students responding tended to make high levels of significance easily attainable; often, significant differences between groups were not at all meaningful. Therefore, for the purpose of this survey, we relied mostly on a visual comparison of differences in frequencies between students at three grade levels—elementary (grades 4–6), intermediate (grades 7–9), and secondary (grades 10–12).

QUESTION 1: *What does it mean to be mentally retarded?*
Children's answers to this question were categorized in terms of learning characteristics, social/emotional characteristics, physical characteristics, neurological impairment, and "helplessness." We did not differentiate answers on the basis of vocabulary level. For example, terms such as "dumb," "low IQ," and "slow learner" were categorized as learning characteristics.

In general, students used more than one trait or descriptive word when answering this question. Therefore, we also assessed the expansiveness of their answers in addition to the *types* of traits they used in their description. Tables 2 and 3 present a summary of children's answers to Question 1.

At all grade levels, students commonly described the mentally retarded child in terms of learning characteristics. The most frequent responses were "acts dumb," "stupid," "can't think right," and "not as bright as other children." The next most common response described the retarded child's physical characteristics, usually facial features, motor behavior and other more general limitations of functioning. For example, children said that a mentally retarded child "can't see," "can't talk," "is clumsy," and "has a distorted face." Surprisingly, approximately 25% of the students mentioned specific types of impairment to the brain in their characterization of mental retardation, for example, "can't use his brain" and "has a brain injury." The least frequent response described social/emotional characteristics. When students did characterize the mentally retarded in this way, they used such terms as "weird," "silly," "doesn't know how to act," "immature," and "crazy."

We observed age trends in the categories of learning characteristics, social/emotional characteristics and, as expected, in the expansiveness of the students' responses. Students at the secondary level were more apt to describe the mentally retarded by using social/emotional characteristics or learning characteristics than were students at the elementary level.

Since approximately 30% of all students gave at least two answers, we decided to assess which types of traits or attributes, if any, were most often grouped together on individual questionnaires. We wanted to know, for example, if and when a child used learning characteristics, would he also necessarily use social characteristics. The findings were contrary to what one would expect, especially among older children. Very few children (15%) described a mentally retarded person by using *both* learning characteristics and social characteristics. Most of the students who gave two or more responses mentioned learning characteristics and physical characteristics. Students who said that the mentally retarded

Table 2. Question 1: What does mental retardation mean to you?

| Grade level | Categories of response |||||
	Learning characteristics	Social/emotional characteristics	Physical characteristics	Brain impairment	Helplessness
4-6	43%	7%	22%	16%	16%
7-9	51%	13%	29%	25%	19%
10-12	61%	19%	21%	26%	21%

NOTE: The column and row totals do not equal 100% because a student's answer can be coded into more than one category.

Table 3. Question 1: What does mental retardation mean to you?

Grade level	Number of responses			
	0	1	2	3 or more
4-6	19%	53%	26%	2%
7-9	13%	46%	32%	9%
10-12	8%	47%	34%	11%

child was "dumb," or "stupid," usually also mentioned some physical attribute or limitation. Students did not attribute negative learning characteristics to brain impairment. When children mentioned brain impairment they did so to the exclusion of all other characteristics in the learning and social areas.

In addition to the characteristics mentioned above, students' descriptions also included comments concerning the care of the mentally retarded. A small group of students in all grades (9%) mentioned that the mentally retarded "need special help" and "can't help themselves." Some younger students (7%) also mentioned that the term "mentally retarded" was an insult. They said that "it is a mean thing to call someone," and "kids call you that because you are dumb."

QUESTION 2: How did you find out about mentally retarded people? Students typically responded to this question by saying that they had contact with a specific person who was mentally retarded. For example: "there is a kid in the sixth grade who is mentally retarded," "my neighbor is mentally retarded," and "I saw them in a hospital." Next to personal contact, the most frequent sources of information were the parents, teachers, and friends of the students. For example: "my mother and father told me about it," "our teacher taught us," and "a friend told me." If children did not have any personal contact or were not informed by another, then they usually heard about it through television, magazines, or books.

Table 4 presents student's source of information categorized according to personal contact, adult explanation, peer explanation, and media. The intermediate and secondary level students definitely had more contact with mental retardation than students at the elementary level. As older students' personal contact increased, their reliance on adult explanations decreased.

There was a great deal of variability in children's source of information within each of the elementary, intermediate, and secondary levels of education. This was caused by many extraneous factors. For example, one group of students in an upper middle class elementary school had recently read *Flowers for Algernon,* a book about a mentally retarded

Table 4. Sources of information about mental retardation

Grade level	Sources of information			
	Personal contact	Personal explanation by adults	Personal explanation by peers	Media (TV, books)
4–6	41%	29%	17%	13%
7–9	54%	18%	18%	10%
10–12	50%	13%	21%	16%

person. In that school, however, there were *no* mentally retarded children for the sampled students to see or be with. In contrast, another group of students sampled from a school in a lower income community had never received any materials concerning mental retardation or had any class discussions on the topic. However, the school contained special classes for the mentally retarded and thus provided the sampled students with much personal contact. Children's source of information appears to depend primarily upon the type of school they attend.

In order to find out if students' sources of information were related to the types of traits they used to describe a mentally retarded person, statistical analyses of the data (chi square tests) were conducted. No significant relationship was found between the type or the number of traits a student used to describe a mentally retarded person and his/her personal contact with a mentally retarded person. The data also showed that students' information from adult explanations, peer explanations, and the media had no effect on their stereotypes about mental retardation.

QUESTION 3: What do you think are the most common causes of mental retardation? To this question, more than 50% of the students in each of the three grade levels mentioned defects that occur at birth. Typical responses were: "accident at birth," and "disease when born." Forty-one percent (41%) of the students specifically mentioned the mother: "old mother having kids," "mother is sick," "mother takes drugs," and "mother did not take care of herself." There were some students (19%) in all grades who mentioned external factors after birth, such as "fell on his head" and "mother didn't take care of the child." Lastly, a small group of students (20%) at the secondary level specifically mentioned hereditary causes.

QUESTIONS 4 AND 5: Can mental retardation be prevented? If you answered "yes," what can be done to prevent mental retardation? The number of students who said yes (46%) nearly equaled those who said no (54%). This was true at all three grade levels. Among those students who answered yes, 43% said that mental retardation could be prevented if measures are taken before or during birth. The methods of prevention included: "mother stopping taking drugs," "doctor giving child drugs," and "having checkups to detect it." Twenty-two percent (22%) thought that mental retardation could be prevented or at least altered through education. For example, they said the retarded child should "go to special schools," "have a separate teacher," "be taught to work," and "be taught how to act 'normal'." Several students said that the most effective treatment was treating mentally retarded boys and girls better: "taking the boy or girl as a person not something else" and "treating them the same as others to give them confidence in themselves."

QUESTIONS 6 AND 7: Do mentally retarded boys and girls look different from other boys and girls? If you answered "yes," describe in your own words how a mentally retarded boy or girl looks. Fifty percent (50%) of the elementary students, 70% of the intermediate students, and more than 80% of the secondary students thought that retarded children looked different than other children. Most of the students at the secondary level who did not say that mentally retarded children were always different, thought they were different at least some of the time. They indicated this by writing "sometimes" on their questionnaires.

Of the students who answered "yes" or "sometimes," the majority (37%) described mentally retarded persons as having abnormal physical features. For example, students said that they have "bigger heads," "crossed eyes," "mongolism," "fat stomachs," "crooked faces," "tongues hanging down," and "big eyes." A smaller portion of the students (27%) described retarded children as physically awkward and, to a lesser extent, socially awkward. The students said they "were slow at doing things," "walked funny," "talked funny," and "had a stupid look on their faces." Only students at the secondary level described mentally retarded persons as socially awkward. They were also more apt than elementary level students (60% versus 20%) to state that mentally retarded persons do not all look alike. They said "some look a certain way and others look another way." One elementary level student's answer provided insight into why so many students believe that mentally retarded persons look different: "I think if you know a person is retarded, you think he looks it."

QUESTION 8: How do mentally retarded boys and girls feel? Only a small number of students (16%) thought that retarded children feel normal. Most of the students (48%) said that retarded boys and girls have negative feelings, that they feel "unhappy," "depressed," "sad," "sorry for themselves," and "afraid." Students also used negative terms such as "lonely," "misplaced," and "not wanted" to depict a mentally retarded child's social situation. At different grade levels students attributed these disagreeable feelings to different factors. Most elementary level students thought them due to how "normal" people treat them. For example, they said "kids make them feel bad and sad and not wanted," "they think 'why does everybody hate me,' " "they feel bad because most people stare at them," and "they're left out because nobody likes them." Twice as many secondary level students as elementary level students attributed the retarded child's feelings to the actions of others. However, some secondary level students described a mentally retarded person's unfavorable feelings as being self-imposed: "they feel sorry for themselves," or "they are afraid of other people."

Intermediate and secondary level students tended to describe a mentally retarded child's feelings in terms of his/her academic behavior. They thought he *felt* "dumb," and "inferior in work." There were also several students at the intermediate and secondary levels who described a mentally retarded child as being unaware of his/her problem. For example, they said, "he doesn't realize what others think," and "doesn't seem to even know that he is different from other people." Overall, in response to Question 8, students described the feelings of retarded children as different from those of other boys and girls. While students at all three grade levels depicted a mentally retarded boy's or girl's feelings as bad in general, the reasons for the negative feelings varied.

RESULTS OF THE ADULT SURVEY

In addition to the children we questioned, we also surveyed 150 adults who directly or indirectly affect the lives of mentally retarded children. This group consisted of 40 special education teachers, 60 regular education teachers, and 50 prospective regular education teachers.

Special Education Teachers

We asked 40 special education teachers who had worked with retarded children to "describe a child who is mentally retarded." Questions dealing with causation, prevention, appearance, and feelings were not on the questionnaire because we wanted to obtain spontaneous stereotypic images of mentally retarded children. The participants were 5 males and 35 females ranging in age from 23 to 61 with a mean age of 35.

To analyze the data, the traits and attributes listed by the special education teachers were classified into the categories of learning characteristics and social-emotional characteristics. We sought to determine if the teachers described learning characteristics in a general or specific way and if they mentioned language or motor functioning. For social functioning, we tried to find how often the teachers used terms that describe children's appearance, behavior, and feelings. In addition, we created categories for answers that referred to the special help the retarded child needs and to the severity and cause of retardation.

Most of the special education teachers (84%) described a mentally retarded child in terms of learning characteristics. The most common response was a simple description of cognitive ability. That is, 38% of the special education teachers' responses provided no more information than that a retarded child "suffers retardation in mental development" or "is lacking intelligence." The rest of the teachers who mentioned learning characteristics were more specific in their responses. Sixteen percent described the mentally retarded child in terms of IQ level: "IQ between 50 and 79," and "low IQ" are examples. Only 20% of the special education teachers described their specific cognitive limitations in areas such as memory, e.g., "difficulty dealing with memory," and abstract thinking, e.g., "inability to grasp concepts visually or auditorily." Special education teachers seldom mentioned language impairment or motor impairment.

Some of the teachers (16%) compared the learning characteristics of the mentally retarded child to the "normal" child. They said he/she was "a child who learns slower then the average child." Other teachers (32%) did not use the "normal" child as the yardstick, but instead, described the mentally retarded child in terms of a low expectancy level for achievement. For example, they said he/she was "limited in the knowledge he can acquire" and "never able to learn higher level conceptual skills."

The majority of teachers who described a retarded child's learning characteristics used a deficit model. That is, they specified his limitations as opposed to his abilities. There were several exceptions, however. Some mentioned that retarded children "can learn life skills," "can function on a daily basis," and "can be very rational and concrete in their thinking." We were surprised to find that only three special education teachers described a mentally retarded child in terms of the type of special education and training that the child needs. They said that "MRs can learn simple tasks and possibly learn to read" and "they need to learn through small sequential steps and much repetition." Teachers obviously were referring to the education of moderately retarded children as opposed to educably retarded children.

Only a small number of special education teachers (22%) described retarded children by referring to their social/emotional characteristics. Some mentioned that a mentally retarded child "had little self-control," "was in a daze," or "was overly sensitive." Others included in their description the affective feelings of the mentally retarded person. They used words such as "angry" and "sad" and attributed these feelings to the actions of others who "ridicule or stare at them."

Few special education teachers (16%) mentioned the cause of mental retardation. They attributed learning dysfunctions to either brain injury or genetic disorders, for example, "brain damage," and "genetic problems."

Missing from the teachers' descriptions was an indication that all mentally retarded children are not the same. Only 15% mentioned that there are different forms or levels of mental retardation. Several specifically used such terms as "educable" and "trainable," while others used the more antiquated terms "imbecile" and "idiot." Only one commented that "there is no typical mentally retarded child."

Regular Education Teachers

We asked 30 regular education teachers who had very little or no contact with mentally retarded children to "describe a child who is mentally retarded"—the same question we had asked special education teachers.

The 30 teachers were from schools similar to those from which the student sample had been selected. There were 6 males and 24 females ranging in age from 25 to 52 years with a mean age of 34. The regular education teachers' answers were analyzed by categorizing their responses according to whether they described learning or social-emotional characteristics.

Most of the regular education teachers (77%) responded with very general references to a mentally retarded child's learning characteristics. For example, they said he/she "learns very slowly," and "is limited intellectually." Several referred specifically to IQ: "below 80 IQ," "70 IQ or under," and "an extremely low IQ." Several teachers also described specific cognitive and motor limitations, such as "behind in memory," "cannot understand cause and effect relationships," "unable to perform most abstract processes," "uncoordinated," and "slow in physical activities."

As did special education teachers, regular education teachers employed a "normal" standard when depicting the mentally retarded child. For example, teachers wrote that a retarded child "will learn more slowly and not as much as other children," and "has capabilities of mental functioning which are below normal level for his age group." When discussing learning problems, some teachers mentioned such causes as "neurological reasons for being retarded," "significant impairment in the CNS," and "not having a normal brain." These teachers only cited "problems with the brain" as reasons for the child's learning problems.

After learning characteristics, the social characteristics of retarded children were the next most frequently mentioned by regular education teachers. Of the 23% who referred to a retarded child's social characteristics, most mentioned his/her behavior, in general, as being different from "normal" children. They wrote about "the small amount of eye to eye contact," "infantile behavior," "trying hard to please," and "usually sweet, happy, and good natured dispositions." These last trait descriptions indicate that teachers view a mentally retarded child as qualitatively different than a "normal" child. That is, they are not using academic standards in evaluating the mentally retarded child as they tend to do when evaluating a "normal" child.

In addition to describing the retarded child with negative social traits or extremely positive affective traits, teachers also portrayed the child as having a deviant appearance: "he is disheveled" and "he appears young for his age." Only one teacher stated that the mentally retarded child does not look different than a normal child: "his physical appearance and development are normal."

Very few regular education teachers described a mentally retarded child in terms of the special instructional needs of the child. Teachers who did mention the educational consequences of mental retardation were totally divided in their prognosis. Two said that a mentally retarded child "can have the capacity to be educated" and "can learn to perform routine jobs and support himself." In contrast, several other teachers had a negative expectancy, stating "he cannot function in a classroom situation," and "he cannot be expected to learn to cope with any kind of teaching or instruction."

Regular Education Teachers (Revised Questionnaire)

To obtain a better understanding of teachers' stereotypes of mental retardation, we decided to ask a question that provided more structure for answers than did our original question: "Describe a child who is mentally retarded." In our second questionnaire we asked, "How does a mentally retarded child act, look, and feel?" We administered this new questionnaire to a group of 30 regular education teachers (19 female, and 11 male), who ranged in age from 23 to 50 and had a mean age of 29. They had little or no contact with mentally retarded children.

More than one third of the regular education teachers in our second survey said that a mentally retarded child looks normal. However, most of them clarified their "normal" statement by adding a reference to the severity of the mental retardation: "he looks normal or different depending on the degree of retardation" and "most except Mongloids look completely average." Other teachers only mentioned Down's syndrome or described the characteristics peculiar to Down's syndrome. The remaining teachers were less specific in their descriptions, saying, for example, that a retarded child "looks out of it," "has a blank expression," and "has different facial features."

Few teachers (10%) described how a retarded child acts by specifying the learning characteristics of the child. They used more general terms, such as "uncoordinated," "slow," and "slow to respond." Some teachers were even more vague, saying only that retarded children were "different," "retarded," and "engaged in inappropriate behavior."

The majority of the teachers (80%) described how a mentally retarded child acts by referring to his/her social behavior. They made special note of the differences between the behavior of a mentally retarded child and that of a normal child. They described the child as "hyperactive," "immature," "disoriented," and "not in touch with reality." These last descriptions indicate that the teachers believed that the retarded child is unaware of his/her condition and surroundings.

Some teachers (23%) believed that there is no one typical mentally retarded child. Instead of attributing negative characteristics to the mentally retarded child, the teachers said that retardation either "depends upon severity" or "depends upon child." While these teachers implied that there were differences among the mentally retarded, they did not use any of the existing categories, such as "educable" or "trainable," in their descriptions. This was the first indication that some teachers differentiate mental retardation according to degree of severity.

In response to the question, "How does a mentally retarded child feel?," 20% of the regular education teachers said that he/she "has all sorts of emotions as a normal child does" and "has normal ups and downs." Others thought the child felt "happy" and "fine." However, most teachers (40%) described the mentally retarded child as "rejected and isolated" but did not give any reason for the child's social condition.

Prospective Regular Education Teachers (Revised Questionnaire)

Using the same questionnaire that was used in the second regular education teacher survey, we questioned 50 prospective regular education teachers (10 males and 40 females) who were students at a college in the Boston area. Their ages ranged from 18 to 36, with a mean age of 22.

Most prospective teachers (44%) indicated that a mentally retarded child *sometimes* looks normal depending on the severity or cause of the retardation: "he probably looks normal unless he's profoundly retarded" and "he may look like a normal child unless he has Down's syndrome" were typical answers. Only a few undergraduates described the appearance of a mentally retarded child as "average" or "like a human being" without these qualifying responses.

There was a small group of prospective teachers who described a retarded child's appearance by using vague terms such as "different," "weird," "abnormal," and "distorted in appearance." The rest of the teachers referred to Down's syndrome or mentioned the characteristics of a Down's syndrome child, for example, "chubby," "short, stubby hands and fingers," and "eyes slightly slanted." A few teachers even described the retarded child as hydrocephalic ("large heads, small bodies") and one response actually included that clinical term.

Similar to regular education teachers in the field, few prospective teachers (8%) mentioned learning characteristics in their descriptions of a retarded child's behavior. Those prospective teachers who did said that the child "is uncoordinated," "has a short attention span," and "has a speech impediment." Other prospective teachers were more vague, using such terms as "weird," "stupid," and "retarded." Most of the prospective teachers (92%) used social traits to describe the retarded child's behavior, depicting them as "hyperactive," "uncontrolled," and "loud";

some, however, said that they were "reserved," "quiet," "shy," and "afraid to answer questions." In general, students used negative social traits to depict either an extremely active or an extremely withdrawn child.

Prospective teachers also depicted the mentally retarded child as socially immature. For example, they said that a retarded child "is younger than his CA," "acts like a baby," and "acts like a 4-year-old when he is 15 years old." Some even characterized the mentally retarded child's behavior as being overly "good"; they were depicted as "loving," "affectionate," "playful," and "liked by all."

When asked how a mentally retarded child feels, several prospective teachers (16%) said that a retarded child is unaware of his/her feelings. "He is not aware of deviation," "he is oblivious," and "he doesn't worry about what others think since he cannot understand" were typical responses. In contrast, however, the same number believed that the retarded child *is* aware that he/she is different saying that "he is frustrated with society's outlook on him," "angry that others treat him different," "insecure," and "feeling inferior watching other children do things he can't." Most of those who did not mention awareness only said that a retarded child "feels different." Two unique responses to this question underscored our reasons for doing this survey: "A mentally retarded child's feelings depend on how others around him understand the handicap," and "his feelings depend upon the attitudes that society has toward him."

Prospective teachers did not mention the causes of mental retardation as did regular education teachers, nor did they describe the retarded child in terms of his special educational needs. With one exception, the prospective teachers did not use labels such as "educable," "mild," "severe," or "profoundly retarded" in their descriptions. Perhaps most importantly, most did mention that all mentally retarded children are not alike.

SUMMARY AND DISCUSSION

From the results of our survey, we see that children's and teachers' conceptions of mentally retarded children contain accurate as well as inaccurate components. In the following summary, our most salient findings are discussed and the answers we received from the different groups of people we surveyed are compared. Our concluding remarks address the misconceptions that children and teachers still have.

Responses of the Children

Many children correctly described a mentally retarded child in terms of his/her learning difficulties. The only age trend observed in the children's descriptions was in their expansiveness—older children told us more. Older children referred more to the social characteristics than did younger children.

Misconceptions most frequently occurred when children were describing a retarded child's appearance and feelings. They often confused mental retardation with sensory handicaps such as blindness and deafness. They also tended to view moderately to severely retarded children (such as those with Down's syndrome) as typical of the entire retarded population. Overall, the retarded children that they described would not be capable of functioning in a regular classroom. Perhaps this is due to the fact that a child is only aware of retardation that is apparent to the eye. Mild retardation, which may not be reflected in appearance, may go unnoticed. This could account for children's overly negative descriptions of retarded children's appearance.

No relationship was found between the type of contact children had with retarded children and the type or the expansiveness of their descriptions of such children. Children who had direct personal contact with retarded persons, for example, had no more accurate a description of a retarded child than did those who had only learned of retardation through adults or media presentations. This finding is somewhat discouraging since we hoped to find increased direct contact leading at least to accurate information. Before we can call this finding definitive, however, more research has to be done. Future research must define more clearly the nature of the contact and must also examine the outcome of the interaction. If children have had a positive experience with a retarded person, they may be apt to remember more, or at least may be willing to talk more, about him.

One of the more potentially troublesome misconceptions our survey uncovered was that mothers are often the cause of mental retardation. Many students thought that either through negligence or accidents, mothers brought on retardation before, during, and after childbirth. Mothers' carelessness can lead to retardation, but it is certainly not the most common cause. This incorrect belief sows the seeds of unnecessary guilt for many women who give birth to mentally retarded children.

Some students thought that mental retardation could be cured, or at least helped along, by proper educational approaches and healthy attitudes on the part of those in the retarded person's social environment. Most students had an accurate conception of what the social situation is for a retarded child. They were aware of the loneliness, isolation, and rejection the child faces. This awareness has not been documented before although we have known for a long time that children's attitudes toward retarded children are negative.

Responses of the Teachers

Teachers' perceptions of mentally retarded children tended to consist of accurate descriptions of moderately to severely retarded children. Frequently, what we found interesting about their answers was what they did not say or did not develop. The simplicity of our questions may have been partly responsible for certain omissions. Nevertheless, the fact remains that different groups of teachers did respond slightly differently to the same question. Special education teachers and one group of regular education teachers received one type of questionnaire while another group of regular education teachers and a group of prospective regular education teachers received a revised questionnaire. For the purposes of comparability, we discuss together only the groups that had the same questionnaire.

Initial Questionnaire Special education teachers and regular education teachers responded similarly to the initial questionnaire in that most answered with a clinical definition of a mentally retarded child: one who learns slowly and has a low IQ. This definition was sufficiently general so that a reader could not tell if they were referring to a mildly, moderately, or severely retarded child. They failed to differentiate between different types of retardation and did not label the child. Social traits were only mentioned occasionally as brief afterthoughts.

The two groups of teachers differed in that special education teachers never mentioned the educational implications of retardation. Perhaps this was because they took such implications for granted. Regular education teachers not only mentioned more often the special help retarded children need, but also referred more to their cognitive, motor, and language inadequacies. They also presented a "loving and happy with infantile emotions" stereotype of the retarded child more than special education teachers. This misconception seems rooted in people's image of a severely retarded child as one who, although not able to function properly, is still happy and loving because he/she is not aware of his/her condition. Teachers who did view the mentally retarded child as aware described the child as having negative feelings.

Revised Questionnaire In response to the second questionnaire, regular education teachers and prospective regular education teachers both tended to depict a severely retarded child (usually with Down's syndrome). Regular education teachers were far more likely to mention specific undesirable social traits that a retarded child might have. While prospective teachers' social descriptions were more vague, they were also more negative than the regular education teachers' descriptions. They often depicted the mentally retarded child as either keenly aware or blissfully ignorant of his/her social situation. They also differentiated among the different levels of retardation far more than did regular education teachers.

Comparison of the Responses of Children and Teachers

When the children's and teachers' answers in this study are compared; only certain general statements can be made because of the differences in age, experience, and literacy, which caused the use of different questionnaires. The teachers did have a better knowledge of what it is like to be mentally retarded than did the children. Several of the children's misconceptions are absent from the teachers' responses. However, both groups did tend to picture a severely retarded child when asked to describe only a mentally retarded child. Although this is not necessarily a misconception, it is a negative exaggeration that has possibly harmful consequences for more mildly retarded persons. Only 8% of the mentally retarded population is classified as moderately to severely retarded. Because they *appear* retarded, the entire retarded population becomes identified with them (Hollinger & Jones, 1970; MacMillan, Jones, & Aloia, 1974). As a result, mildly retarded persons suffer from the low expectations and stigmatizations people reserve for more severely retarded persons. On the positive side, our survey revealed that most teachers and many children are not only aware of the social challenges facing the retarded child, but are also mindful of the role that others must play in making him/her feel at home in new surroundings.

CONCLUSIONS

The misinformation that our survey has revealed among teachers and students is significant. Our findings indicate that there are certain facts that should be made clear to all teachers and students:

1. Down's syndrome and other severe forms of retardation affect only a small percentage of the mentally retarded population.
2. Mentally retarded children can participate meaningfully in classrooms.
3. Blind and deaf people are not usually mentally retarded, and vice versa.
4. Mothers are usually not to blame for a child being mentally retarded.
5. A wide range of abilities exists among mentally retarded people.
6. It is usually impossible to tell if a person is mentally retarded by only looking at him.
7. Mentally retarded people do have feelings and are usually aware of their condition.

The final three statements correct misconceptions that have been present in America since at least 1926 when the National Committee on Mental Hygiene documented the nine most prevalent misconceptions about feeblemindedness. The other misunderstandings they cited may still be present today, but our surveys did not address them directly and they were not mentioned spontaneously by our respondents.

Teachers' misconceptions indicate the extent to which many of them are not equipped to work with mentally retarded children. Their failure to describe mentally retarded children accurately can be traced to the failure of their teacher training program to require any courses on the mentally retarded or exceptional child. The present rush to retrain teachers, already in the field, to deal more effectively with the educational and emotional needs of the mentally retarded child attests to the lack of adequate preservice training.

In the past, teacher education programs were designed around the outmoded assumption that the handicapped child is not to be considered a member of the regular classroom program. The present courses of study that prepare regular education teachers still do not provide the necessary instruction to meet the demands of mentally retarded children.

The need for continued reform and reappraisal of our teacher preparation program and inservice training program is mandatory if mainstreaming is to work. As Martin (1974) has suggested, "if...we don't plan today for those societal patterns of response to the handicapped, we will be painfully naive, and I fear we will subject many children to painful and frustrating educational experiences in the name of progress." Teachers need to be helped to recognize their misconceptions about and subsequent feelings toward mentally retarded children and to understand the significant effect their feelings have on their actions in the classroom.

Although there may never be a time when everyone can give a precise definition of mental retardation, it is time for people's ideas to reflect as closely as possible the reality of what it is like to be a mentally retarded person. This is especially true for teachers and children as school systems integrate retarded children. We need to replace all false stereotypes with information about how mentally retarded persons really look, act, and feel. We have documented children's and teachers' perceptions of the mentally retarded child here in order to help those who are committed to bringing about this type of change.

REFERENCES

Appell, M. J., Williams, C. M., & Fishell, K. N. Interests of professionals in fields of exceptionality. *Vocational Guidance Quarterly,* 1963, *12,* 43–45.

Baldwin, W. D. The social position of the educable mentally retarded in the regular grades in the public schools. *Exceptional Children,* 1958, *25,* 106–108.

Bandura, A., & Walters, R. H. *Social learning and personality development.* New York: Holt, 1963.

Brophy, J. E., & Evertson, C. M. *Learning from teaching: A developmental perspective.* Boston: Allyn & Bacon, 1976.

Brophy, J. E., & Good, T. L. *Teacher-student relationships, causes, and consequences.* New York: Holt, 1974.

Condell, J. F., & Tonn, M. H. A comparison of MTAI scores. *Mental Retardation,* 1965, *3,* 23–24.

Copeland, A. P., & Weissbrod, C. S. Differences in attitudes toward sex-typed behavior of nonretarded and retarded children. *American Journal of Mental Deficiency,* 1976, *81,* 280–288.

Dentler, R. A., & Mackler, B. Mental ability and sociometric status among retarded children. *Psychological Bulletin,* 1962, *59,* 273–283.

Efron, R. E., & Efron, H. Y. Measurement of attitudes toward the retarded and an application with educators. *American Journal of Mental Deficiency,* 1967, *72,* 100–107.

English, R. W., & Palla, D. A. Attitudes towards a photograph of a mildly and severely mentally retarded child. *Training School Bulletin,* 1971, *68,* 55–63.

Feshbach, N. Variations in teachers' reinforcement style and imitative behavior of children differing in personality characteristics and social backgrounds. *CSEIP Technical Report No. 2.* Los Angeles: The University of California at Los Angeles, 1967.

Gallagher, B. The effect of teacher attitudes on children's response to defective articulation. *Journal of Educational Research,* 1967, *60,* 456–458.

Gottlieb, J. Attitudes toward retarded children: Effects of labeling and academic performance. *American Journal of Mental Deficiency,* 1974, *79,* 268–273.

Gottwald, H. Public awareness about mental retardation. Council for Exceptional Children Research Monograph, 1970.

Heber, R. F. A manual on terminology and classification in mental retardation. *Monograph Supplement of the American Journal of Mental Deficiency* (2nd ed.), 1961.

Hollinger, C. S. & Jones, R. L. Community attitudes toward slow learners and mental retardates: What's in a name? *Mental Retardation,* 1970, *8,* 19–23.

Johnson, G. O. Social position of mentally handicapped children in regular grades. *American Journal of Mental Deficiency,* 1950, *55,* 60–89.

Johnson, G. O., & Kirk, S. A. Are mentally retarded handicapped children segregated in the regular grades? *Exceptional Children,* 1951, *17,* 65–68.

Jordan, J. E. *Attitudes toward educational and physically disabled persons in eleven nations.* Latin American Studies Center, Michigan State University, 1968.

Kleck, R. E., Richardson, S. A., & Ronald, L. Physical appearance cues and interpersonal attraction in children. *Child Development,* 1974, *45,* 305–310.

Kvaraceus, W. C. Acceptance-rejections and exceptionality. *Exceptional Children,* 1956, *22,* 238–331.

Lapp, E. R. A study of the social adjustment of slow-learning children who were assigned part-time to regular classes. *American Journal of Mental Deficiency,* 1957, *62,* 254–262.

MacMillan, D. L., Jones, R. L., & Aloia, G. F. The mentally retarded label: A theoretical analysis and review of research. *American Journal of Mental Deficiency,* 1974, *79,* 241-261.

Marge, D. K. The social status of speech-handicapped children. *Journal of Speech and Hearing Research,* 1966, *9,* 165-177.

Martin, E. D. Some thoughts on mainstreaming. *Exceptional Children,* 1974, *41,* 150-153.

Monroe, J. D., & Howe, C. E. The effects of integration and social class on the acceptance of retarded adolescents. *Education and Training of the Mentally Retarded,* 1971, *6,* 20-24.

Panda, K. C., & Bartel, N. R. Teacher perception of exceptional children. *Journal of Special Education,* 1972, *6,* 261-266.

Polonsky, D. Beliefs and opinions concerning mental deficiency. *American Journal of Mental Deficiency,* 1961, *66,* 12-17.

Rosenblith, J. F. Learning by imitation in kindergarten children. *Child Development,* 1959, *30,* 69-80.

Rosenblith, J. F. Imitative color choices in kindergarten children. *Child Development,* 1961, *32,* 211-223.

Rosenthal, R., & Jacobson, L. *Pygmalion in the classroom.* New York: Holt, 1968.

Ross, D. Relationship between dependency, intentional learning, and incidental learning in preschool children. *Journal of Personality and Social Psychology,* 1966, *4,* 374-381.

Rucker, C. N., Howe, C. E., & Snider, B. The participation of retarded children in junior high academic and nonacademic regular classes. *Exceptional Children,* 1969, *35,* 617-623.

Semmel, M. I. Teacher attitudes and information pertaining to mental deficiency. *American Journal of Mental Deficiency,* 1959, *63,* 566-574.

Siperstein, G. N., & Gottlieb, J. Parents' and teachers' attitudes toward mildly and severely retarded children. *Mental Retardation,* 1978, *16,* 321-322.

Skrtic, T. M., Sigler, G. R., & Lazar, A. L. Attitudes of male and female TMR teachers toward the handicapped. *Journal for Special Educators of the Mentally Retarded,* 1975, *11,* 171-174.

Strong, E. K. *Change of interest with age.* Palo Alto: Stanford University Press, 1931.

Warren, S. A., Turner, D. R., & Brody, D. S. Can education students' attitudes toward the retarded be changed? *Mental Retardation,* 1964, *2,* 235-242.

Whiteman, M., & Lukoff, I. F. Attitudes toward blindness in two college groups. *Journal of Social Psychology,* 1964, 53, 179-191.

Winthrop, H., & Taylor, H. An inquiry concerning the prevalence of popular misconceptions relation to mental deficiency. *American Journal of Mental Deficiency,* 1957, *62,* 344-348.

CHAPTER 9

Advocacy Through the Eyes of Citizens

Stephen S. Strichart and Jay Gottlieb

Services to many handicapped individuals are currently undergoing a metamorphosis in which emphasis is shifting from providing services in segregated environments to helping individuals assume a productive place in the environmental mainstream. We see increasingly the impact of the normalization principle at work. The removal of physical barriers restricting the handicapped person's access to buildings and activities is a result of Section 504 of the Rehabilitation Act of 1973 and the enactment of PL 94-142 (Education for All Handicapped Act of 1975) allows increasing numbers of handicapped children to be educated with nonhandicapped peers to the greatest extent appropriate. The deinstitutionalization process has been in existence for several years so that the phenomenon of individuals with even moderate or severe handicaps living in the community is as typical as not. The movement of developmentally disabled persons into the community has brought with it attendant problems of ensuring that they are able to function effectively in the face of new complexities and demands. Many of the handicapped persons involved in the deinstitutionalization process are mentally retarded, who, by definition, have impaired social adaptability. An innovative response to the problem of impaired social adaptability has been offered by Wolfensberger (1973) in his conception of citizen advocacy.

DEVELOPMENT OF CITIZEN ADVOCACY PROGRAMS

Wolfensberger (1973) defines a citizen advocate as "a mature, competent citizen volunteer, representing, as if they were his own, the interests of another citizen who is impaired in his instrumental capacity, or who has major expressive needs which are unmet and which are likely to remain unmet without special intervention" (p. 11). By specifying that the citizen advocate is a volunteer, Wolfensberger advances a role distinguished from that of the ombudsman, who is an appointed official (Mallory, 1977). Wolfensberger believes that in order to represent someone's interests as one's own, one must be free of conflicts of interest. Thus, the role of the advocate cannot effectively be exercised by persons employed by agencies that normally provide services to the impaired person (i.e., protégé), because, as advocates, such persons would frequently find themselves in situations in which the service they naturally might want to extend to the protégé would be contrary to the interests of the agency in which they are employed.

Wolfensberger sees an advocate fulfilling two needs of handicapped persons: instrumental needs and expressive needs. Instrumental needs are those needs that deal with the practical and material problems of everyday life, and expressive needs are those needs that involve the exchange of affection; i.e., meeting needs for relationship, communication, warmth, love, and support. The differentiation of instrumental and expressive needs results in a number of possible advocacy roles.

Specific advocacy roles emerge depending on which of these needs is to be fulfilled. Primarily instrumental roles include conservator, trustee, curator, instrumental guide-advocate, and instrumental guardian. A primarily expressive role is that of advocate-friend. Some roles are combinations of instrumental and expressive functions, such as the instrumental-expressive-guide-advocate, the foster parent, the instrumental-expressive guardian, the tutor, the adoptive parent, the parental successor, and the instrumental-expressive spouse.

Wolfensberger's concept of a citizen advocate interacting with a developmentally disabled protégé was first put into practice, during 1970, by the Capitol Association for Retarded Citizens in Lincoln, Nebraska. A survey conducted in 1975 by the National Association for Retarded Citizens (NARC) revealed that a total of 117 local and 10 state citizen advocacy programs operated in 30 states (National Association for Retarded Citizens, undated). Approximately 5,000 pairings of advocates and protégés were established. Local association for retarded citizens units were responsible for approximately 75% of the programs, suggesting that the majority of protégés were mentally retarded individuals. The growth of the programs was in large part accounted for by a child advocacy project launched by NARC in 1972 with federal funds.

Despite the proliferation of citizen advocacy programs during the last few years, there has been a lack of information describing the advocates, their motivations, and the roles they assume when interacting with their protégés. Kurtz (1975) noted this lack of information, but little published information has appeared in the interim to fill the void. The purpose of the study of the Florida Citizen Advocacy Program was to obtain some of this information. The general purposes of this study were: 1) to obtain descriptive information regarding people who volunteer to become advocates, 2) to determine advocates' reasons for volunteering, and 3) to examine advocates' perceptions of the effects of the advocacy program on the protégés and on themselves.

THE FLORIDA CITIZEN ADVOCACY PROGRAM

The development of the Florida Citizen Advocacy Program was initiated in 1970, and the first demonstration project was begun in 1973 (Florida Association for Retarded Citizens, 1976). Although the initial emphasis was on instrumental advocacy, the *Citizen Advocacy Manual* (Florida Association for Retarded Citizens, 1976) states that the advocate-protégé relationship "should be designed to meet the need (or needs), be it expressive or instrumental or a mixture of both..." (p. 3). In January 1977, the Florida Association for Retarded Citizens contracted with the Florida Retardation Program Office to plan and carry out the state system in accordance with Section 113 of Title II of the Developmental Disabilities and Rights Act (PL. 94-103). Florida's program is thus typical of those across the nation because it is within the jurisdiction of an association for retarded citizens.

Procedures for the Study of the Florida Citizen Advocacy Program

A questionnaire was designed to tap a variety of current areas of concern to the citizen advocacy movement. The areas of concern were: 1) the reasons people gave for becoming advocates, 2) the advocates' perceptions of their protégés, 3) the nature of interaction between the advocates and their protégés, 4) the effects of the advocacy program on the advocates, 5) the effects of the advocacy program on the protégés, and 6) the advocates' perceptions of the Citizen Advocacy Program.

With the assistance of their local advocacy offices, 170 citizen advocates who were actually matched with protégés were identified and mailed questionnaires. The 83 (49%) advocates who returned the completed questionnaire constituted the subjects of this investigation.

Table 1. Occupations of advocates as determined by the Turner scale

Occupational category	Number of advocates
Unskilled laborers and service workers	0
Semi-skilled laborers	3
Skilled laborers and foremen	6
Clerical workers and sales clerks	11
Small business owners and managers and retail salesmen	3
Semiprofessionals	9
Business agents and managers	1
Professionals	16
Large business owners and officials	0
College students*	31
Housewife*	3

*Not included in Turner (1964) scale.

In addition to data obtained from the questionnaire, in-depth home interviews were conducted with 19 advocates by one interviewer, a graduate special education student, in order to obtain more detailed information regarding selected area of information tapped by the questionnaire.

Characteristics of Advocates

The age distribution of the 83 advocates, 67 were females, was as follows: 18 advocates were under 21 years of age (22%), 44 were between 21 and 30 years of age (54%), 8 were between 31 and 40 years of age (10%), and the remaining 11 were 41 years of age and older (14%). The sample of advocates in this study was well educated, for the most part. Thirty-three (40%) advocates were college graduates and 12 (14%) held a graduate degree. In addition, another 31 (37%) advocates had attended college. Only three advocates (4%) had not completed high school.

The occupations of the advocates ran the gamut from semi-skilled laborers (there were no unskilled laborers in the sample) to professional workers, as determined by the Turner (1964) scale. The largest number of advocates were college students ($N=31$). Professionals were the most frequently represented group of those who were employed. Other occupations well represented in the sample were clerical workers and semi-professionals. (See Table 1.)

Only 25 advocates in the study were married, 50 advocates had never been married and 6 were divorced. Two persons did not indicate their status. Of the 83 advocates, 66 did not have children, and of those 17 who did, only 2 reported having retarded children. Three other advocates reported that other members of their immediate family were retarded.

Seventy-four advocates provided estimates of their annual income. Six (8%) reported earnings of over $15,000, 26 (35%) reported incomes of

$10,000-$15,000, and 42 (57%) stated that they earned less than $10,000. The high percentage of students in this sample must be considered when interpreting the income data.

Fifty-two advocates stated that they had experience with mentally retarded persons before becoming an advocate. Twenty-eight of these advocates had experience with retarded persons as a result of their professions, e.g., teachers and social workers, and 31 advocates had served as volunteers at one time. At the time of data collection for this study, advocates had been paired with their protégés for an average of 9.6 months (SD = 5.6 months).

In order to obtain an estimate of the representativeness of our sample, we compared it with a larger sample reported in the nationwide survey conducted by NARC, which comprised 53% of the ongoing citizen advocacy programs at that time. That survey reported that the preponderant number of advocates were between 20 and 29 years of age, were female, and were either white collar workers, students, or persons working in their homes. High frequency occupations reported were teacher, social worker, secretary, and salespersons (National Association for Retarded Citizens, undated). The present sample compares favorably with the national sample reported by NARC on the dimensions of chronological age, sex distribution, and occupations.

Characteristics of Protégés

Eighty-four (84) mentally retarded persons were protégés in the present investigation. This number is one greater than the number of advocates because one advocate had two protégés. Forty-four (53%) protégés were female. The age distribution of the group was as follows: 43 (53%) protégés were under 21 years of age, including 8 who were below the age of 8, 31 (38%) were between 21 and 30 years of age, 6 (7%) were between 31 and 40 years of age, and the remaining 2 (1%) were 41 years of age or older. The ages of two protégés were not reported.

The protégés were representative of a range of levels of mental retardation. Thirty-one (41%) protégés were mildly retarded according to records maintained by the citizen advocacy office, 35 (47%) were functioning in the moderate level, and 9 (12%) were severely retarded. Level of retardation was not reported for nine protégés.

Place of residence was varied for the sample. Twenty-three (28%) of the protégés resided at home either independently or with their family, 10 (12%) resided in foster homes, 21 (26%) lived in group homes in the community, and 28 (35%) were in an institution. Place of residence was not reported for two protégés. Thus, it may be seen that the thrust of the Florida Citizen Advocacy Program is directed toward protégés living in the community.

Again, the Florida sample may be compared with data reported by NARC. The NARC survey found that the majority of the citizen advocacy programs served both children and adults, involved protégés whose major disability was mental retardation, and directed their efforts toward protégés living in the community at large rather than in institutions. The present sample compares favorably with these characteristics.

FINDINGS OF THE STUDY

Reasons for Becoming an Advocate

An important goal of citizen advocacy programs is to identify the reasons why people volunteer to become advocates. As the citizen advocacy movement continues to expand, professional workers in the field of mental retardation will face an increasing need to recruit appropriate volunteers who can provide retarded persons with a variety of successful experiences they otherwise would find difficult to obtain. If motives for becoming advocates can be identified, public awareness campaigns can be developed and tailored to accommodate the needs and desires of potential advocates. Furthermore, given that it is important for matches between advocates and protégés to persist at least long enough for the effects of the relationship to emerge, such knowledge could allow advocacy programs to function in ways in which advocates will receive sufficient gratification to keep them involved in the program. Toward these ends we attempted to identify the most frequently stated reasons why people volunteered to become advocates.

In the Florida study the reason most often stated for becoming an advocate was a general desire to help mentally retarded persons or to help a specific mentally retarded person whom the advocate knew ($N=31$). Examples of this altruistic behavior are the 25-year-old teacher who "was interested in helping the retarded in a nonacademic manner" or the 24-year-old foreman who indicated that he decided to become an advocate because "I cared about this person." Other frequent reasons stated by the advocates included a desire to fill spare time in a meaningful way ($N=12$), to meet unfulfilled personal needs ($N=10$), and a general desire to support the goals of the citizen advocacy program ($N=10$). Twelve of the advocates indicated that they had become involved in the program as a result of exposure to the nature and goals of citizen advocacy in their college courses. The present data compare favorably with the data reported by Jennings (undated) in his evaluation of reasons why people became involved as advocates in the Austin, Texas Citizen Advocacy program. His respondents cited a variety of personal reasons and many expressed their belief in a general need for advocacy.

The reasons expressed by the advocates in the present study for becoming advocates fall into two general categories. One set of responses, other-oriented, expressed a nonspecific, unstructured desire to help retarded people. The other category, self-oriented, was for people who wanted to fulfill some void in their own lives. While some advocates gave responses that fell into both categories, the majority of advocates' responses fell into one category or the other.

It would be desirable to know whether other-oriented advocates differ in systematic ways from self-oriented advocates in the manner that they approach their responsibilities as advocates. Unfortunately, our data do not allow us to answer this important question. It does appear reasonable to expect, however, that the continued long-term success of citizen advocacy programs could very well be contingent upon the extent to which programs were structured to meet the needs of the advocate, and not only the needs of the protégé. In other words, citizen advocacy programs can be viewed as having two groups of clients: protégés and advocates. In the case of other-oriented advocates, attention can focus primarily on the needs of the protégé. However, in the case of self-oriented advocates, equal attention may have to be directed to their needs as well as to those of the protégé.

A third group of advocates represent a special case by virtue of the fact that they volunteered as a result of exposure to the citizen advocacy program during college classes. For these advocates, we could not clearly determine whether they were primarily self- or other-oriented. Their motivation in some cases may have been related to a desire to obtain a good grade in their course.

To the extent that the data from the present investigation are generalizeable, it is possible that large numbers of advocates could be recruited on college campuses through the simple device of a lecture and/or discussion. Our data do not permit us to make statements regarding characteristics of the recruiter that would be optimal for such an endeavor. Furthermore, we were unable to assess whether the relatively youthful advocates recruited from the campus are as effective as the older, more mature individuals.

Advocates' Perceptions of their Protégés

How do the advocates view their protégés? We attempted to explore some areas of advocates' perceptions of protégés, especially their perceptions of the protégés' functioning as members of society.

Previous reports of the daily lives of mentally retarded persons presented a picture of the retarded person in the community consumed by his stigma (Edgerton, 1967) and totally dependent upon the beneficence of another person to survive the daily rigors of life. However, in a follow-up study, Edgerton and Bercovici (1976) indicated that approximately 10 years after retarded persons are released from institutions they do not feel as overwhelmed by their self-perceived stigma as they did when they were first released from the institution. How important then is the notion of stigma and community attitudes toward retarded persons to the success of citizen advocacy programs? Do the perceived stigma and the negative attitudes pose such serious threats to the daily lives of protégés that the advocates should be trained in methods of dealing with this problem? Or, has the notion of stigma and community rejection been overemphasized?

Sixty-eight advocates responded to the question of whether they believed that their protégé felt stigmatized by his/her condition of mental retardation. Only 19% answered affirmatively. The relatively low percentage of advocates who viewed their protégés as being stigmatized by their retardation is supported by the advocates' perceptions of community attitudes. Only 26% of respondents believed that their protégé was the victim of negative community attitudes.

As a result of their experiences with their protégé, 68 advocates (78%) had become more optimistic about their protégé's chances for leading an independent or semi-independent life in the community. Excluding protégés under 18 years of age and/or living in an institution, 64% of the advocates regarded their protégés as not at all self-supporting, 32% saw their protégés as partially self-supporting, and only 4% perceived their protégés as fully self-supporting. Yet, the overwhelming majority of this group of advocates (87%) did not believe that their protégés were too dependent on them in their relationship.

Overall, these data do not portray so unfavorable a picture of retarded persons' daily lives in the community, at least with regard to society's view of them as reported by the advocates. The comment of one advocate reflects the feelings of many others:

> I originally thought that it (community attitude) would be very negative. I thought that people would react quite suspiciously and quite negative towards myself and (protégé). But I felt quite the contrary.... I was really taken by the way the community, or those that I have encountered in the community, have accepted or have at least worked around with him.

Another advocate indicated that "They liked her. No problems. All my friends accepted her, which is great." However, not all of the advocates reported that positive community attitudes were expressed, particularly by older people or by children. One advocate, in talking about the older generation, said that "...they think differently of retardation.... They still have the thought that people belong in an institution."

The comments of another advocate indicated the severity of negative reactions that on occasion can be experienced: "Every time we went out, there were people staring and pointing and really hurting her feelings and I would like to come back with something like... I want to protect her because she does have rights...."

In sum, however, the general pattern of data with regard to society's reactions to the mentally retarded person in the community is not unfavorable. However, instances of negative reaction do arise—usually in the form of staring, pointing, or taunts—sufficiently often so that advocates should be made more aware of these during their training program and perhaps be offered additional techniques for responding effectively. Overall, perhaps the statement of one advocate who said that "people were fair" best sums up the community's reaction to the protégés.

In addition to questioning advocates on community attitudes, stigma, and dependency, the advocates were asked their feelings regarding marriage and children for their protégés. Advocates whose protégés were under 18 years of age were excluded from this analysis. The remaining advocates were fairly evenly divided on the matter of marriage. Fifty-two percent (52%) responded positively with regard to their protégé marrying a normal person. Interestingly, only 42% responded positively when the potential marriage partner was another retarded person. To a large degree, however, it appears that the issue in the advocate's mind is more one of whether a protégé should marry rather than whom he/she should marry.

The attitudes of these advocates were fairly similar regarding the matter of whether or not the protégés should have children as a product of their marriage. To that question, 43% responded that they should, 47% responded negatively, and 10% were undecided. Apparently, where an advocate viewed marriage as a viable possibility for his/her protégé, there was no concern that the additional responsibilities incurred by caring for children might be too much of a burden on the protégé. This conclusion is speculative, however, since our data did not address this issue directly.

The fact that advocates were fairly evenly divided on the issues of marriage and children suggests that there was no overriding single stereotypical notion of the retarded that operated in the minds of the advocates. Rather, protégés were evaluated in terms of their own unique set of characteristics that might render them suitable as a marriage partner or parent.

The diversity of advocates' perceptions of protégés is also mirrored in their responses to a question asking them to list their protégés' major strengths and weaknesses. Forty-nine different strengths and 49 different weaknesses were identified, showing again that no single stereotypical notion was operating. Among the most often-cited strengths were the desire to learn, determination, warmth, consideration, friendliness, and outgoing personality. On the negative side, characteristics most frequently cited were lack of self-confidence, unrealistic expectations, poor speech and communication skills, and low frustration tolerance.

The final question that advocates were asked concerning their perceptions of their protégé was whether their protégés were receiving the services they required. One-half of the 68 advocates who responded to this question indicated that they felt they were not. Those services seen as most frequently lacking were: psychiatric and counseling, vocational training, education, and dental and speech correction. The present findings were very similar to those of Jennings (undated). His sample of advocates most frequently reported attempting to procure needed medical, dental, and speech therapy services for their protégés.

To summarize the advocates' perceptions of the protégés, most advocates felt that community attitudes were not negative and that the issue of stigma was not problematic for their protégés. Furthermore, there was no evidence of stereotypic thinking toward protégés; protégés were seen as unique individuals with their own configuration of strengths and weaknesses. Feelings were mixed concerning whether protégés should marry and have children. Finally, the need for additional services in many cases was reported.

Nature of Interaction Between Advocates and their Protégés

The crux of the citizen advocacy movement obviously concerns the nature of interaction between the advocates and the protégés. The activities that are engaged in will, in large part, dictate whether the protégé will have a successful experience. But what exactly do the advocates do when they are with their protégés? How frequently do they get together?

Because the citizen advocacy office in Dade County, Florida (the largest of the three citizen advocacy sites participating in this investigation) suggested to the advocates that they get together with their protégés once a week (Dade County Association for Retarded Citizens, undated), we wanted to corroborate whether, in fact, the advocates did meet with their protégés at least this often. Our data indicate that one-half of the advocates (52%) met with their protégés at least once a week. Eighty percent (80%) of the advocates indicated that they phoned their protégés at least once a week, and 87% indicated that the protégés were told that they could call them when they had a particular problem. Of those advocates who saw their protégés less than once a week, 14% stated that they saw their protégés once a month or less. These data suggest that some monitoring of advocates by the citizen advocacy office may be necessary to ensure that the advocate-protégé match is sufficiently active.

What do advocates and their protégés discuss when they get together or talk on the phone? Excluding protégés under 14 years of age from the analysis, we found that certain subjects were very frequently discussed. Leisure time activities were discussed by 93% of the advocates, and 79% discussed financial matters. On the other hand, only 47% of the advocates discussed the protégés' family problems and only 39% discussed matters of sex. In the latter instance, it is interesting to note that protégés initiated the discussion 60% of the time. Discussion of vocational matters occupied a middle position; 56% of the advocates discussed this with their protégés. These data suggest that advocates tend to shy away from discussions of personal and/or sensitive matters, focusing instead on the more general social aspects of their protégés' lives.

What do the advocates report doing when they are with their protégés? To gain a perspective on this question, we first asked advocates to indicate what they usually did when they were with their protégé. Responses to this question were coded as reflecting *instructional* activities (e.g., tutoring in school subjects), *social* activities (e.g., visiting the advocate's home), or *recreational* activities (e.g., going for a ride). The most common form of activity by far was social, with 83% of the advocates reporting that they engaged in social activities with their protégé. Forty-nine percent (49%) of the advocates engaged in recreational activities, and only 10% reported that they provided instructional activities.[1] Analysis of these data indicates that the majority of advocates performed expressive functions (i.e., friendship and emotional support) as opposed to instrumental functions (i.e., practical assistance in coping with everyday situations and problems). As such, these data are consonant with the findings reported by NARC (undated), which indicated that the majority of advocates (54%) performed expressive functions exclusively and that only a small minority (8%) performed instrumental functions exclusively. Further evidence of the expressive role played by advocates was furnished by Jennings (undated) who reported that protégés stated their most frequent interactions with their advocates to be eating out, traveling, and going for rides, all in the expressive rather than instrumental sense. Similarly, Jennings' advocates reported that protégés preferred expressive interactions such as sports and shopping.

It is important to compare the activities that the advocates state they engage in and the activities that the citizen advocacy office recommends (McGlamery & Malavenda, 1977). McGlamery and Malavenda suggested that citizen advocates should: 1) provide friendship, guidance, and

---

[1] Numbers exceed 100% because advocates could respond to more than one category.

emotional support; 2) monitor programs and services; 3) provide opportunities for socialization and community exposure; and 4) secure legal assistance when necessary. These guidelines suggest that advocates should fulfill both instrumental *and* expressive functions, while our data suggest that advocates usually fulfill only the latter. That is, we found that advocates most closely personified what Wolfensberger (1973) referred to as the advocate-friend role, whereas the citizen advocate office suggested that their advocates fulfill the instrumental-expressive guide-advocate role.

To the extent that an important goal of the citizen advocacy movement is to encourage advocates to engage in both expressive and instrumental roles with the protégés, our data, coupled with the national data reported by NARC and that of Jennings, suggest that additional training will have to be provided in the area of instrumental functioning. On the assumption that it is naturally easier for advocates to perform expressive roles than instrumental roles, citizen advocacy offices may have to offer more supportive services than they are presently providing if instrumental roles are to be performed adequately. Another possibility is that the role of the citizen advocate should be redefined as including only expressive functions, leaving instrumental functions to professionals who are trained to offer practical assistance to handicapped persons. This latter redefinition, however, runs counter to the prevailing philosophy of citizen advocacy, which minimizes professional involvement in the belief that professionals are invariably placed in a position of conflicting loyalties between the agency they serve and their protégé. Hence, to be consistent with the philosophy of citizen advocacy as espoused by Wolfensberger (1973), it is incumbent upon citizen advocacy offices to place additional stress on training instrumental role development among advocates. Formal training procedures may have to be devised by citizen advocacy programs, or they may need to look to training institutions for this function.

Because the advocates reported that they primarily engaged in social functions with their protégés, we wished to determine the specific kinds of activities in which they participated. An analysis of interview data with 19 advocates revealed a considerable degree of consistency in the activities that advocates engaged in with their protégés. Most advocates took their protégés to the beach, bowling, shopping, to restaurants, and to the park for an afternoon, etc. The flavor of these activities is well represented by one advocate who reported:

> Well, we do a lot of recreational activities, such as going out to the beach, to Cape Florida to go swimming. We've been on a few cookouts. We go to wrestling matches. We've been to football games. We've been to miniature golf. He's come over to my house for a Christmas party. We've done some

shopping together; he had to pick up a watch for himself and a couple of albums. He's gone down and bought lunch out of a public supermarket for us. So we kind of just do regular things that two people when they get together would do.

While these activities do have instrumental aspects, it is important to realize that these are implicit. The explicit intent of the activities is of an expressive nature. It will be recalled that we previously indicated that one-half of the advocates felt that their protégés were not receiving all of the professional services that they required. Now we wished to determine whether the advocates were actively recruiting these services on behalf of the protégés. Sixty-five percent (65%) of the total sample of advocates reported that they had actively contacted persons or agencies responsible for providing professional services for the protégés. Close inspection of these responses, however, revealed that advocates' contacts with professionals were primarily to obtain information about their protégé rather than to secure additional services for their protégé. The information requested by the advocates was intended to enable them to improve their relationships with protégés by affording more detailed understanding of the background and preferences of the protégés.

To summarize the advocates' interactions with their protégés, we found that discussions between advocates and protégés concentrated mainly on general social concerns and tended to avoid personal, sensitive areas such as sex and family matters. In their activities with the protégés, advocates functioned mainly in the social and recreational domains as advocate-friends. Finally, even in their contacts with professionals concerning their protégés, advocates tended to seek general information about their protégés rather than to attempt to modify the nature of the services that were being offered.

Effects of Advocacy Experience on the Advocates

Although the primary intent of citizen advocacy programs is to assist the handicapped person in his daily encounters in the community, an important secondary concern is to provide advocates with learning experiences about handicapped people. McGlamery and Malavenda (1977) stated that "Citizen advocacy provides an opportunity for citizen advocates, their friends, families, neighbors, and co-workers to learn about people with developmental disabilities; to learn that people with developmental disabilities are unique individuals who cannot be labeled, categorized, or stereotyped."

Accordingly, we asked the advocates to indicate the changes in their attitudes and feelings toward mentally retarded persons that occurred as a result of their citizen advocacy experiences. Advocates' responses fell into two categories: 28% indicated no change in their attitudes and feelings, and 72% indicated a positive change as a result of their experiences with the protégés. Examples of these changes include advocates who came to recognize the handicapped as persons with individual needs and wants ($N=8$), who developed an appreciation of their "human" qualities ($N=6$), who acquired greater understanding of their situation ($N=15$), who developed greater tolerance of handicapped persons ($N=7$), and who became more at ease in their presence ($N=3$). Importantly, not a single advocate stated that his/her feelings and attitudes changed for the worse. Clearly then, the citizen advocacy program produces positive changes in the expressed attitudes of the advocate and fulfills the goals stated above. The fact that positive changes in attitudes developed does not necessarily signify that advocates did not experience some frustrations. Indeed, many advocates were frustrated by aspects of their experiences. These frustrations often stemmed from the advocates' desire to obtain additional services for their protégé in the face of a sea of red tape that constantly seemed to work against the protégé. Other frustrations resulted from the pain of sharing failure experiences when both the advocate and the protégé wanted the latter to achieve a particular goal, only to find that he/she lacked the skills to do so.

These frustrations were amplified in our interviews with the advocates, as is evident from one advocate who, in trying to get social security for the protégé, complained:

> I mean this has been a fight from beginning to end. It took about 9 months to get a social security card in his (the protégé's) own name. Now that they finally got it in his own name, they are sending it to the wrong address. All these bureaus are unbelievable. The red tape involved. Then, of course, the VA reassessed him and wanted to cut off his benefits. I called the doctor and said, 'Look, social security is willing to go along and give him a chance to rehabilitate. He spent 20 years out of 23 of his life in an institution. He still isn't working and if he gets a job he's going to need supplemental because you can't live today on the money you make, especially just starting out.' So they said they didn't know if he was eligible and they would take it into consideration. So far, he's still getting both of the checks. So we fought for that with him, and, of course, they don't know if it's going to last for too long. But at least it is still coming through.

Or, from a second advocate who was frustrated because

> He's not able to grasp anything or improve himself, whether it be bowling or anything else. I think it's only a natural thing to see him better himself, no matter what he does. And you try to repeat the same thing over again so that he can get a better concept of what you're trying to do. And I guess that's part of the frustration, that he doesn't seem to grasp what I'm trying to teach him.

And, a third advocate who felt the frustration of not knowing how to help her protégé:

> (Protégé) had a speech problem and he also had a problem with his attention span, which was extremely short. I didn't know how to handle this, how to cope with this, how to improve the situation. I think that was the most frustrating thing. It's not so much helping him or not helping him, it's not knowing how.

These last observations are again suggestive of the relative inability of advocates to provide instrumental assistance to protégés, even when they want to do so.

To summarize the effects of the advocacy experience on the advocate, this experience is perceived to have a salutary effect for a high proportion of the advocates. While approximately one-quarter of the advocates reported no change of attitudes toward handicapped individuals, the remaining three-fourths expressed positive changes, although some also expressed considerable frustration over many aspects of their encounters. However, these frustrations did not diminish their generally favorable attitudes and feelings.

Effects of the Citizen Advocacy Program on the Protégés

The main purpose of the citizen advocacy program is to match developmentally disabled persons with citizen volunteers in order to meet the needs of handicapped persons and to promote better community understanding and acceptance of them. We wished to determine how the citizen advocacy program affected the protégé, as reported by the advocates.

Sixteen advocates (19%) stated that they could not observe any changes in their protégés that could be attributed to their participation in the citizen advocacy program. One advocate reported that as a result of the interactions, the protégé regressed and became more dependent. Aside from this one negative comment, all of the advocates who noted changes reported positive changes in the protégés' behavior.

Among the more frequently mentioned changes in the protégés' behaviors were greater confidence ($N=7$), improved language skills ($N=13$), more outgoing ($N=7$), relates better to people ($N=8$), more independent ($N=5$), and happier ($N=4$).

Interviews with the advocates revealed additional details regarding perceived changes in protégés' behavior. One advocate expressed that she saw her protégé:

> Develop from when she was very shy and into herself and kind of aggressive, because she didn't have much confidence in herself, to the point where she

now is calmer. I think that was a big accomplishment that she gained more respect for other people and she came out of herself socially.

And another advocate, reported that his greatest satisfaction was:

When he talked to me after a month and a half of not talking to me or looking at me. They thought he didn't have any speech at all when they referred him there. It was just locked within his shell and he wouldn't talk to anybody or trust anybody so it took me a while to gain his trust.

These two illustrations highlight the kinds of positive changes in daily behavior that the advocates observed in their protégés as a result of the citizen advocacy program.

Advocates' Perceptions of the Citizen Advocacy Program

As previously observed, one of the most critical needs for the survival of the citizen advocacy movement is to ensure an adequate number of appropriate persons who volunteer to become advocates. If we are to continue to recruit advocates we must understand the gratifications that advocates receive in their role. To this end, we asked advocates directly what reason they would use as an inducement to potential advocates, based on their own experiences. The responses were consistently similar, with the majority of advocates stressing either the "good feeling" that occurs from being an advocate, or the worthiness of helping someone less fortunate. Responses to this question were consistent with those discussed earlier where advocates were asked the reasons why they became advocates. Those reasons were categorized as representing either a self-oriented motivation or an other-oriented motivation, and the present responses can be similarly categorized. The data suggest that the reasons why people volunteered to be advocates initially were the same ones that they would subsequently offer others who contemplate volunteering. As such, it appears reasonable to conclude that advocates' initial expectations were being fulfilled. It must be borne in mind, however, that all questions posed were post hoc and that advocates could have selected the reasons they would give to others primarily as a means to justify their own initial expectations for themselves.

Taken as a whole, the major inducement for potential advocates is in the affective domain. Efforts to recruit advocates should profitably stress the good feeling that results from being an advocate and helping others who are less fortunate.

CONCLUSIONS

Results of the study have indicated that advocates volunteered because they wanted to help a handicapped person or because they wanted to fulfill some void in their own lives. We characterized these two types of responses as other-oriented and self-oriented, respectively. It was further found that advocates did not report many negative community attitudes toward their protégé, nor did they perceive that the protégés felt stigmatized by their condition of mental retardation. Furthermore, during their interactions with protégés, advocates discussed mostly general social concerns and tended to avoid discussions involving intimate matters, such as sex and family problems. Advocates tended to function mainly as advocate-friends, interacting with the protégé in a predominantly expressive manner. In addition, the advocacy experience had salutary effects on approximately three-fourths of the advocates, with the latter figure representing the proportion of advocates who reported positive changes in attitudes toward the handicapped as a result of their experiences as an advocate. While some advocates' attitudes remained the same, none reported more negative attitudes as a function of their advocacy experience. The overwhelming majority of advocates expressed the opinion that the citizen advocacy program was beneficial to the protégés, describing positive changes in the daily behavior of their protégés. Finally, it was found that the reasons cited by the advocates for recruiting other advocates were the same as the reasons they gave for becoming advocates themselves. This suggested an overall satisfaction of their experiences as an advocate.

Although this investigation was only a preliminary attempt to gain some insights into the nature of advocates' perceptions of the citizen advocacy program, and it did not actually observe the interactions between the advocates and the protégé in order to validate the advocates' verbal responses to our questions, it appears that both the advocates and the protégés benefited from their experiences.

It should be considered, however, that the present sample of subjects may be somewhat biased in that they represented only one-half of the advocates who were asked to participate in this investigation. The respondents may have been those who generally were supportive of the citizen advocacy program and experience. We do not know whether similar results would have been obtained had a larger number of advocates participated. Furthermore, there is the additional potential problem of a response set bias operating in this study. Since all respondents completed the questionnaire at their leisure, it is conceivable that they made deliberate attempts to provide internally consistent responses to the questions, rather than provide their "true" feelings.

Finally, our data suggest that the benefits that appear to derive from the citizen advocacy program are the result of the expressive functions that the advocates perform, as opposed to the instrumental functions. One of the clearer findings was that the advocates appeared to feel more comfortable in expressive functions rather than in assisting the protégés in the practical aspects of daily living. If there is any one good way to illustrate this expressive function, it is in the words of one advocate who, when describing his experiences, said:

> I think the pinnacle is just to see the protégé's face. He just smiles so much. When we go out together and just drive in the car, I'll tell him to look at something and he gets so excited. He doesn't speak, but just to see him facially communicate and smile and hug me. That, I think, is really the most exhilarating part of the citizen advocacy program.

This is close to Wolfensberger's (1973) sentiments when he wrote: "At a certain point, a person needs a friend and not a law, and no law can create, nor any amount of money buy the freely-given dedication of one person to the welfare of another" (p. 10).

DIRECTIONS FOR FURTHER RESEARCH

The importance of the citizen advocacy concept and the lack of research regarding its viability call for investigations to facilitate its optimal implementation on behalf of handicapped citizens. The Florida study suggests a number of questions that merit examination. These may be grouped into clusters concerning advocates, protégés, and the nature of their interaction.

Research Concerning Advocates

An initial question concerns whether or not volunteers can effectively meet the varied needs of handicapped persons. Specifically, how much training do volunteer citizen advocates require to be effective, what form should the training take, and who should do the training? It may be that despite Wolfensberger's belief that only volunteers can fulfill the advocacy role, the needs of the handicapped in the community may be so complex that professionals are needed to fulfill them. The extent of training that would be required might be so great as to be prohibitive, and it could be that highly sophisticated trainers are needed in terms of experience and instructional skills. These concerns must, however, be considered in the realization that advocates are not expected to fully meet all needs of their protégés, but to supplement the efforts of professionals, and, furthermore, that advocates are encouraged to consult with their citizen advocacy office as problems arise that are beyond their capabilities.

Specific questions occur regarding the ability of citizen advocates to change negative attitudes held by some community members toward their protégé, particularly attitudes of older persons and children, to improve weak aspects of their protégé that they perceive, and to procure apparent needed services for their protégé. Effective training procedures for advocates in these regards need to be formulated, designed, and implemented.

What are the most important characteristics of an advocate? Relevant characteristics appear to include level of education, occupation, personal attributes, and motivation for being an advocate. Research efforts should be directed toward identifying the optimal advocate profile.

Finally, once this profile is identified, ways to recruit and retain such advocates must be developed. In the special case of college students, we need to determine whether they have the experiential maturity to be successful advocates, and if so, how do we get them to remain as advocates beyond the confines of their college course.

Research Concerning Protégés

The present study was primarily directed to understanding the citizen advocacy experience as it impacts on the advocate. What about the effects of this experience on the protégé? Our results indirectly suggested positive outcomes for the protégé. These results need to be substantiated and differentiated directly. Interviews with protégés, and observation and ratings of their behavior should be used to study the effects of the citizen advocacy program on its clients in such areas as academic and vocational skills, emotional growth, and interpersonal abilities. For example, do protégés achieve more material success in the community, foster a more positive self-concept, or make more friends as an effect of their interaction with an advocate?

Research Concerning Advocate-Protégé Interaction

Our results indicate that the primary quality of the advocate-protégé relationship is an expressive one. Is this desirable? If so, how can we improve its structure? If not, what type of relationship should be encouraged and supported?

Regardless of the exact nature of its relationship, what of its parameters? How long should the advocate-protégé match last if the desired effects are to occur for both participants, and how should termination be effected? How intense should it be (i.e., how frequently should advocates and protégés interact?). How do we establish the best pairings of the advocate and the protégé based on characteristics of each? Finally, it is more beneficial for a protégé to experience a deep, extended relationship with a single advocate, or to be exposed to the varied aspects of several advocates for shorter periods of time.

Answers to these and other related questions are vital if the spirit of Wolfensberger's concept of citizen advocacy is to prevail and flourish.

REFERENCES

Dade County Association for Retarded Citizens. *The citizen advocate handbook*. Miami: Author, undated.

Edgerton, R. *The cloak of competence.* Berkeley: University of California Press, 1967.

Edgerton, R. B., & Bercovici, S. M. The cloak of competence: Years later. *American Journal of Mental Deficiency,* 1976, *80,* 485–497.

Florida Association for Retarded Citizens. *Citizen Advocacy Manual* (Rev. ed.). Tallahassee: Author, 1976.

Jennings, P. *An evaluation of the Austin, Texas citizen advocacy program.* Austin: The University of Texas at Austin, Center for Social Work Research, undated.

Kurtz, R. A. Advocacy for the mentally retarded: The development of a new social role. In M. J. Begab & S. A. Richardson (Eds.), *The mentally retarded and society: A social science perspective.* Baltimore: University Park Press, 1975.

Mallory, B. The ombudsman in a residential institution: A description of the role and suggested training areas. *Mental Retardation,* 1977, 15–17.

McGlamery, J., & Malavenda, R. *Memo to Florida ARC Citizen Advocacy Steering Council,* March 25, 1977.

National Association for Retarded Citizens. *Characteristics of citizen advocacy programs in the United States.* Arlington, Texas: Author, undated.

Turner, R. H. *Social context of ambition: A study of high school seniors in Los Angeles.* San Francisco: Chandler Publishing, 1964.

Wolfensberger, W. Citizen advocacy for the handicapped, impaired and disadvantaged: An overview. In Wolfensberger, W. (Ed.), *Citizen advocacy and protective services for the impaired and handicapped.* Toronto: National Institute of Mental Retardation, 1973.

IV

Classroom Applications

CHAPTER 10

Using Research Findings for Classroom Programming

Edward L. Meyen and Warren J. White

> We are challenged daily to provide the handicapped children in our charge with the best education possible. To achieve this goal, we need both skill in teaching and knowledge upon which to base our efforts. The knowledge that we need is frequently obtained through the process of research (Prehm & Altman, 1976, p. 5).
>
> I have, for some time, been of the belief that the procedures and materials, indeed most of the practices of special education classes, should to a great extent, be supported by research. Unlike many of my opinions, I have almost universal support on this point (Lovitt, 1978, p. 5).
>
> It has often been asserted that a 50 year gap exists between knowledge gained in basic research laboratories and application of that knowledge to problems which exist in classrooms (Whelan & Haring, 1966, p. 281).

If the methodologies employed by teachers should be supported by research, and if the research literature represents a resource to teachers in resolving instructional problems, then why do so many teachers view research as being of little value; something carried out primarily by researchers on esoteric topics? It has been the experience of the authors that teachers often equate research with theory and, when possible, avoid participation in structured research. Teachers are also reluctant to develop their own research skills. Even a casual review of educational research reports and journal articles would support the perceptions of teachers. The dilemma increases in significance for teachers of the mentally retarded. Their students present more complex instructional problems and less is known about their learning characteristics. At the same time, there is a growing concern on the part of parents and the public in general for accountability in the education of the handicapped.

This chapter is based on the premise that research is integral to sound instructional planning and that instructional planning is basic to quality education for the mentally retarded. Teachers, as well as researchers, share in the responsibility for making research results applicable to instructional decision making. Inherent in these premises is a concern for research and instructional planning as separate but interrelated processes. Prehm and Altman (1976) define research as the process of asking questions and obtaining answers to those questions using objective, repeatable, and systematic procedures. This definition provides a meaningful frame of reference for the teacher. It suggests a focus on the formulation of questions, but it does not infer a restrictiveness on the type of questions researched. It does, however, emphasize the importance of asking "good" questions and knowing how to translate observations into researchable questions. The reference to "objective, repeatable, and systematic procedures" makes the definition by necessity restrictive. While intuition, trial and error, and personal bias may serve to resolve some problems, they are not research strategies. Unfortunately, they are often resorted to under the guise of problem solving. Instructional planning, on the other hand, is a process which makes use of research results or at least the results of good questioning procedures. Meyen (1978) has specified the following goals for instructional planning:

1. To make use of available information on learner characteristics and instructional options in planning specific teaching activities
2. To establish short-range objectives within a long-term plan that can be implemented as intended, often by persons other than the teacher responsible for the original planning
3. To allow for collecting evaluative evidence that illustrates the pupil's cumulative performance
4. To provide a base for instructional decisions regarding programs for individual pupils (pp. 113-114)

The teacher skills required in effective instructional planning are highly compatible with those of the researcher. If teachers are to utilize research results and data derived from research behaviors in making instructional decisions, they need to gain access to the research literature and be able to differentiate information of practical value from theoretical or less appropriate information.

At least two major problems inhibit the effective utilization of research results in instructional planning by teachers. The first centers on the commitment of teachers to instructional planning. The second relates to the context in which research results are made available to consumers. Although logic would suggest that instructional planning would be a high priority for teachers and administrators responsible for educational programs serving the mentally retarded, experience reveals that such has not been the case. Planning obviously has occurred, but formalized and systematic planning procedures have been the exception rather than the rule. A major reason for this has been the failure of administrators to provide teachers sufficient time for planning. A contributing problem has been the complacency of many administrators in accepting general daily lesson plans as evidence of instructional planning. The individualized education program (IEP) requirement of PL 94-142 has dramatically altered the emphasis placed on instructional planning for the handicapped. The mandate specifies that IEPs be developed on all handicapped children and details the manner in which the IEPs are to be developed and the information that is to be included. School districts are currently engaged in implementing instructional planning procedures to comply with the IEP requirements. Implementation has taken two forms, i.e., the design of planning systems and the provision of inservice training to assist teachers in developing their planning skills. Thus, this domain of the problem may be resolved in the future. Consumer access to the research element of the problem continues with no primary solution in sight. Access to research by consumers is complicated primarily by the traditions, motives, and reinforcers that operate to influence the way in which research is reported. Researchers tend to write to other researchers. It is reasonably safe to say that few researchers have the teacher in mind when they prepare manuscripts based on the results of their research. They are more inclined to be sensitive to the expectations of other researchers and the review criteria set by editors of professional journals. While such an approach enhances communication among researchers, it accomplishes little in terms of the dissemination of research to practitioners. A by-product of the reporting behavior of researchers is that most research results are published in journals and sources not routinely read or subscribed to by teachers. Although this is consistent with the underlying motives of researchers, it does not enhance the utilization of research results by teachers. Progress is being made by funding agencies in redirecting the dissemination efforts of researchers. Some professional organizations have responded to this issue by initiating new journals that provide avenues for reporting to consumers with more applied interests. A recent example is the organization Phi Delta Kappa, which has recently initiated a new publication called *Practical Application of Research (PAR)*.

There is a trend toward making researchers and the publishers of research results more responsive to the needs of practitioners. While this response needs to be encouraged, the body of existing literature accumulated over many years will remain in a state that is not easily tapped by teachers and other consumers. Altering the situation will require a change on the part of teachers. Instead of blaming researchers for ineptness in reporting, teachers need to recognize the realities of the situation and develop skills allowing them to at least efficiently search the literature and glean usable information. It is unreasonable to assume that the existing body of research will at some time be transformed into easily readable and well organized information or that someone, through computer technology, will summarize existing research. If teachers are to expand the resource of research, they will need to individually assume some responsibility.

INSTRUCTIONAL PLANNING GUIDELINES

Although the emphasis of this chapter is not on instructional planning techniques, efficiency in the use of research results by classroom teachers necessitates that they be skilled in the process of planning. Most teachers by virtue of having to communicate with parents, principals, and fellow teachers adopt some form of instructional planning. Too often the lack of time for planning results in their strategies being sufficient for communication purposes but insufficient as an approach to effecting change in pupil behavior.

The individualized education program (IEP) requirement of PL 94-142 is having a dramatic impact on the attention given to instructional planning and on the value placed on planning by administrators. Because the IEP represents a primary source of evidence of the services provided by the schools to a handicapped child and a basis for assessing the student's performance, it is essential that teachers and administrators be skilled in instructional planning and that they make use of related instructional research. This presents the additional problem of accessing the literature and being able to incorporate research results into instructional planning.

Space does not permit a detailed discussion of instructional planning. However, instructional planning is the primary context in which research results are used. From this perspective, teachers are encouraged to refine their planning skills as a prerequisite to expanding their efforts in the use of research results. Effective instructional planning helps the teacher identify situations in which research results are applicable and enhances the use of research results.

The following suggestions by Meyen (1978) represent general guidelines for instructional planning. They are not rules, but they have been derived from observing teachers engaged in successful instructional planning.

Systematizaton The purpose of instructional planning is to assure that instructional decisions about a student's program consider all information pertaining to the learner's needs. This requires systematic planning. The relative severity of learning problems exhibited by exceptional children dictates further that planning be continuous and not occur only when the child's problem is interfering with instruction.

Detail No plan can describe all of the skills, concepts, and information that a child will or should be taught. Even if this were possible, it would not be desirable. Learners vary in their responses to tasks, and the risk is present that a teacher may adhere to a detailed plan when evidence shows that the plan should be altered to meet the child's changing needs. Planning must allow for "on the spot" decision making.

On the other hand, sufficient planning time on the part of the teacher is important to success of the plan. Decisions must be made on how detailed a plan should be regarding skills, activities, and materials. The more serious the learner's problem, the more precise the planning required. Another major consideration pertains to whether or not persons other than the teacher will be involved in carrying out the plan. The plan should contain sufficient information to assure appropriate interpretation and implementation.

Format The content and provisions for remediation, not the plan's organizational format, determine its appropriateness for a particular student. The organization and recording format of instructional plans, however, do influence how well planning efforts succeed. An organized plan simplifies the matching of instructional options to learner characteristics.

To ensure uniformity, districts often adopt or design a particular planning system. Some advantages accrue in having all teachers use a similar format: A uniform approach simplifies the administrator's role in evaluating the effectiveness of teacher planning; and uniformity in format enhances communication among teachers. In most cases, forms are designed to make planning more convenient and to reduce the amount of time involved.

Program Emphasis In developing instructional plans, teachers have a tendency to refer only to the child's most immediate problems. Certainly, more specific planning is required to remediate obvious serious learning problems, but a program or curriculum emphasis also must be maintained. For example, a visually impaired child who is skilled in math may be experiencing difficulty in social studies because of slowness in reading by the braille method. Planning attention must be given to the student's needs in mathematics and other subjects, even though more short-term planning may be involved in developing the student's braille reading speed and alternatives for acquiring experiences in social studies.

Intensiveness Once a teacher has developed a program in which a child progresses satisfactorily, the time and effort (intensity) allocated to planning can be reduced. This does not mean that the teacher stops recording plans, collecting performance data, or conferring with other teachers. It means that less detailed planning is required and more planning time can be devoted to students for whom a satisfactory plan has not yet been developed.

Because of the amount of time required in effective instructional planning, the teacher must make judgments regarding how much time to devote to planning for each student. If evidence suggests that a student is progressing satisfactorily, planning becomes less formal and the emphasis shifts to program monitoring.

Evaluation Unless planning includes the evaluation of short- and long-term objectives, the benefits will be minimal. Because specific evaluation tasks are sometimes difficult to design and not generally available in commercial form, some teachers tend to resort to available achievement measures or other standardized tests. Although standardized tests have certain advantages, they generally are not appropriate for measuring student performance on specific tasks included in routine instructional plans.

Teachers need to carefully determine when standardized measures are appropriate and when they need to consider other options. Teachers must evaluate their instructional planning, but they must use evaluation measures that relate directly to the student's instructional program. This generally results in teachers' having to design at least part of their evaluation tasks. When incorporating evaluation tasks into instructional planning, attention must be given to the relationship of the evaluation task to the instructional activity, the time required for the teacher to design the task, the time required by the student to demonstrate task performance, and the value of the information derived in this process.

Procedures In deciding upon instructional planning procedures, two primary factors must be considered—the impact of instructional planning on student programming, and the demands which the planning process places on teachers. The previously outlined guidelines (systematization, detail, format, program emphasis, intensiveness, and evaluation) combine to influence programming for students. But they also create time demands on teachers. If the procedures are too complex and time consuming, the teacher may not be able to plan and teach effectively. If the plan is too simple, little is gained in terms of pupil benefits.

The initial goal is to design procedures that allow for efficiency on the part of the teacher and enhance instructional decision making specific to student's needs. The ultimate goal is to employ planning procedures which result in benefits for the learner.

Teachers should assume leadership in developing planning procedures. Administrative concerns do not always contribute to teacher efficiency or pupil benefit, and administrators often answer general program questions by expanding instructional planning requirements. If program questions can be answered by an instructional planning process that does not add substantially to the teacher's workload, that process should be considered. The primary emphasis, however, should be on instructional planning for specific students, and the emphasis must be on developing *workable* planning procedures. (pp. 115-118)

RESEARCH AND INSTRUCTIONAL PLANNING

It could be argued that the use of research findings should be an explicit step in any planning process. It has already been stated that the learning problems of mentally retarded children and youth complicate the instructional decision making of teachers and add to the scope and difficulty of their teaching mission. If this is true then the reader may question the lack of detailed emphasis on using research results in instructional planning. In the previous discussion on instructional planning guidelines no reference was made to research. The reason relates to the authors' perspective that the use of research results is an inherent behavior of good teaching and, as such, is not restricted to the process of instructional planning. Teachers should approach their teaching, i.e., instructional decision making, in much the same manner that a good researcher approaches the design and conduction of a research study. For example, teachers should be able to:

1. Determine the problem
2. Identify the variables involved
3. Design an intervention
4. Structure procedures for measuring effects
5. Implement the intervention
6. Assess the effects
7. Determine the consequences of effects

In the process of working through these phases, a researcher must become familiar with the findings of other researchers concerned with the same and/or similar problems. Information that is learned from the works of others may influence the researcher, and in some cases result in a decision not to carry out the study. The researcher's knowledge must go beyond the understanding of the problem and the familiarity with appropriate design and analysis techniques. The researcher must be efficient in drawing on the works of others to avoid researching problems already solved or perpetuating errors in design or analysis that others have already corrected or found to be unresolvable. The teacher's situation is highly similar. He/she, too, must draw on the works of others. It is not only inefficient but somewhat naive to approach each new teaching task on the assumption that you are the first to encounter the problem or that you can independently solve it. Teachers must, as a part of their teaching routine, be able to examine an instructional situation, to determine the nature of the problem, to recall sources of information, and to employ behaviors that will result in viewing the problem pragmatically.

In many ways the use of research results is an attitudinal form of a teaching strategy. The teacher must be conscious of the learner's performance and response to techniques, materials, and situations. When the learner's behavior suggests an instructional need, the teacher must be sensitive and, as part of his/her response, intuitively begin to deal with the problem in a methodical manner. While these instructional decisions cannot be treated as a separate case study or research problem, the process the teacher applies can approach a logic similar to that of the researcher. For example, the teacher can:

1. Describe the learner's problem
2. Determine the factors that are contributing to the learner's problem
3. Apply techniques that the teacher has found successful in similar situations
4. Gain access to sources of assistance and information, e.g., consultants, materials, and colleagues
5. Structure a plan based on information that he/she understands
6. Establish baseline data on the student's performance in the problem area
7. Implement a program
8. Monitor effects of the program
9. Make decisions as to whether or not additional resources are necessary in order to enhance the learner's performance in the problem area.

Unless a teacher integrates into his/her teaching style an informal but methodical way of approaching the resolution of instructional problems, it is highly probable that existing options will not be considered and that the learner will be subjected to the effects of trial-and-error teaching. Even the teacher who is adept at analyzing instructional problems and is familiar with resources will not be consistently successful in solving the problems presented by learners. Having approached a problem in this manner the teacher has made use of available resources and will be in a better position to use resource people. The use of resource people requires a more refined description of the problem and of the responses of the learner to instruction.

Merely employing a logic analogous to that of a researcher is not sufficient as a teaching strategy. The teacher must also have in his/her repertoire of teaching skills and techniques a knowledge of research findings as well as information on sources that can be utilized as a means of gaining access to research results. A teacher who has invested in developing a base of information on research applicable to teaching will be more successful in employing the logic previously described primarily because he/she will have more options to draw on in attempting to resolve specific instructional problems. While a person could formalize a teaching strategy to the point of specifying discrete steps that a teacher might carry out in attempting to resolve an instructional problem presented by a student, it is not feasible to present such a formal approach for assisting teachers in expanding their knowledge of research. Teachers have a basic responsibility to gain access to research information applicable to their particular teaching situation. This view is offered in spite of the realization that the odds are not in favor of a teacher easily gaining access to research information. Certainly there are a number of factors complicating the teacher's study and understanding of the research literature. However, these circumstances have existed for some time and the teacher cannot assume that they are going to be corrected in the near future. The reality is that there is a wealth of research information available to teachers and that it is incumbent upon teachers to pursue existing avenues. At the same time, researchers and members of the education profession generally must address the question of how research results can be made more accessible to classroom teachers. Teachers who do not invest in reading the education research literature, as well as in studying instructional and curriculum materials specific to their area of teaching responsibility, are restricting themselves in terms of the instructional options available to them. This has the effect of lessening their impact on the performance of the learners for whom they are responsible.

Teachers routinely make instructional decisions by applying techniques and using materials that are products of research without knowing the research basis. They may merely consider their action as "using good common sense" or they may credit a methods course or professor with the useful idea. Whether it is important that a teacher know the source of a method or technique as a condition of using it is questionable. The critical concern is that teachers employ effective teaching techniques in appropriate situations. This necessitates having access to educational research results and the ability to understand the implications of the results. Such a statement is easy to write, but accomplishes little. The authors are aware of this but feel that it warrants inclusion in any discussion on the use of research results in program planning. Certain realities exist that will not change during the careers of most teachers presently in the field. For example, the research literature specific to the education of mentally retarded children currently existing today will still represent the primary source of research information 30 years from now. The format in which the research literature is couched is not likely to change substantially in spite of new and emerging technologies. Granted, research results may be abstracted, may become available upon demand through computerized retrieval systems, and may be correlated with materials, but observation of the student's instructional problem, description of the problem, and understanding of the information provided will remain the personal responsibility of the teacher.

The educational enterprise is obviously wrought with problems in the transformation of research results into instructional practices. The problem has many facets, each of which is identifiable. It is possible to relate elements of the problems to various members of the education profession. Having done this, it remains clear that teachers constitute the bottom line in terms of whether or not the results of educational research impact on the performance of children. Unless the teacher is motivated to use available resources, the efficiency of retrieval systems is of little consequence.

Although it is not reasonable to expect teachers to be self-sufficient in the application of research results to their teaching and instructional planning, teachers can develop considerable proficiency in gaining access to research information specific to their teaching interests. They can also become skilled in deriving usable information from the reading of research reports. Suggestions for the reading and analysis of research reports are presented in the next section. Familiarity with sources of educational research is of little value if the ability to use the information efficiently is lacking.

READING RESEARCH REPORTS FOR PRACTICAL VALUE

The more a person knows about a subject, the easier it is to read research in the area. If a teacher is highly knowledgeable on a particular topic, then he/she will probably not feel a need to devote time to study and research in the area. More emphasis will likely be given to those areas in which teachers are less knowledgeable and, in turn, less equipped to solve problems presented by their students. In the reading of reports on educational research there are generic content and skill areas in which a teacher needs to be proficient in order to glean information that will be of practical value in instructional planning. These content and skill areas may not be directly related to the information being sought on a particular instructional problem, but unless teachers are proficient in these areas they will not be efficient in reading research reports or even reasonably accurate in interpreting the results that they do read.

Teachers are often reluctant to read research articles and reports because they lack a background in statistical analysis. Certainly, individuals who are sophisticated in statistical analysis and research design will find the study of research manuscripts easier. The lack of such background, however, does not preclude a person from gaining usable information from research reports. If an understanding of statistics and specific terms is necessary in studying a report, interpretation can be obtained from a person with appropriate skills. A researcher who is concerned with communicating results to consumers of educational practices will attempt to report results in a manner that is straightforward and not complicated by the use of statistical terminology. The important consideration for the teacher is to know how to locate the studies appropriate to his/her interest and then to derive from the report information that is of practical and usable value. Many research reports do not hold value for the classroom teacher. This does not mean that they are poor studies or ineffectively reported. It may be that they are intended for other audiences and are concerned with theoretical issues that are not instructional research problems. Too often, studies are unfairly criticized by practitioners because they are perceived by the reviewer as impractical when they were not designed to be practical. Instead, the studies were addressing theoretical problems. On the other hand, some researchers do study practical problems but overdignify their results by unnecessarily resorting to statistical terms in reporting. In the process the significance of their research is lost and the results have little impact.

When one buys a book at the airport newsstand there is a set of expectations that operate. The selection may result from the recommendation of a friend or from familiarity with reviews on the book. On the other hand, a book may be selected merely because the person is seeking something to read for purposes of relaxation and the book jacket offers an appealing description. The goal may not be related to acquiring information, but an expectation of pleasurable reading prevails. While the reader brings to this reading experience certain expectations, the responsibility for holding the reader's interest is shared by the author. If the book proves to be dull or if the plot is vague and the reader loses interest, the consequences are not necessarily great. The reader may begrudge the time spent in determining his/her lack of interest in the book. In this situation the question of who is responsible for the book not meeting the reader's expectations is shared between the reader who made an inappropriate selection, the author who failed to provide appealing reading material, and possibly the publisher who misrepresented the story. The next time a book is selected at the newsstand the person will likely take more care in the selection process.

In selecting educational research reports to study, the teacher is in a somewhat different situation. First of all, the selection process can be greatly improved and second, the reader can rather quickly determine if the content meets expectations. The report need not be read in its entirety in order to decide whether or not it is addressing a problem of interest.

The difference is that the consequence of devoting time to a poor research report is generally greater than having spent the time reading a bad novel. The reason being that research reports are generally read for the purpose of gaining information to solve a problem and the time devoted to reading research is often minimal, and therefore expensive.

In working with teachers in inservice training and graduate courses it has become apparent that the person who appears to gain the most from reading research is a person who knows what he/she is looking for, and not necessarily the person who is most sophisticated in research skills nor the best scholar. The following suggestions are the result of these observations. They do not constitute a recipe, but they have been found to be helpful and are offered in that context.

Know the Reason for Going to the Research Literature

Considerable time is often wasted in the research review process because the reviewer has not taken time to clarify what he/she is looking for. The scope of research studies in education dictates that an investment be made in defining the information sought. Most research reviews, abstracts, and retrieval systems are organized around topics and descriptors. This is done to assist the reviewer in locating desired information. However, the efficiency of the reviewer in using the sources is greatly dependent on their knowledge of the problem being researched. Merely knowing that you are interested in the reading problems of the mildly mentally retarded is not sufficient. In general, teachers develop interests in research data from their experiences, i.e., working with students having specific learning problems which the teacher is unable to resolve with available resources, and observing patterns of performance of several students over a period of time. For example, a teacher may note that students with poor reading comprehension also experience problems with math reasoning tasks. Or the teacher might learn of a new instructional material that employs an unfamiliar technique. Before investing in the material, it would be valuable to know more about the technique. Attention to the following questions is helpful in clarifying a person's reasons for examining the research literature.

1. What is the nature of the instructional problem for which assistance is sought? Be as specific as possible.
2. What are the characteristics of the students for whom the instructional problem applies? Do not expect to locate studies that match exactly the students of concern to you. But knowing the characteristics of your students allows you to make judgments about how closely the subjects of a particular study approximate your target group. It also helps you eliminate studies from your review process.

3. Under what circumstances does the instructional problem of interest occur? In some respects this is an expansion of question 2. Because the delivery models for educating mentally retarded and youth vary, it is not uncommon to find a research study designed to investigate specific techniques in different settings, such as special classes, regular classes, tutorial arrangements, and peer teaching models. Thus, it is important to have in mind the circumstances of interest to you.

This discussion on refining reasons for looking at research literature is not intended to suggest that the results of studies not specific to your interest might not generalize to your problem. This might occur. But the closer the study approximates the problem, the population, and the circumstances of interest, the higher the probability of usable information being located and, in turn, saving time.

Know What Information Is of Practical Value

Obviously what is of most value to a reader depends on the nature of the problem he/she is attempting to solve. However, for the practitioner concerned with instructional problems there are some general guidelines that are helpful.

1. Look for descriptive information on the instructional materials used in the investigation. If the materials were designed by the researcher they would be considered experimental and probably are not available for use. Thus, even if highly successful, they are not of use to you unless you can acquire them. If the materials used are experimental and not available, look for directions or specifications on how to develop them for your own use.
2. Research results are often reported by "level of confidence or significance." For example, a result that is significant at the 0.01 level means that the differences in scores (behavior, time, etc.) observed in the study are likely to occur 99% of the time when the research design is repeated. For your purpose as a teacher this level of prediction may not be important. If you locate a study that is of interest to you, but the results are reported as being rejected, consult someone with expertise in statistics. It may be that the results were negative for purposes of the researcher, but for your purpose the results may be sufficient. The important goal is to locate research that relates to your specific interest and then determine the implication of the design results for your purposes.
3. Most research reports, whether they are monographs, final reports, or journal articles, provide a literature review. The review covers a variety of topics related to the research. Some elements of the review

will not be of practical value. However, if similar studies have been conducted they should be cited in the review. Thus, you will be able to locate additional resources by examining this section of the report.
4. Frequently a researcher will discuss his/her rationale for pursuing the study. Such information may serve as a good check for the teacher (reader). It may be that the teacher's concerns will be answered through the general comments of the researcher.
5. Look for recommendations on needed research and replication. Some researchers are very explicit in discussing the implications of the research. Generally, this discussion is in nontechnical language and can be highly useful for the teacher.
6. In reading a research report don't limit yourself to the design and results. Look for specific examples, techniques, and/or procedures that are applicable to your interest and that may be helpful to you in your own situation. Too often a reader is only concerned with the design details of the study. If a teacher is reading a study for information to help resolve an instructional problem, then his/her purpose for reading the report is different from a researcher who is reviewing the work of another researcher. The teacher is seeking information and need not be concerned only with the rigor of the research study. Learn to skim for useful information.

Know What to Expect from Research Literature Sources

Several types of sources provide access to the research literature. Each is somewhat unique in the amount and type of information provided. Depending on your purpose in seeking information, a particular source will be more appropriate than others. Following is a brief description of sources most commonly used.

Abstract Abstracts include a brief description of the study, the objective, and the population and may cite the basic findings. Generally limited to approximately 100 words, abstracts often precede published articles or teachers reports. Abstracting services publish collections of abstracts systematically organized to assist reviewers wanting merely to identify research in a particular area.

Research Reviews Agencies, individual scholars, and/or research institutions often publish extensive research reviews on topical areas. The reviews generally attempt to summarize the "state of the art" on specific topics. An advantage of most research reviews is that they synthesize research findings and often compare the design and results of studies. Frequently they provide direction on needed research.

Monographs Monographs vary from documents similar to research reviews to comprehensive reports on individual studies. The typical monograph contains a comprehensive discussion on a single study or programmatic research combined with a review of related research. They tend to be highly substantive and probably represent the most complete research source. However, monographs are generally written for a particular purpose and, because they are demanding to produce, are not available on many topics. It has been the authors' experience that most monographs do not address practical applied research topics. Instead they tend to focus on topics of interest to researchers engaged in programmatic research of a more theoretical nature.

Final Reports Most funding agencies require that comprehensive reports to be filed at the completion of research studies. Final reports contain detailed information on the project's design, inclusive of specific information on procedures, analysis, and results. Most reports include copies of instruments and forms used in the study. Final reports are useful, particularly if they relate to your area of interest. The major problem is they are not widely disseminated. However, many are retrievable by systems such as ERIC and therefore can be identified by requesting a search. Researchers frequently publish journal articles and in the article refer to the final report. This is an additional avenue through which final reports may be located. The primary value of the final report versus a journal article on the same study relates to the detailed attention to procedures and the examples of forms and instruments generally included.

Journal Articles Professional journals are probably the most frequently used source of research literature. Journals represent the primary vehicle through which research is disseminated. Most disciplines have several journals in which research findings are reported. To a certain extent quality control measures are applied; each manuscript submitted is reviewed and only a small percent are actually published. Journals also have standards that must be met by the author. An advantage of journal articles over final reports and monographs is the length of the article. In most journals the range is from four to eight pages. The author is forced to be brief but complete. Journals also tend to be organized in a standard format, making it easier for the reader to determine the appropriateness of the article. The typical format for a journal article includes such headings as Introduction, Method, Results, and Discussion.

Publisher's Research Reports A major interest of teachers relates to research done on commonly available instructional products. Some publishers include research summaries in their promotional materials and others cite research references. Too many, however, do not report research data on their products. If research references are not included with the promotional information or mentioned in the instructor's guides, teachers are encouraged to contact the publishers. They may or may not have studies available. It has been the authors' experience that the publishers of the curricular products are able to refer you to the developers, who, in turn, are able to provide at least formative evaluation reports or summaries.

A note of caution that warrants consideration when reviewing research literature pertains to the timeliness of the reports. Journal articles are often published 2 years after they are submitted. Final reports are generally due 6 months after completion of the study and may not appear in retrieval systems or indices for another year. Monographs and reviews depend on research studies being available through journals, etc. Thus, monographs and reviews typically report on "studies" that are at least 3 years old. Reviewers need to recognize that access to current research literature is limited. The best avenue is to identify people or centers doing research in your area of interest and request that your name be placed on their mailing list. Prepublished reports are often distributed among individuals with similar interests.

Know How You Will Use the Information You May Locate

Too often a person reads a research study about a problem of interest and rejects the implications of the findings without giving serious consideration to validating the intervention or treatment through trial. In some cases the reader has sufficient information to make such a decision. In other situations, rejection of the findings as an alternative worth trying is a result of the reader not intending to use techniques or methods reported in the literature regardless of how promising they may be. Again, the authors are suggesting that the attitude of the reader, i.e., teacher or other, searching for answers to instructional problems through the research literature is of prime importance. The odds are against finding an answer to a specific problem, but if one knows what he/she is searching for and is willing to invest some effort in modification of strategies and/or program materials, the probabilities of finding helpful direction are increased. Certainly, the more information the reader has related to the problem area the more efficient he/she will be in finding usable information. But a person can gain substantially from approaching the reading of a research report with an open and receptive attitude. This does not mean that everything one reads should be believed and assumed to be applicable to resolving the problem, but only through looking at an idea or suggested technique from several perspectives can one determine the possible applications. In many cases, a reader designs a variation of a technique that was not suggested in the report by merely testing the idea out in his/her mind and applying a little brainstorming. Coupled with an open and inquisitive attitude should be an expectancy to do something. The reason for reviewing the literature is to seek answers and/or alternatives. Thus, part of the suggested "attitude" should be a commitment to try new approaches. This also means that the teacher must begin his/her search for assistance once the need for assistance has been substantiated. Otherwise, students may be subjected to teaching strategies that only partially solve the problem. Or students may learn to minimally cope with the deficiency, which lessens the need and reduces the usability of the instructional problem. Once this occurs, it is too late to make use of research implications, which earlier in the teaching process would have been helpful.

APPLYING RESEARCH FINDINGS

In order to put the preceding comments in perspective, several examples of using research literature might be helpful.

Helping Students Deal with Failing on the Job

One common problem in using research results in the classroom is finding research relevant to the problem at hand. Consider Ms. A., a work-study teacher. Although Ms. A. has several years of experience in work-study programs and feels she does a good job training and placing students, she now has several students consistently failing at work experiences. In an attempt to find a way to help these students, Ms. A. has decided to consult the research literature.

As a first step Ms. A. must fairly specifically define her reasons for going to the literature. She should state the nature of the problem, the characteristics of the group, and the circumstances in which the problem occurs. In this case, the problem is students failing on jobs. The group she is interested in is the secondary age mentally retarded, and the circumstances are work experiences. Thus, Ms. A.'s reason for going to the literature is "to find ways to help secondary age educable mentally retarded students who are not successful in work experiences." Because abstracting sources use the key words in article titles to organize studies by focus, Ms. A. should also list synonyms and terms related to the key words in her interest area. Her final statement of interest is "to find ways (techniques, methods) to help secondary age (adolescent) EMR students who are not successful in work experiences (vocations, habilitation)."

With the focus of interest area narrowed, Ms. A. encounters a problem common to persons looking for specific types of research studies: getting started!

The most straightforward way to begin looking at the research literature is to find a current abstracting source (*Education Index, Psychological Abstracts,* etc.) and start working back through the issues. This is, however, time-consuming. Another solution is to locate an article reviewing the literature relative to the vocational experiences of the mentally retarded. Typically, reviews of the literature report not only significant studies directly related to the topical area, but also studies in related areas. A review should give Ms. A. several leads to additional studies and will probably also give her a good overview of other types of research she might be interested in. Another tactic Ms. A. could use is to attempt to find one or two researchers identified with research on the vocational experiences of the retarded. Following their work should not only yield valuable information, but the bibliographies of the articles should provide further references. If Ms. A. can find a recent article dealing with her area of interest, she could also check its bibliography for additional references.

After using several of these techniques to locate articles, Ms. A. found the following study (abstracted by the authors).

> Chaffin, J. D. Production rate as a variable in the job success or failure of educable mentally retarded adolescents. *Exceptional Children,* 1969, *35* (7), 533–538.
>
> *Description:* Chaffin paired secondary-age retarded subjects who have been judged as "probably successful" or "probably unsuccessful" on their next job assignment on the basis of the number of previous work assignments, IQ scores, and chronological age. Each pair was assigned to a work placement in the community and their employers were asked to judge the students as successful or unsuccessful following 2 weeks of work. Each pair worked at the same job with the same supervisor in the same work environment. Production records were kept daily on each subject. Following the subject's last day of work, an interview was held with each employer and a work evaluation was completed. During the interview, the employer was asked if he would hire this student as he would the average applicant, provided the job was available. If the employer responded affirmatively, the student was judged to be successful.
>
> A second stage to this experiment examined the effects on employer attitudes of modifying production rates of randomly selected subjects earlier identified as successful.
>
> *Findings:* The results of the first stage of the study indicated a definite positive relationship between the individual's production rate and the employer's judgment of job success or nonsuccess.
>
> Results of stage two indicated that modification of production rate influences employer's judgment of success. Subjects previously labeled unsuccessful by employers were judged successful when their production rate increased.

The sample of subjects used in the study closely corresponds to the students in Ms. A.'s class, i.e., secondary EMR students engaged in work experiences. Because of this the results of the study should have clear implications for her students. In the study Chaffin reports that a retarded worker's rate of production is important to his/her vocational success or failure. To Ms. A., this suggests that more attention may need to be directed toward the training aspects of work situations, i.e., clarifying exactly what is expected of the client in terms of job duties, production standards, and quality of work. Ms. A.'s students who consistently fail at jobs may simply not know what is expected of them. Ms. A. may be able to help the students succeed by meeting with the student and the employer to have the student's job duties and the employer's expectations clearly specified. The study also reports that if a student, judged by employers as unsuccesful, can improve his/her production rate, the employer's rating of the student may improve. By learning the student's specific job task from the employer and by setting up training for the student in the classroom, Ms. A. may be able to increase the student's production rate and his/her job rating.

Social Reasons Why Students Fail on Jobs

In the previous example, Ms. A. was able to solve the problem of her students failing on job experiences by simply increasing their production rates. This techniques does not appear to be relevant for students failing at their jobs, but who are rated as good workers by their employers. Consider the following research report (abstracted by the authors).

> Edmonson, B. T., Leland, H., & Leach, E. M. Social inference training of retarded adolescents at the pre-vocational level. Final report of VRA Project RD-1388-P. Kansas City: University of Kansas Medical Center, 1968.
>
> *Description:* The investigators in this study reasoned that the retardate's lack of social comprehension (i.e., the ability to perceive socially relevant cues in social situations while disregarding irrelevant and peripheral details) contributes to frequent behavioral deviance (and thus to vocational nonsuccess). In this large study the Test of Social Inference (TSI) was developed through a series of pilot trials involving small groups of retarded and nonretarded subjects.
>
> A social comprehension training curriculum was also developed as part of the project. The curriculum consisted of a series of lessons that illustrate adult settings important to the retardate's independent functioning.
>
> *Findings:* The correlations between TSI scores of public school and institutionalized EMR students and scales of social range, social relationships, peer acceptance, and attentiveness were significant at the 0.001 level. Data also indicated that TSI scores of nonretarded pupils exceeded those of retarded pupils; TSI scores of low IQ pupils tolerated within the regular class exceeded those of special class pupils; and that the TSI scores of retarded subjects in public school special class exceeded those of retardates whose behavioral nonadaption had lead to their institutional placement.

Significant gains in social comprehension were made by pupils using the social perceptual curriculum developed in the project.

For the work-study teacher these results are significant. The reasons some students fail on jobs are obvious, e.g., lack of proper work skills and poor or obnoxious social behavior. But for students with adequate work skills and no severe social behaviors the reasons are less obvious. This study suggests that a lack of the ability to perceive and react to relevant social cues in the environment may be a reason these students fail. The study also indicates that social comprehension is measurable and, to a large extent, remediable through training.

Teachers with students such as these may find it helpful to assess the student's responses to subtle social cues and, if necessary, implement a remediation program.

Encouraging Social Development Through Play

Ms. C., an early childhood teacher, has an integrated classroom of preschool handicapped and nonhandicapped children. In the classroom the children socialize and at times play together, but the amount and types of play are not consistent across play areas in the room. In order to develop programs to assist each child's social development, Ms. C. wanted to learn which play areas encourage interaction between children. After looking through several resources she found this article (abstracted by the authors):

> Haralick, J. G., & Peterson, N. L. Influence of social and physical setting on interactions among handicapped children in an integrated preschool. In *Kansas Research Institute for the Early Childhood Education of the Handicapped: Reviews of Literature,* OEO (USOE 300-77-0308). Lawrence: The University of Kansas, 1978.
>
> *Description:* This study examined the play interactions between handicapped and nonhandicapped children within the typical kinds of play areas found in preschool settings. Social interactions of five nonhandicapped children in an integrated classroom setting containing eight handicapped children were studied tracking their interactions in play areas containing 1) handicapped children only, 2) nonhandicapped children only, and 3) combinations of both handicapped and nonhandicapped children. Ages of the children ranged from 3 to 6 years. Play areas examined:
>
> Preacademic table play area (skill-oriented materials such as puzzles, pegboards, lotto, etc.)
> Art or creative play area (crayons, paints, clay, scissors, etc.)
> Manipulative floor play or block play area (wood construction blocks, toy trucks, etc.)
> Kitchen or playhouse area (housekeeping furniture, dolls, dishes, play clothes, etc.)
> Physical education or gross motor area (indoor ladder and slide, rocking board, rocking horse, etc.)

Free play area (books, flannel board, busy boxes, etc.)

Findings:
1. Manipulative floor play or block play area had the highest frequency of play by all children.
2. The frequencies with which handicapped or nonhandicapped played with each other and the type of play that occurred between them differed across areas. Combinations of children were most frequently observed in the manipulative floor play area and secondly in the kitchen area. The area which most frequently contained groups of handicapped children only was the table play area.
3. The greatest amount of overall cooperative play occurred in the block play area. The least occurred in the art play area. Except for the block play area, parallel and isolate play was the most frequently observed form of play across play areas and groups of children.
4. Play behavior between handicapped and nonhandicapped children did not differ in the table play area when nonhandicapped children played with handicapped peers or with other nonhandicapped peers. In the art play area, however, only nonhandicapped children play cooperatively.
5. More cooperative exchanges between handicapped and non-handicapped were observed in the physical education area than between groups of only nonhandicapped children (Peterson, 1978).

Although this study is well designed and written, and the results seem relevant to her interest, the study presented so much information that Ms. C. had trouble interpreting it. After consulting a colleague, she made the following interpretations based on her desire to include more social development activities:

1. The block play area seems to encourage interaction between handicapped and nonhandicapped students; therefore, social development might be enhanced by scheduling more activities there.
2. Class isolates, children new to the class, and handicapped children who tend to interact only with other handicapped children should be scheduled for as many integrated physical education activities as possible.
3. The table play area frequently contained only groups of handicapped children. An effort should be made to integrate more nonhandicapped children in the area.
4. The art play area does not encourage interaction between groups; games and other high interest activities may be needed to stimulate cooperative play in this area.

Techniques to Increase Listening Skills

Mr. D. is a special education teacher in an elementary school resource room. Over the past several months he has observed that several of his students are becoming increasingly inattentive to what he says to them. Even though they appear to be listening, frequently they cannot even repeat the questions just asked of them. Frustrated by this lack of attention, Mr. D. finds an article reporting techniques to increase listening skills (abstracted by the authors).

> Ross, D. M., & Ross, S. A. The efficacy of listening training for educable mentally retarded children. *American Journal of Mental Deficiency,* 1972, *77,* 137-142.
>
> *Description:* Retarded and nonretarded primary age school children were taught listening skills within the context of small-group games. The 10-week training program included intentional teaching, peer modeling, and tangible, social, and symbolic rewards. The retarded children were matched on a number of variables and randomly assigned to experimental and control groups. The nonretarded group (called the average group) was also used as a control group.
>
> *Findings:* The data provided strong support for the efficacy of listening training for young EMR children. Posttest scores of the experimental group exceeded those of the control group on 8 of 10 criterion subtests, exceeded those of the average group on one subtest, and equaled the average group on three subtests.

The study not only gave Mr. D. examples of listening skills training, but also gave him something more important. In the discussion section of the article, Ross and Ross caution that many times the performance deficit often seen in EMR children may be partly due to teachers reinforcing appropriate listening postures (nodding at appropriate times, attentive expressions, etc.) while not requiring objective evidence that the children are listening. Mr. D. observed his interactions with the students having problems and found that he was, in fact, reinforcing their attending behaviors, but not their attention. Instead of instituting a program of listening skill training, Mr. D. simply began reinforcing the students' attending behaviors *and* their attention to his classroom instruction.

Selecting an Appropriate Teaching Method

Mr. B., an elementary school special education teacher, has in his class an EMR child having difficulty learning sight vocabulary words. Because the child, Ted, has several good friends in the room, Mr. B. often has him practice sight words with one of them. This practice, however, has not been successful. While searching for a teaching method to help Ted, Mr. B. found the following article (abstracted by the authors):

> Hartup, W. W. Friendship status and the effectiveness of peers as reinforcing agents. *Journal of Experimental Child Psychology,* 1964, *1,* 154-162.
>
> *Description:* Performance on a marble-dropping task of 36 nursery school children (ages 4-5) was the dependent variable used in this study. Friendship status ("liked" or "disliked") was the independent variable.

The 36 children were randomly assigned to either the LP (reinforced by liked peer) group or the DP (reinforced by disliked peer) group. Both the LP group and the DP group were then divided at their respective median ages; thus, four subgroups were constituted for the experiment (LP 4-year-olds, LP 5-year-olds, DP 4-year-olds, and DP 5-year-olds). Each subject in each group was given a picture sociometric test to ascertain which children in the class he/she liked and disliked.

The LP group children were individually taken to a room and instructed in the marble-dropping procedure. Base rates were taken, then a "liked peer" was introduced as a reinforcing agent in the procedure (the liked peer had previously been trained by the researcher to give verbal approval as the reinforcer). The number of marbles dropped through the holes in a bin during each minute of the 6-minute session were recorded by an observer. The base rates were subtracted from the number of marbles inserted during each minute, furnishing six different scores for each subject.

Similar procedures were used with the DP group of children.

Findings: Liked and disliked peers differentially affected performance. Performance was better maintained in the DP group than in the LP group and by 5-year-olds rather than 4-year-olds. (Performance was enhanced among the 5-year-old DP group, whereas in all other subgroups performance deteriorated during the session, more so under the LP condition.)

The results of this study have direct implication for Mr. B.'s classroom. The sharp difference in the scores for the liked peer group suggests that the presence and comments of liked peers interfered with the task. It appears that liked peers evoked friendly approach responses and bids for attention (which, in turn, interfered with performance), while disliked peers did not. Also, anxiety may have affected performance. If disliked peers elicited more anxiety in the text situation than liked peers, than the mere presence of disliked peers may have resulted in improved performance.

For Mr. B., this means that using Ted's friends to help him practice sight words may actually be interfering with the learning of the words. Mr. B. should discontinue using Ted's friends to help him practice; instead, he should try using a disliked peer. Just the presence of the disliked peer in the practice situation may improve Ted's performance. If Ted's success at learning the words is still low, Mr. B. could teach the disliked peer to socially reinforce Ted's performance. If, after a period of time, this does not work, Ted's performance may be improved by grouping him with several disliked peers in a sight word task or game. A key element here is Mr. B.'s willingness to attempt variations of the procedure in order to find one that works successfully for him and for his students.

CURRICULAR SOURCES OF RESEARCH INFORMATION

A significant source of research information often overlooked by teachers is the literature reporting major curriculum development efforts. Although curriculum development is frequently not considered "research" by many teachers, most major curriculum development projects do utilize research designs and methodology to evaluate and field test their curricula. Reports from these projects not only provide teachers information on researched teaching strategies that can be used in the classroom, but also offer a wealth of related information. For example, most major curriculum development efforts operate from a clearly specified rationale. If the rationale for developing the curriculum closely resembles the teacher's concern for going to the literature, the report may offer 1) references to additional relevant research, 2) information on similar curriculum development projects that may more closely fit the teacher's needs, 3) ideas on the teaching environment not presently considered by the teacher, and 4) examples of successful and unsuccessful teaching methods used by the project (formative evaluation reports are excellent sources for these). In addition, statements of rationale or position papers presented by curriculum projects are usually substantive and well documented.

Literature from major curriculum development projects is generally not found in research journals. Although some projects occasionally do publish in journals, most of the literature is contained in project reports, newsletters, and working papers. This can be a disadvantage to some teachers because, typically, these sources are not as readily accessible as research journals. These sources can usually be found in instructional material centers, university department libraries, ERIC, some public school professional libraries, and directly from the projects and the publishers of curriculum products.

Some examples of major curriculum development projects for the mentally retarded that have produced products and that represent sources of curriculum information are:

1. *Biological Science Curriculum Study (BSCS)* Directed by William Calahan and William V. Mayer at Boulder, Colorado, BSCS is a comprehensive curriculum development center concentrating its studies in the field of science. The science curricula developed by BSCS are designed for the mildly mentally retarded and include *Me Now, Me and My Environment,* and *Me and My Future.* BSCS also publishes the BSCS Journal (formerly BSCS Newsletter). Information can be obtained from BSCS (P.O. Box 930, Boulder Col.) or Hubbard Scientific Company (P.O. Box 104, Northbrook, Ill.).
2. *Debbie School Program* Designed to be used as an early intervention program for infants or profoundly retarded individuals, the

Debbie School Program was developed by William Bricker and Diane Bricker and their staff, Laura Dennison, Richard Iacino, Jacques Davis, Linda Kahlin, Gisela Chalelanat, and Betty Vincent. Information can be received from the Mailman Center for Child Development, University of Miami, Miami, Florida.

3. *I CAN* I CAN is directed by Dr. Janet A. Wessel and staff. It is a developmental curriculum concentrating on physical education materials for mentally retarded children and youth from preschool through 14 years of age. I CAN is designed to be used by special education teachers, physical education specialists, theraputic recreation specialists, and curriculum specialists. Information can be obtained from Dr. Wessel, Department of Health, Physical Education, and Recreation, Michigan State University or from Hubbard Scientific Company.

4. *Programmed Environment Project* Directed by Dr. James W. Tawney, the Programmed Environment Project is a behavioral curriculum designed to train specific behaviors, such as grasp and pull motions, to establish simple responses to stimuli, and to promote generalization of responses in severely mentally retarded individuals. Information can be obtained from Dr. Tawney, Department of Special Education, University of Kentucky, Lexington.

5. *Project MORE* James R. Lent, George Peabody College for Teachers, Nashville, Tennessee, was the director for this behavioral task analysis curriculum designed to teach daily living skills to moderately and severely mentally retarded persons. Programs can be used by professionals, paraprofessionals, parents, aides, or volunteers. Information can be obtained from Dr. Lent and from Hubbard Scientific Company.

6. *Social Learning Curriculum* The Social Learning Curriculum (available for both primary and secondary age students) was developed at the Curriculum Research and Development Center in Mental Retardation at Ferkauf Graduate School of Humanities and Social Sciences, Yeshiva University. The center is directed by Dr. Herbert Goldstein. The Social Learning Curriculum concentrates on social development, but it also emphasizes skills and concepts related to language, math, and motor development. Information can be obtained from Charles E. Merrill Publishing Company, Columbus, Oh.

SUMMARY

The manner in which researchers report their research results has made it difficult for teachers to gain access to or to make use of research results. Too often researchers write for fellow researchers and fail to report their results in a form usable by teachers. For the classroom teacher, instructional planning represents the context in which research results are applied. This dictates an investment by teachers in developing planning skills and in techniques for searching and analyzing research results. The state-of-the-art in terms of research results will not likely change, but hopefully in the future researchers will become more sensitive to the needs of consumers. Teachers, as consumers of research, must also recognize the importance of research in instructional planning and be willing to make the necessary investments.

RESEARCH RESOURCES

Sources of Information in Abstracted Form

Child Development Abstracts and Bibliography
Current Index to Journals in Education (CIJE)
Dissertation Abstracts
DSH Abstracts (Deaf, Speech and Hearing)
Educational Resources Information Center (ERIC)
Education Index
Exceptional Child Education Resources (formerly *Exceptional Child Education Abstracts*)
Mental Retardation and Developmenal Disabilities Abstracts (formerly *Mental Retardation Abstracts*)
Psychological Abstracts
Research in Education

Selected Periodicals that Include Research Articles Relating to the Mentally Retarded

AAESPH Review (American Association for the Education of the Severely and Profoundly Handicapped)
American Educational Research Journal
American Journal of Mental Deficiency
American Journal of Occupational Therapy
American Journal of Psychology
American Sociological Review
Asha (A Journal of the American Speech-Language-Hearing Association)
Behavior Therapy
Behavioral Science
British Journal of Mental Subnormality
Bulletin of the National Association of Secondary School Principals

Bulletin of Prosthetics Research
Career Education Quarterly
Child and Family
Child Psychiatry and Human Development
Childhood Education
Day Care and Early Education
Developmental Psychology
Education and Training of the Mentally Retarded
Educational Researcher
Exceptional Children
Exceptional Parent
Generic Psychology Monographs
Harvard Education Review
Journal of Abnormal Child Psychology
Journal of Abnormal Psychology
Journal of Applied Behavior Analysis
Journal of the Association for the Study of Perception
Journal of Career Development
Journal of Career Education
Journal of Child Psychology and Psychiatry
Journal of Consulting and Clinical Psychology
Journal of Creative Behavior
Journal of Education
Journal of Educational Psychology
Journal of Educational Psychology and Measurement
Journal of Educational Research
Journal of Experimental Child Psychology
Journal of Experimental Education
Journal of Language, Speech, and Hearing
Journal of Mental Deficiency Research
Journal of Music Therapy
Journal of Negro Education
Journal of Nervous and Mental Disease
Journal of Pediatrics
Journal of Personality and Social Psychology
Journal of Personality Assessment
Journal of Psychology
Journal of Social Issues
Journal of Special Education
Journal of Speech and Hearing Disorders
Journal of Teacher Education
Mental Retardation

Perceptual and Motor Skills
Personnel and Guidance Journal
Physical Therapy
Psychology in the Schools
Reading Research Quarterly
Rehabilitation Digest
Rehabilitation Research and Practice Review
Review of Educational Research
School Psychology Digest
Vocational Guidance Quarterly

REFERENCES

Chaffin, J. D. Production rate as a variable in the job success or failure of educable mentally retarded adolescents. *Exceptional Children,* 1969, *35* (7), 533–538.

Edmonson, B. T., Leland, H., & Leach, E. M. Social inference training of retarded adolescents at the pre-vocational level (Final report of VRA Project RD-1388-P). Kansas City: University of Kansas Medical Center, 1968.

Haralick, J. G., & Peterson, N. L. Influence of social and physical setting on interactions among handicapped and nonhandicapped children in an integrated preschool. In Kansas Research Institute for the Early Childhood Education of the Handicapped: Reviews of Literature, OEO (USOE 300-77-0308). Lawrence, The University of Kansas, 1978

Hartup, W. W. Friendship status and the effectiveness of peer as reinforcing agents. *Journal of Experimental Child Psychology,* 1964, *1,* 154–162.

Lovitt, T. Blending research and practice. *Journal of Special Education Technology,* 1978, *1*(1), 5–11.

Meyen, E. L. *Exceptional children and youth: An introduction.* Denver: Love Publishing Co., 1978.

Prehm, H. J., & Altman, R. *Improving instruction through classroom research.* Denver: Love Publishing Co., 1976.

Ross, D. M., & Ross, S. A. The efficacy of listening training for educable mentally retarded children. *American Journal of Mental Deficiency,* 1972, *77,* 137–142.

Whelan, R. J., & Haring, N. G. Modification and maintenance of behavior through systematic application of consequences. *Exceptional Children,* 1966, *32* (5), 281–289.

Index

American Association on Mental Deficiency, 184
Antecedents, see Variables, independent
Applied behavior analysis
   arithmetical analysis of results in, use of, 100
   dependent and independent variables in, 76
   designs of, 78
   and education, comparison of, 74
   goals of, 74
   group and single-subject designs, difference between, 78
   observational reliability in, discussion of, 79-81
   single-subject designs in, 74
      advantages and disadvantages of, 78-79
      purposes of, 81
      types of, 82-99
   statistical analysis of results in, use of, 100
   traditional group designs, 74, 77
   visual analysis of results in, use of, 100-101
   see also Changing criterion designs; Multi-element designs; Multiple baseline designs; Reversal designs; Single-subject designs; Variables
Association for Retarded Citizens (ARC), 134
   see also National Association for Retarded Citizens

Bayley Scales of Infant Development, 115-116

Behavior
   as dependent variable, 76
   differential reinforcement of other, 87, 89
   of teachers, toward EMR children, see Teacher attitudes; Teacher behavior; Teacher expectancy
   see also Applied behavior analysis
Biological Science Curriculum Study (BSCS), 276
Boehm Test of Basic Concepts, 139, 140, 141
Bruininks-Oseretsky Test, 139, 140, 141
Bureau for the Education of the Handicapped, 152, 153, 189

California decertification program
   background of, 191-193
   interpretation of, 198-199, 202
   Keogh et al. study, 197
   Meyers et al. study, 193-197
Capitol Association for Retarded Citizens, 232
Changing criterion designs
   advantages and disadvantages of, 99
   baseline phase in, 97, 98-99
   explanation of, 97
   setting criterion level in, 99
   studies using, 97-98, 99
   see also Applied behavior analysis; Multi-element designs; Multiple baseline designs; Reversal designs; Single-subject designs

281

282 Index

Citizen Advocacy Programs, 231–250
  advocate/protégé interaction, 248–249
  citizen advocate, defined, 232
  development of, 232–233
  in Florida, *see* Florida Citizen Advocacy Program
Consequences, *see* Variables, independent
Court cases, instrumental, in mainstreamed education movement, 5, 179, 185, 191, 192, 193, 194
Critical thinking
  as component of social competence, 154
  elements of, 157–158
  see also Independent action; Inductive teaching method; Social competence; Social Learning Curriculum (SLC)
Curriculum development
  curriculum, defined, 152
  versus research, 148–150
  Social Learning Curriculum, 153–175
  sources of research information in, 276–277
  see also Educational research; Inductive teaching method; Instructional planning; Social Learning Curriculum

Debbie School Program, 276–277
Denver Developmental Screening Test, 114
Developmental Disabilities and Rights Act (PL 94-103), 233
Diana v. *School Board of Education*, 5, 185, 191, 192, 193, 194
Differential reinforcement, *see* Applied behavior analysis; Behavior
Down's syndrome, 222, 223, 225, 226, 227
  forms of, 112
  historical background of, 110–111
  recent literature on educability of children with, 111–114

Down's syndrome children
  early education programs for, 116–147
  language education studies of, 115–116
  see also Expanding Developmental Growth through Education (Project EDGE)
Down's Syndrome Congress, 144

EDGE Language Sample Test, 139, 140, 141
Education, mainstreamed
  court cases instrumental in movement toward, 5, 179, 185, 191, 192, 193, 194
  evaluating programs of
    paradigms for, 47–72
    single-subject designs for, 73–105
  historical background of, movement, 4–6, 177–186
  programs for young children with Down's syndrome, 109–147
  and the "quality of life" issue, 65–67
  research in large-scale curriculum development for, 148–175
  review of issues concerning, 176–206
  students' and teachers' perceptions of the mentally retarded child, 207–230
  teacher attitudes toward, 3–23, 188–189, 209–211, 219–224
  teacher expectancies and their implications for, 24–44
  using research findings for classroom programming in, 253–280
  see also Environment, least restrictive; Quality of life
Education for All Handicapped Children Act (PL 94-142), 3, 4, 6, 14, 109, 179, 185, 186, 193, 203, 208, 209, 231, 255, 256
Educational research
  application of, for classroom programming, 253–280

curricular sources of information, 276–277
versus curriculum development, 148–150
curriculum-directed and curriculum-related, comparison of, 150–152
defined, 254
literature sources, 266–268
problems in use of, for instructional planning, 255–256
reading reports for practical value, 262–269
resources, 278–280
use of, in instructional planning, 259–262
using the literature, examples of, 269–275
see also Applied behavior analysis; Curriculum development; Down's syndrome children; Expanding Developmental Growth through Education (EDGE); Inductive teaching method; Instructional planning; Social Learning Curriculum (SLC); Test of the Hierarchy of Inductive Knowledge (THINK)
Efficacy studies
defined, 178
problems of
evaluation of achievement and adjustment, 181–183
failure to specify treatment in, 183
misapplication of findings to mainstreaming, 183–184
sampling procedures of, 179–181
unit of analysis, 183
EMR children, 176–203
see Mentally retarded persons
Environment, least restrictive, 4, 6, 176–177, 185, 186, 208
see also Education, mainstreamed; Quality of life
Environmental Language Inventory (ELI), 115
Evaluation paradigms
classification of, data within MPE context, 56–58
the concept of validity under different, 53–54
discussion of, 47–48
the dominant paradigm, 49–51
multiple perspective evaluation (MPE), 51–54
shift in
implications of, 55–59
necessity of, 52
SPE versus MPE paradigms, 60–61
see also Education, mainstreamed
Expanding Developmental Growth through Education (Project EDGE)
caregiver/child interaction in program, 125–126
characteristics of children and families participating in, 135–138
communication stimulation in program, 126–127
conceptual development framework for, 117–119
future research related to program, 141–145
goals of, 117
impact of hearing impairments on IQ scores in, 142
instructional augmentation in program, 128–130
instructional materials used in, 117, 118
preschool program, 131, 132
program lessons
educational principles incorporated in, 125–131
management and logistics of, 121, 124
parent-participant rating of, 120–121, 122–124
planned variations in, 130–131
selection of control and experimental groups for, 132–135
see also Down's syndrome; Down's syndrome children

Florida Association for Retarded Citizens, 233

Florida Citizen Advocacy Program
  advocates and protégés, interaction between, 240-243, 247
  advocates in
    characteristics of, 234-235
    effects of program on, 243-245
    reasons for becoming, 236-237, 246-247
  advocates' perceptions of, 246, 247
  development of, 233
  procedures for study of, 233-234
  protégés in
    advocates' perceptions of, 237-240
    characteristics of, 235-236
    effects of program on, 245-246
Florida Retardation Program Office, 233
Functional relationship, *see* Variables

Hobson v. Hansen, 5

I CAN Program, 277
Illinois Index of Self Derogation, 183
Illinois Test of Psycholinguistic Abilities (ITPA), 115
Independent action
  as component of social competence, 154, 158
  see also Critical thinking; Inductive teaching method; Social competence; Social Learning Curriculum (SLC)
Individualized education programs, 255, 256
Induction, *see* Inductive teaching method; Social Learning Curriculum (SLC); Test of the Hierarchy of Inductive Knowledge (THINK)
Inductive teaching method
  assumptions underlying
    age-relatedness, 157, 162-163
    hierarchy, 156-157, 161
    social competency, 157-158, 163
  background and sources of, 155
  dimensions underlying levels of, 163-164

  explanation of, 153-156
  implementation of, studies of, 166-172
  induction, discussion of, 153
  related to levels for scoring THINK test, 160
  see also Social Learning Curriculum (SLC); Test of the Hierarchy of Inductive Knowledge (THINK)
Inservice training, 15
  see also Teacher attitudes; Teacher behavior; Teacher expectancy
Instructional planning
  curricular sources of research information for, 276-277
  goals of, 254
  guidelines for, 256-258
  problems in using research results in, 255-256
  reading research reports for practical application in, 262-269
  use of educational research in, 259-262
  using research literature, examples of, 269-275
  see also Curriculum development; Educational research
Iowa Test of Basic Skills, 194

Language training, of children with Down's syndrome, 115-116
  see also Down's syndrome children
Least restrictive environment, *see* Environment, least restrictive
Larry Mills, 5
Larry P., 179, 185, 194

Mainstreaming, *see* Education, mainstreamed
Mental age, as a guide to projecting educational goals for EMR children, 37-38
Mental retardation
  children and teachers' knowledge of, comparison of, 227

children's knowledge of, survey of, 211–219, 224–225
defined by AAMD, 184, 208–209
teachers' knowledge of, survey of, 219–224, 226–227
see also Down's syndrome
Mentally retarded persons
care of, background/history, 73
as co-designers of educational systems, 68
see also Education, mainstreamed; Mental retardation; Teacher attitudes; Teacher behavior; Teacher expectancy
Metropolitan Achievement Tests (MAT), 194, 195–196
Minnesota Teacher Attitude Inventory, 17
Mongolism, *see* Down's syndrome; Down's syndrome children
Mongoloid Development Council (MDC), *see* National Association for Down's Syndrome
Multi-element designs
advantages and disadvantages of, 97
explanation of, 95–96
studies using, 96–97
see also Applied behavior analysis; Changing criterion designs; Multiple baseline designs; Reversal designs; Single-subject designs
Multiple baseline designs
across behaviors, 91, 92
across settings, 91–92, 94
across subjects, 91, 93
advantages and disadvantages of, 94–95
baseline phase in, 89
demonstration of functional relationships in, 88–89, 90
intervention sequences in, 89, 91
see also Applied behavior analysis; Changing criterion designs; Multi-element designs; Reversal designs; Single-subject designs

Multiple Perspective Evaluation (MPE)
funding problems related to, 63–65
training the MPE evaluator, 62–63
Multiple Perspective Evaluation (MPE) paradigm, 51–59

National Association for Down's Syndrome, 133
National Association for Retarded Children (NARC), 232, 233, 235, 236, 241, 242
National Committee for Mental Hygiene, Inc., 208, 228
Normalization, principle of, *see* Education, mainstreamed; Environment, least restrictive; Quality of life

Paradigms, evaluation, *see* Evaluation paradigms
PARC, 5
Peabody Picture Vocabulary Test, 115
PRIME, *see* Programmed Re-entry into Mainstream Education
Programmed Environment Project, 277
Programmed Re-entry into Mainstream Education (PRIME), 8–9, 11, 14, 15, 17, 18
achievement and adjustment data of, 191
background to, 189
program characteristics of, 189–190
Project EDGE, *see* Expanding Developmental Growth through Education
Project MORE, 277

Quality of life
and the mainstreaming movement, 65–67
as systems design, 68–69
see also Education, mainstreamed; Environment, least restrictive

Rehabilitation Act of 1973, 231
Reversal designs
  ABA design, 82, 83, 84
  ABAB design, 84, 85
    advantages and disadvantages of, 87–88
    variations on, 86–87
  baseline phase in, 82–84
  common characteristics of, 82
  see also Applied behavior analysis; Changing criterion designs; Multi-element designs; Multiple baseline designs; Single-subject designs

Self-concept theory, 30–31
Setting events, see Variables, independent
Single-subject designs, in applied behavior analysis, 74
  advantages and disadvantages of, 78–79
  difference between, and traditional group designs, 78
  purposes of, 81
  types of
    changing criterion design, 97–99
    multi-element design, 95–97
    multiple baseline, 88–95
    reversal design, 82–88
  see also Applied behavior analysis; Variables
Social competence, components of, in instructional theory of Social Learning Curriculum, 154, 157–158
Social Learning Curriculum, 277
  implementation of, studies of, 166–172
  inductive teaching method used in, 153–156
  social competence as defined by instructional theory of, 154
  see also Inductive teaching method; Test of the Hierarchy of Inductive Knowledge (THINK)
Social Learning Curriculum Classroom Observation System (SLC-COS)
  purposes of, 166
  see also Social Learning Environment Rating Scale (SLERS); Social Learning Interaction System (SLIS)
Social Learning Environment Rating Scale (SLERS)
  factor analysis compared to THINK performance, 170–171
  factor analytic examination of, 168–170
Social Learning Interaction System (SLIS), 166, 167, 168
Social Learning Observation Record (SLOR), 170, 172
Stanford-Binet Test, 139, 140, 141, 180, 192
Supportive services
  inservice training, 14, 15
  for regular teachers in mainstreamed education of EMR children, 14–16
  see also Education, mainstreamed; Teacher attitudes; Teacher behavior; Teacher expectancy

Teacher attitudes, 19
  and teacher perception of children's behavior, 19–20
  toward EMR and TMR children, comparison of, 11–12
  toward mainstreaming of EMR children, 3–23, 201, 209–211
    beliefs concerning placement of EMR underlying, 16–17
    effect of available supportive services on, 14–16
    effect of general educational attitudes on, 17–18
    factors underlying, 10–18
    feelings of incompetence underlying, 13–14
    lack of knowledge of behavior of EMR children underlying, 11–13

optimism, 12–13
  studies of, 7–10
  see also Education, mainstreamed; Teacher behavior; Teacher expectancy
Teacher behavior
  changing biased, 38
  general instructional strategies, 21–22
  and teacher expectancy, correlation between, 27–29
  toward EMR children, 20–21
  see also Education, mainstreamed; Teacher attitudes; Teacher expectancy
Teacher expectancy
  biased, 26
  defined, 25
  effect of handicapped label on, 33–35, 36
  effects of assumptions about, 27
  factors influencing, 33
  function of normal, in teaching/planning process, 25–26
  implications of, for teachers of EMR children, 39–41
  problems in projecting education of EMR children, 36–37
  as "self-fulfilling prophecies," 26
  and student behavior
    failure to demonstrate correlation between, 30
    studies of, 26–29
  see also Education, mainstreamed; Teacher attitudes; Teacher behavior
Teachers, classification of, in terms of expectancies, 29–30
Test of the Hierachy of Inductive Knowledge (THINK), 158
  assumptions underlying
    age-relatedness, 157, 162–163

  hierarchy, 156–157, 161
  social competency, 157–158, 163
  dimensions underlying levels of 163–164
  factors underlying, and traditional IQ tests, comparison of, 164–165
  operational definitions of levels for scoring, related to ITM levels, 160
  overview of interview (testing) procedure, 159
  problem-solving performance, compared to SLERS factor analysis, 170–171
  social learning concepts tested by, 158
  see also Inductive teaching method; Social Learning Curriculum (SLC)
Texas PRIME Project, *see* Programmed Re-entry into Mainstream Education

Validity, and evaluation paradigms, 53–54
Variables, dependent and independent
  in applied behavior analysis, 76
  in education, 75
  functional relationships between, 76, 100
    rules for identifying, 79
  the relationship between studies of, 75–76
Variables, independent, classification of, 76–77

Wechsler Intelligence Scale for Children, 161, 192